STRAIGHT TALK ABOUT

Starting
AND
Growing
YOUR
Business

Starting
AND
Growing
YOUR
Business

**SMART ADVICE
FOR ENTREPRENEURS
FROM
ENTREPRENEURS**

SANJYOT P. DUNUNG

McGraw-Hill

New York / Chicago / San Francisco / Lisbon / London / Madrid / Mexico City
Milan / New Delhi / San Juan / Seoul / Singapore / Sydney / Toronto

The *McGraw·Hill* Companies

1 2 3 4 5 6 7 8 9 10   FGR/FGR   0 9 8 7 6 5

ISBN 0-07-142727-9

This publication is designed to provide accurate and authoritative information in regard to the subject matter covered. It is sold with the understanding that neither the author nor the publisher is engaged in rendering legal, accounting, or other professional service. If legal advice or other expert assistance is required, the services of a competent professional person should be sought.

> —*From a Declaration of Principles jointly adopted by a Committee of the American Bar Association and by a Committee of Publishers.*

McGraw-Hill books are available at special quantity discounts to use as premiums and sales promotions, or for use in corporate training programs. For more information, please write to the Director of Special Sales, McGraw-Hill Professional, Two Penn Plaza, New York, NY 10121-2298. Or contact your local bookstore.

This book is printed on recycled, acid-free paper containing a minimum of 50% recycled, de-inked fiber.

Library of Congress Cataloging-in-Publication Data

Dunung, Sanjyot P.
  Straight talk about starting your own business / by Sanjyot P. Dunung.
     p.   cm.
  Includes bibliographical references.
  ISBN 0-07-142727-9 (pbk. : alk. paper)
  1. New business enterprises—Management.   2. Entrepreneurship.   I. Title.
HD62.5.D865   2005
658.1'1—dc22

2005006146

To Shanth, Yash & Anand

Find your own special star and reach for it.
Follow your hearts and true passions.

* * *

To My Fellow Entrepreneurs

"Do not go where the path may lead, go instead where there is no path and leave a trail."

—*Ralph Waldo Emerson*

CONTENTS

ACKNOWLEDGMENTS AND AUTHOR'S NOTE

Books like *Straight Talk* come from years of collective experiences and discussions. There are many, many people whose wise counsel and insight I have benefited from and who have directly and indirectly contributed to this book. I am grateful to all of these people who have through the years touched my life and my businesses. While it may be difficult to thank everyone personally, there are few special thank yous, which I note below.

I also want to express my sincere gratitude to the people who worked for, with, advised, or invested in my companies. The concept for this book came as I navigated the entrepreneurial opportunities, bumps, and challenges. Over the years, many of you also experienced the same entrepreneurial cycles with me and generously shared your insight, wisdom, enthusiasm, professionalism, and above all, friendship. Thank you.

This book would not have emerged in its current form if it weren't for the inspiration and input of some wonderful fellow entrepreneurs and friends. Their stories bring to life much of the lessons of *Straight Talk* and follow in the pages hereafter. All of their personal experiences, attitudes, passions, and enthusiasm highlight what attracts so many to the intriguing world of entrepreneurship.

I want to extend a special thank you to Karen See for sharing her wisdom and experiences, as well as providing extensive input and contributions on Chapter 4, "Marketing and Sales." She gave the chapter much of its "marketing meat." I've enjoyed our own informal peer mentoring group and sharing similar "tales from the trenches" over the past few years. Our early swapping of "stories and experiences" helped me see the need and potential for a book like this.

I also want to extend a special thank you to Rosalind Resnick, Liz Elting, and Adrienne Plotch for the informal peer mentoring over long meals, occasionally with much-needed cocktails, and warm friendship that helped give shape to the stories, lessons, and experiences in the pages ahead.

I would like to extend a very warm thank you to Gail Koff and Martha Daniel for sharing their rich and insightful entrepreneurial experiences, challenges, and successes, all of which add color and depth to the chapters ahead.

I have deep, special gratitude to Patrick Owen Burns and Mark Edmiston, both of whom provided much-needed wise counsel and contributed significantly to both my knowledge and experiences in the world of venture and investment capital.

I want to give sincere thanks to Steve Lindstrom, Jim Holden, and Jim Moore for their respective insight on venture capitalists, the financing industry, and entrepreneurial experiences.

I am grateful to Nancy Prager Kamel and Mark Segall for their enduring and patient friendship and wise business counsel as I navigated through my own entrepreneurial peaks, valleys, and bumps; and to Nancy, a special thanks for *frequently* reminding me that mistakes were permissible, just not the same ones. To Lue Ann Eldar for her enduring support, faith, and friendship, thank you.

My sincere thanks to Stephen Isaacs, my editor at McGraw-Hill, for his patience with my schedule and his early input. No book can get off the ground without an early and productive editorial brainstorming effort. My deep gratitude to Ann Wildman, my first editor at McGraw-Hill, for her early interest and brainstorming efforts as I put the concept for this book together. I also want to extend a grateful thank you to Nicole Walker for weaving through my manuscript with her expert editorial skills and for working with my schedule, which wasn't always the most convenient.

My heartfelt and warmest thanks to Susan Lestingi for many years of close, dependable, kind, and enduring friendship, as well as her essential wise business- and people-related insight at just the right times. To Lynne Byrne Williams and Dolores Santos, I extend my warmest gratitude for their close, insightful, and warm friendship and advice. My warmest gratitude to Joyce Coit, a valued personal and business confidante, with whom I have the odd twist of fate to share the same cast of financial characters. To Tony Leroy, I want to extend my warmest gratitude for his very unique insight and kind friendship. All of you have been instrumental as I navigated the gray, fuzzy space between professional and personal worlds that each of us must come to terms with at various junctures in our lives.

To my husband Deepak, I'm deeply grateful for the experiences that we've shared that have contributed significantly to my growth and learning. We have been very fortunate to have been blessed with kind, wonderful, and supportive family and friends to whom we extend our heartfelt gratitude.

To my wonderful boys, Shanth, Yash, and Anand, thank you for your patience in letting me spend the nights and weekends needed to finish this book. Your contagious giggles, hugs, and antics provided inspiration at just the right times. You give my days, my work, and my life meaning, purpose, and enormous joy. I hope that as you grow, you will each find your own special star and reach for it. Follow your hearts and true passions on your own life journeys.

To my parents, Prafulla and Vaijayanti, a most heartfelt thank you, which somehow doesn't seem adequate enough, for always providing me with enormous spiritual support and unconditional love; being there at the times in my life when it was needed most; and embodying the lifelong values of hard work, passion, kindness, integrity, discipline, and generosity of heart and spirit. For many decades, you have both lived exemplary lives and you continue to do so.

Author's Note:

There are a lot of experiences, stories, facts and opinions in this book. I'd like to clearly state that the opinions in this book, if not directly attributed to a fellow entrepreneur, are mine or as a direct result of research I've conducted. I bear full responsibility for any inaccuracies and/or omissions of all that follows in the pages ahead.

I hope that this book provides you with insight and essential information on your own entrepreneurial journey. I'd love to hear from fellow entrepreneurs and those who work in the worlds of entrepreneurship, including employees, VCs, investors, advisors, and customers. If you'd like to submit a potential "Tales from the Trenches" for the next edition or just have an interesting or really great personal story, please send it to me at spdunung@straighttalkbusiness.com. Please note that while I can't acknowledge receipt for all stories, no experiences will be used without the sender's final permission.

Thank you for making this book part of your entrepreneurial journey! I hope it provides you the necessary insight as you commence or continue to navigate the entrepreneurial peaks, valleys, and bumps.

INTRODUCTION

Like many entrepreneurs, when I started my first company, I didn't know any other entrepreneurs. My frame of reference was the corporate world, in which I had cut my professional teeth, so to speak. As I progressed, I found myself facing all sorts of opportunities and challenges that I would have been able to navigate much more smoothly had I had the knowledge I do now. It was not until I was well into my second company before I began to meet fellow entrepreneurs whose companies were at similar stages of growth. Once we began to share experiences, I realized that I was not alone and that my experiences were not unique.

One of the most difficult challenges entrepreneurs face is the feeling of aloneness when facing all of the business issues of starting, growing, and running their own company. The reality is that while many of the challenges that entrepreneurs face are unique to entrepreneurship, individual entrepreneurs are certainly not alone. Many entrepreneurs feel as though no one else has made a certain mistake or faced a particular challenge, when in truth many have.

After many coffees and cocktails with fellow entrepreneurs, I realized that there were no sources any of us could turn to to read about "real-life" experiences. All of the books on entrepreneurship were written by journalists or consultants and lacked a real understanding of what it was like to be "in the trenches."

Also, most entrepreneurial books profile only enormously successful entrepreneurs or companies, thereby bypassing much of the common entrepreneurial experience. Not every company can be a Dell or Microsoft, yet thousands of entrepreneurs happily achieve a high level of success far beyond the sole-proprietorship stage. My focus is on the millions of entrepreneurs looking to find success in this range.

As entertaining and inspiring as the rags-to-riches stories may be, it is important to focus on the opportunities, the challenges, the mistakes, and the bumps in the road. It's important to know what the early years of highly successful companies were really like on a day-to-day basis. There's a prevalence of PR-generated images of young entrepreneurs in garages or dorm rooms, which then fast-forward to a very success- ful post-IPO world. The decade or more in between is a vague blur and rarely referenced, yet every company and entrepreneur faces many of the same challenges during those growth years. Even the most suc- cessful entrepreneur experiences bumps in the road, and may need to fold several companies before finding the right "recipe" for success.

Further, the reality is that most entrepreneurs have no guarantee of success. Clearly, you feel optimistic about your possibilities or you wouldn't be engaged in your current project. However, you can't know for sure. You just believe and hope that you're right. Michael Dell and Bill Gates didn't wake up one morning in their early years and know for sure that they would create multibillion-dollar companies within one or two decades. Few focus on the fact that it's passion, not a clairvoyant guarantee of success, that fuels the entrepreneur on a daily basis.

As an entrepreneur, I found that there were too few easy-to-access resources on how to start and grow a business beyond the sole-proprietor stage. Of the multitude of entrepreneurial books, few address the operat- ing issues of actually running a young or small company. Most are writ- ten for people deciding whether to start a business and rarely address the ongoing operating challenges or steps for how to best handle them. As a result, most entrepreneurs find themselves wondering what others did in similar business situations and having few places to go for insight and expe- rience sharing.

There's lots of information out there, much on the Internet, so much so that it can at times seem overwhelming. However, most books or resources don't focus on the issues you experience after start-up and usually between years 1 and 5. What I have tried to do is to bring out the salient stages of the entrepreneurial process.

This is the handbook I wish I'd had when I began my first business. In it, I've tried to incorporate all the knowledge I gleaned from having had several businesses. Often, the most frustrating quandary for entrepreneurs, and for people in general, is that they don't know what questions to ask, because they don't know what they don't know.

In this book, I've tried to highlight the range of key issues that you need to consider every step of the way. Of course, we have all had a little entrepreneurial optimistic arrogance at one point or another and thought we could handle everything just fine. As we get more seasoned, we realize that while that may be true in some situations, it would be much less stressful to be able to anticipate and be prepared for opportunities, challenges, and bumps in the road.

Entrepreneurship is a spiritual journey where you learn as much about yourself as you do about your business, products, and customers. What I hope will make this book useful is that it provides relevant facts while nourishing the entrepreneur's spiritual journey.

Those who think it's just hard facts, business, and dollars and cents have probably never met a real entrepreneur. I am not just talking about the human side of a company and the problems it can cause—something all organizations encounter. I am referring to the intense soul-searching an entrepreneur goes through when asking himself or herself a slew of questions every day while encountering opportunities and obstacles. It's about the passion and believing all the way deep into your gut and soul. For that reason, you'll find that I'll talk at times about the things you'll need to reflect on at different stages of the start-up and growth. I've also given the topic its own chapter, "Keeping the Faith," Chapter 8, where I talk about handling the tough days and even rapid growth. It is important to stay balanced and true to your vision.

I was moved to write this book because of my personal experiences. I'm on my third company as a career entrepreneur. Through all three I've made a good number of mistakes and many smart moves, some as a result of careful planning and strategy and others from luck and timing. Entrepreneurship encompasses all of it—the successes, the challenges, the mistakes, and the comebacks. I wanted to write a book for novices as well as for seasoned career entrepreneurs, for companies with revenues of six figures as well as companies of nine figures. I've also written this book for potential entrepreneurs, for people thinking of starting their own companies, to help them understand what they may encounter along the way. I have personally ridden the entrepreneurial roller coaster, and it's a great ride for those who are ready for it.

My entrepreneurial experience started quite early in my life. Even as a child, I was always starting a business of some sort. As I was I was not content to have just another lemonade stand, my "business" was a successful little Sunday-morning camp for neighborhood kids. I charged a mere 50 cents per child for two hours—quite a bargain in today's terms—and I soon realized I had much to learn about pricing. It was the first of many ideas, and I gradually learned, as many entrepreneurs do, that it's a long way from a great idea to tangible success.

My first company sort of fell into my lap—which is how many entrepreneurs find their first firm. In my case, my first company was offered to me by a friend who wanted to move to the new Czech Republic and needed to "sell" her business, which was in essence one client. I jumped at the opportunity. I bought the "business" and her fax machine for $500. The client didn't make much money, and sales were very low by my heady expectations. I knew I needed to expand, and again, "the entrepreneurial opportunity" found me. It was the early nineties and Asia was starting to boom. Sensing the opportunity, I expanded into providing companies with cultural training services and products to enter and operate in the Asian market. At the same time, we helped Asian companies learn about and enter the American market.

We grew quickly until the Asian economic crisis of 1997 started to unravel our key overseas partners and our sales plateaued. I then realized, along with some key customers, that taking our training methodology, materials, and know-how to a technology platform would be highly beneficial for them and profitable for us. It was the beginning of the dot-com period, and although we weren't a dot-com, we certainly rode the early wave.

By this point, after a decade-plus in the "culture" business, I was deeply passionate about the need for great products to help people of all ages learn about different cultures. I had always wanted to run my own firm, and I wanted to grow one from a unique idea or vision that I knew was germinating deep within. This was an approach that worked well for me. I had discovered a market need, developed ideas, and my life's passion was born.

Despite my enthusiasm and the advantage of external funding, my second company was a bit ahead of its time and fell victim to the post-9/11 economic collapse and a disincentivizing capital structure, which I'll talk more about in Chapter 3. It's taken me till company three to get the right formula and timing to create a growing and profitable education company. Through it all, my vision has stayed fairly consistent, only evolving with market opportunity and demand. This has enabled me to continue building my knowledge, network, and experience. I'll talk more about keeping the faith in Chapter 8.

Most entrepreneurs erroneously assume that typical management books will teach them everything they need to know about operating and managing their own companies. However, more often than not, typical business books do not address the kinds of opportunities and challenges that entrepreneurs face. These books assume access to a base level of resources, including both people and money. Most entrepreneurs are usually low on both of those resources and require different strategies and tactics to succeed. This book will highlight those innovative tactics and strategies and profile some real-life tales from the trenches.

Many people are surprised to learn that successful entrepreneurs do not always have a perfect business plan and marketing and sales strategy in place before launching their businesses. In fact, many often deviate so significantly from the original plan that the business is unrecognizable. Instead, what seems to be the mark of a successful entrepreneur is the ability to adeptly navigate the daily, weekly, and monthly bumps, twists, and turns in the life of a young or small company.

We live in a world of instant gratification. People want instant success along with everything else. There are no prepackaged sure paths to successful entrepreneurship. You'll notice from the title that this book does not promise a get-rich-quick scheme. This book is about building growing, sustainable businesses and the experiences that most entrepreneurs go through.

I'll relay one of the more sound pieces of advice I have received: Start a business for what you can get out of it this year, not three to five years down the road—because you're not likely to make it to that future point if you can't take care of today. Pay yourself a salary and strive for profitability.

If you're looking for a how-to book with a step-by-step outline for guaranteed success, don't look here. You won't find that in this book. In fact, you won't find it anywhere, and you should be wary of those who promise such formulaic approaches. There is no guaranteed formula for success. The path to successful entrepreneurship is unique in every circumstance. The product, the market, and the timing are all unique. Something that works in one mix may not work in another. What's similar is the *spirit* that bonds entrepreneurs.

I'm not going to suggest that I have all the answers and have figured out this entrepreneurship thing to a science. What makes a successful entrepreneur is 50 percent ingenuity, 50 percent luck and timing, and 100 percent hard work. If you're quickly doing the math and ready to write to my editors about a typo, it's intentional. Entrepreneurship is not an exact science; it's an art. I've often heard that luck is defined as preparedness meets opportunity.

Launching a successful business requires vision and passion. Some have tried to make it a science, hence the preponderance of VC incubators, which are insulated breeding labs for taking an idea and hiring a management team to take the idea and make it an enduring and growing company. The reality is that these incubators have produced limited success. They're missing the key ingredient, the zealous entrepreneur, who's convinced that his or her idea IS the next best thing to sliced bread and is ready to go for broke—in some cases literally. Cherry-picking a bunch of successful professionals and asking them to launch a new venture is like a soda without the fizz. It's missing the key ingredient—the entrepreneur's passion. It's the passion that helps the entrepreneur keep the faith during the start-up phase and the difficult times and eventually successfully navigate the entrepreneurial opportunities and bumps along the way. I'll talk more about navigating your company to success and keeping the faith in Chapters 6 and 8.

When I decided to write this book, I had some initial qualms. To be of value, this book needed to be honest, which meant the necessity of admitting and publicly analyzing both my successes and my failures. The Japanese have a cultural concept called *honne/tatemae*, which means *real* truth as opposed to the "public" truth. I realized that as entrepreneurs we needed a *honne* book, in other words a real-truth book. We want to know what it's really like to experience the stages of growing a young company, from dealing with venture capitalists to employees to customers.

When I speak on entrepreneurship, I often find that audiences are more interested in the challenges, pitfalls, problems, and failures. The successes are, of course, very important, but everyone is willing to share those. What's lacking is a candid discussion of entrepreneurship by entrepreneurs. We often learn more about business not through the successes, but through the analysis and soul-searching of failures.

I'm not going to talk in detail about what kind of businesses you should consider starting. If you have not yet determined that, there are a number of books, some even industry-specific, that talk about the details of starting and operating certain structural and market-focused businesses. However, I'd recommend that you read this book, as you'll need to think about things like those noted in Chapter 1 in order to select the best opportunity for yourself, as well as use the other chapters to chart your company's route to success.

Seasoned entrepreneurs will also find great value in this book. The presented situations and experiences are real, and most people can relate to the challenges and opportunities. First-time entrepreneurs will certainly find value as well, but the experiences presented in this book will ring a bit more true after you've started down the entrepreneurial road. In this book you'll find real-life experiences from entrepreneurs and myself. These Tales from the Trenches help to illustrate a point in the relevant chapter.

I can't, despite my best intentions, reduce entrepreneurship to 10 easy steps as if there were some mechanical formula. Life should be so easy. We'd have a heck of lot more successful entrepreneurs. This is more about what to look for along the way. No one can predict his or her path with any surety; all you can do is prepare for the range of "wild animals" and "weather conditions." Pursuing entrepreneurship needn't be difficult, but you need to understand that it's also not formulaic. There is no perfect business plan, no perfect amount of start-up funding, no perfect organizational structure, and so on. Rather, it's a combination of what works for you. As you navigate the world of entrepreneurship, this handbook will provide you with the range of options, experiences, and strategies to help you start and grow a very successful company.

STRAIGHT TALK ABOUT

Starting
AND
Growing
YOUR
Business

ARE YOU READY FOR ENTREPRENEURSHIP?

O kay, so you think you want to be an entrepreneur. Up until the late 1990s, most people equated the word "entrepreneurship" with people who were risk-takers or nonconformists, usually unable to work in a corporate environment. It was a small segment of the population who were willing to take what most perceive as very high risks.

Suddenly the Internet era created a whole new breed of wanna-be entrepreneurs. Entrepreneurship was in vogue, and everyone wanted to be one. However, most of these newcomers were more intrigued by the prospect of instant riches than with creating new products or services or uncovering new ideas and markets. When the Internet bubble burst, the shift reversed and people sought the surety of corporate life again.

Most people believe that entrepreneurs are risk-takers. In truth, that is far from the reality. Entrepreneurs are certainly an adventurous group, but most would not describe themselves as aggressive risk-takers. More often they are passionate about an idea and carefully plan how to put it into effect. Most entrepreneurs are more comfortable with managed risk than with dangerous get-rich-quick schemes.

Entrepreneurship came into high profile in the late 1990s with the dot-com era. That period shaped the expectations and perceptions of an entire generation of potential entrepreneurs. It also made the world of venture capital more commonplace and accessible.

Personal Philosophy and Goals

First, What Makes You Tick?

When you start a business or assess how to grow it, you first need to think about your personal priorities and values—these will influence every aspect of your business whether you like it or not. Your business is an extension of you and will need to complement your personal goals and values, not challenge them.

You need to think carefully about what motivates you. What makes you happy and fulfilled? In essence, what makes you get up in the morning? What would you like to be doing in a year? In five years? What does a fulfilling day look like?

Having a personal philosophy to guide you is essential. Most of us have core values that have been shaped since childhood. Our values have helped shape our personal philosophy, which may evolve over time as we face opportunities and challenges.

Our personal philosophy helps us, among other things, to determine how we define success. For some it's material gain, for others it's artistic expression, and for others it might mean making a difference. The key is to determine your own unique philosophy. If you try to adopt others' philosophies, you'll find yourself bending whichever way the wind blows. It may sound a bit like a self-help guide, but it should come as no surprise when you look at the range of successful business books that many are looking for the professional spiritual guide. Entrepreneurship is a spiritual journey. It's a path for not only reaching your vision and potential, but for many people it brings a sense of purpose to their professional existence.

If you're objective and honest with yourself, entrepreneurship can help you better understand your own character, as well as give you greater insight into others' characters and human nature in general. You may find that people relate to you or respond to situations differently than you anticipated. More importantly, you'll likely discover new sides of your own professional personality, for better and worse, more often the former. As you experience the successes and the challenges, you'll hone your skills and goals and find that you're able to attack issues with laser focus.

As you consider becoming an entrepreneur, you'll need to ask yourself a host of questions starting with

1. Why you would you like to have your own business?
2. What resources do you have access to?
3. What personal resources are you willing to commit?
4. What kinds of operating and management experience do you have?
5. Are you a product or service business kind of person?
6. What existing relationships do you have that you can leverage to get customers, capital, advice, and so on?
7. What's your end goal?
8. How do you define success? How do key people in your life define success? If their definition differs from yours, can they accept your definition?

The key is that there are no right or wrong answers to questions like these. Each of us has to choose our own path. Be sure that you understand what motivates you and why you want to pursue entrepreneurship.

Some of you may also be career entrepreneurs, people whose chosen profession is to start new ventures. You may have both successes and non-successes under your belt. Everyone can benefit from refreshers and new insight. That's why I relish the opportunity to meet with fellow entrepreneurs, formally and informally. In Chapter 6, I'll cover peer networks. In this chapter, I challenge you, whether you're a first-time or a career entrepreneur, to always keep asking yourself why you're an entrepreneur. Review your personal philosophy and goals every so often. It's okay if they change and evolve, and quite frankly, they should, as we all pass through the various stages of life. The answers are actually less important than the self-discovery process. The process will help keep your personal goals and objectives clear and enable you to make decisions that are consistent with those goals.

Why Do People Want to Become Entrepreneurs?

There's certainly no one-size-fits-all answer to this question. People's motivations range from money to flexibility to vision and all combinations of these.

The Vision Thing

Candidly, most entrepreneurs I know would say that while money certainly motivates them, it's not the primary goal. For most, it's pursuing a vision for a new or better product or service. Many entrepreneurs are competitive, and once they have started on their venture, it's about the win as well. Developing a new way of doing things or a new product and selling it to its fullest potential is what makes the sun rise in their world.

Most people decide to start a business because they have a great idea for a product or service. This is usually the best place to start, as it usually invokes the level of passion needed to sustain you through the ups and downs.

If you think you have a great idea and it has been nagging at you for a while, I urge you to at least go through the exercise of Chapter 2's planning process and put together a plan. Even if you can't commence your venture right away, you'll have the information you need to make an informed decision as to when and how you can start your venture.

In Your Blood

For some people, being an entrepreneur is simply following in the family footsteps. If your family consists of a few entrepreneurs, you may feel inspired early on to follow their lead. Many people join family businesses and find themselves in a position to expand and grow them beyond the original scope and plan.

For many career entrepreneur people, being an entrepreneur is in their blood. I knew since I was very little that I wanted to have my own company, although I had no idea in what industry. As I noted in the Introduction, entrepreneurship was in my blood, even though both my parents preferred the professional route of working for a company.

Some entrepreneurs develop their first company and stick with it, whether or not it grows. Others of us are career entrepreneurs who create multiple companies, some successful, some not. Over time, most of us accumulate wealth by either successfully earning money through our companies or through the process of selling them and starting again.

It's the thrill of success that motivates. Don't assume that your first company will be your only company. It might be or it might be one of several building blocks toward lifelong success.

Money, Money, Money

A good number of people say that they're most focused on money and making lots of it. That's a fine enough goal and, of course, very important, but having that as your sole goal can get you into trouble. You need to combine it with another personal goal tied to the business. Does having the best product or service in the market jazz you? Most entrepreneurs will tell you that your business needs to stir more in you than just the money passion to be successful.

Having said that, there's probably a good number of successful entrepreneurs for whom money was the sole goal. Just assess how you'll feel if you don't make "enough" money. More importantly, how do you define "enough"? For many people, the definition of "enough" changes over time as they confront other issues like control and fulfillment. I will talk more about that as I discuss lifestyle businesses.

Part of understanding your definition of "enough" is determining how long you will keep going in a venture that's profitable but isn't bringing you oodles and oodles of money. You'll need some other passion to sustain you at that point. In all three of my companies, I loved what I was doing so much that I probably would have done the same thing even if I wasn't paid, and in my second company, there were a few years of that. However, money was always an important driver, and when there wasn't enough of it in terms of my personal definition, I faced the music and moved on.

Making a Difference

Many people decide to pursue their idea or vision on a full-time basis because they want to create something lasting. People grow tired of dead-end jobs and want to make a difference. By that I am not referring only to life-saving products and services, but to those that allow people to enhance their lives in the broadest sense of the word.

Many businesses have a social mission, from beauty product companies that do not test on animals to uniquely inspired child care facilities. There's even a social venture group (www.svn.org) dedicated to facilitating interaction among socially conscious companies and entrepreneurs.

Be Your Own Boss

Some people just want to work for themselves. That's a good motivation, but again, like money, it won't generate the innovative ideas and creativity required to get a business off the ground. Recognize that success in one industry or function does not ensure that you'll be successful in another. If you want to work for yourself, decide if you only want to deal with yourself or if you want to be the final authority and have people work for you. Buying an existing business or franchise is often a great option for those who are looking to running their own show but aren't sure they have a unique or marketable product or service idea.

Life Transition

Some people choose entrepreneurship to make a change in their lifestyle. This is not necessarily the creation of a lifestyle business, which I'll discuss later. If you're looking to adjust your schedule so you can take care of children or other family members, starting your own business can provide more flexibility than the corporate world, although you may find that you end up working more hours, just not always during the traditional 9-to-6 workday.

The reality is that most entrepreneurs are motivated by a combination of priorities. Collectively, these motivations fuel the entrepreneurial passion. Now some will tell you that businesses should be kept sterile and you shouldn't get too attached to your business so that you'll know when to exit. I disagree. I think the passion is what makes entrepreneurs successful, especially considering that *every* business will experience successes *and* failures and only passion and vision can sustain you through the challenges. Talk to any successful entrepreneur and you'll see their eyes light up at the mention of their product or service. Listen to the passion in their voice. You better believe that their customers are seeing and hearing that passion too.

I'd like to clarify a point here. Passion and vision should not be confused with blindness. Many early entrepreneurs often don't know when it's time to exit a business or cut their losses. Make sure your passion and vision, as well as internal or external factors like capital structure, don't prevent you from making the right business decisions. I have been one of those entrepreneurs whose capital structure made it difficult to transition a business at the right time, although I eventually did. Those who minimize passion and vision focus on these sorts of issues, but most successful entrepreneurs are able to eventually have both the vision and passion as well as the ability to make the right business decisions at the right time. We'll talk more about exit strategies and transitioning both a business and yourself in Chapters 8 and 9.

Forms of Entrepreneurship

Before we continue to talk about entrepreneurs, let's review commonly accepted perspectives of small businesses, early-stage companies, and growth companies. These aren't so much actual definitions as they vary widely from economic to social definitions. The SBA defines small businesses often by the number of employees—for example, under 500 people. Banks may add a financial definition, including revenues and net worth. The finance world and the government also like to differentiate businesses by revenues. This works for finance-related purposes, but the definition goes much deeper. There's a difference in the way the founder and management perceive the company's resources, options, and outlook. The truth is that there is no clear definition that's accepted by everyone—vendors, suppliers, financiers, and entrepreneurs.

For some, the difference between an early-stage or growth company and a small business depends on the stage of the business and perhaps the attitude of the entrepreneur. For this group, a small business is one that's likely to have been around for a number of years and has been at the same size in terms of revenues, numbers of employees, and so on. It's not likely to have a steep growth projection. An early-stage company is one that is relatively young in terms of the number of years it's been established and operating, usually under five years. It often has very strong growth projections. And, perhaps most relevant, its entrepreneur still expects the company to grow aggressively. The challenge is that the differences in the common perception, including government resources such as the SBA, make it difficult to lump these into one simple category, and efforts to address "small business" needs with a one-size-fits-all program usually fall far short.

Early-stage companies are generally considered engines of growth. Some people adhere to the traditional definitions of small, medium, and large enterprises, but that doesn't quite work in today's service-oriented economy. Do you differentiate based on sales, market capitalization, number of employees? Compared to other small businesses, what stage of growth is the company at?

Regardless of the type of entrepreneur you choose to be, realize that the entrepreneurial lifestyle is not likely to provide you with a standard 9-to-5 professional existence. Most entrepreneurs are constantly and consistently thinking about sales, products ideas, and market opportunities. Random events can trigger thoughts and ideas. This is just part of the entrepreneurial spirit. There are three basic ways to be an entrepreneur: sole proprietorship, lifestyle business, and growth company.

Sole Proprietorship

A sole proprietorship is just what it sounds like. You're running the company on your own and are often the only key employee. Consultants, artists, and others fit this category, as they are the company's product or service. This structure works well for people who may want to work from home for family or personal considerations.

Lifestyle Business

This category can be very misleading. Most people are quick to assume that these are very small companies, almost like sole proprietorships, and are not likely to have employees, structures, and so on.

"Lifestyle businesses" really refers to moderate growth, not always the size of the company. The entrepreneur has decided to opt against aggressive expansion or more rapid growth, usually for personal reasons, even if market conditions warrant it. Alternatively, some businesses may not have prospects for rapid growth as a result of a smaller market, even though the venture is profitable.

A lifestyle business can generate annual revenues of $100,000 or $30 million or even more. It's not the size of the company, but the approach of the entrepreneur and owner that distinguishes a lifestyle business. Many entrepreneurs start by assuming they will grow aggressively, but somewhere along the way they realize that reaching a certain revenue level affords them ample financial flexibility to meet their personal goals and objectives. Some may make the decision to accept more moderate growth for control reasons. They decide against expanding because they prefer to own everything and are content to be relatively debt free. Revenues may be $10 million, and if they are bringing in $1 to $2 million net to themselves, some may decide that it's the perfect operating level for them. Lifestyle businesses are still very focused on revenues and profitability, but they may not have the same exponential expectations as a fast-growth company.

Whether a lifestyle business is right or wrong for you really depends on your personal philosophy and goals, and how they evolve over time. There are hundreds of thousands of lifestyle businesses in existence, many below our radars, as we don't focus on them. Think about successful businesses in your community that may have been founded by their owners 10 or 20 years ago, and you're likely to discover a handful of lifestyle businesses.

One colleague represents this market well to me. She started an ad agency in California in the 1970s. In the first five years they experienced rapid growth and had two offices in San Francisco and Los Angeles. At that point, she and her husband, who assisted with parts of the business, had achieved their lofty financial goals. They had also started a family. She could have grown through acquisition, which would have required outside capital and investors to deal with, but opted against it. She had several homes, a private jet to commute between the offices, and was living a very comfortable lifestyle. She enjoyed her clients and her team and could achieve a happy balance between home and work. She opted at that point to grow moderately and pursue her venture as a lifestyle business. Being a $50 million agency was acceptable to her. She was no longer seduced by rapid expansion and all of the opportunities and headaches it might bring. She loved getting up every morning and going to work, and, even more, she relished the lack of outside investor involvement, which she felt might be a distraction. I'll talk more about investors and control issues in Chapter 3.

In my opinion and observation, lifestyle businesses are an underrated category filled with successful companies run by entrepreneurs fulfilling both their professional and personal goals. It's hard to anticipate what you will want in 3, 5, or 10 years after you start your venture. You need to be open to the options and not create rigid expectations that can't be modified as you progress.

The key is determining how big is big enough? The answer to this question is very personal and individual. You need to be sure that you allow yourself the personal flexibility to change your mind along the way, just as the California ad entrepreneur did.

Most of us start our ventures with huge dollar signs in our eyes, and let's face it, it sounds much more ambitious and professional to aim for high financial heights. But along the way, many of us realize that it's much more enjoyable to be able to reap the benefits of your venture and not worry prematurely about control or exit strategies. Most of us just want to keep doing what we do because we love it.

Growth Company

What sets a growth company apart from being a sole proprietor or lifestyle business is severalfold. First is the scope of the product or service. Some businesses just can't grow beyond the original founder and maybe one or two employees. Growth companies, as the category suggests, are poised for significant expansion. Second is the personal philosophy and goal of the entrepreneur. Third is how the entrepreneur manages the company's financial strategies. I am not just referring to whether or not he or she raises money, but at some point cash is needed to grow, whether it's to get larger space, hire more employees, or invest in some R&D or marketing and advertising. It requires more creative negotiations with customers, suppliers, lenders, and maybe even investors.

Expansion is a key component of growth. It's very challenging to go from being a small concern to a midsize business. Several issues impact every aspect of the business (we'll cover them more in Chapter 6), but the decision to expand or not to expand and the timing for any resulting expansion is critical for an entrepreneur. Becoming a $30 million company over 10 years is moderately paced growth. Achieving sales of $30 million in three to five years is aggressive growth and not achievable by most companies unless they have a unique product and/or outside investor support.

Should You Become an Entrepreneur?

Whatever your reasons for becoming an entrepreneur, understand and be clear about your personal motivations. This will help you enormously, as you need to make decisions and choices along the way.

As you go through the personal decision-making process, try to talk to as many people as you possibly can. Seek out others who have tried entrepreneurship, both those who have been successful and those who have not. Talk to people in your industry, including colleagues, friends, and potential advisors. You'd be surprised how open people can be about their experiences, good and bad. Of course, read lots of books and get a variety of opinions. You're not trying to get people's "permission" to be an entrepreneur, nor are you looking to give yourself permission. What you should strive for is to understand the factors critical to success and see if you're comfortable with them. There are no right or wrong answers. As I noted earlier, that's one of the reasons I decided to write this book and include "Tales from the Trenches," profiling real entrepreneurial experiences. Only another entrepreneur can tell you what it's like to lie awake at night stressing about whether you'll make payroll that month—we all have. But at the same time, it's the same entrepreneur who can tell you what successful strategy worked to make payroll that month as well as overcome the other challenges that creep up time and time again. It's not the issues that define you as an entrepreneur, but how you respond to those issues.

As you consider entrepreneurship, you need to assess whether it will provide you with the ability to support yourself and your family, both in the beginning and later on, when you eventually achieve your personal financial goals. Are you comfortable with the time it may take to grow and sustain your business? Many people start companies expecting them to grow aggressively in financial terms and then find that they are actually quite content with a profitable lifestyle business that allows them the ability to pursue other personal goals.

Think about what kind of growth you're comfortable with. Do you want a lifestyle business or an aggressive growth business? Both are commendable choices, and only you can make that decision.

As you decide to become an entrepreneur, take a look at your professional and personal support systems, particularly the latter. Are they supporting you or thinking you're off your rocker? Even if you are comfortable with the risks, uncertainties, and challenges, a spouse or other key family member may not be. Negative whisperings can cascade into thunder and rock the very confidence that's required in entrepreneurship. Be wary not only of your own demons, but also those of others around you.

Attitude is a key factor. If, deep down, you're happiest as a sole proprietor but talk about growing a company because it sounds so much better, then guess what? You're likely to stay a sole proprietor and defeat yourself subconsciously. Not only will you not grow your company, but you'll be unhappy and unfulfilled, even if your company is successful by financial and market definitions. Get in touch with what you really want and how you define success. Be comfortable and confident with the answers you arrive at for yourself. Confidence is a key component, as it will draw success to you by way of customers, investors, and supporters.

You also need to assess how you handle stress. How determined are you to succeed? Starting a business isn't always easy, and with the wrong support system, you may have more naysayers than coaches around you. Many businesses fold in the second year despite the fact that the next year might have been the turning point. Most entrepreneurs will tell you that they hit a key milestone of sustainability around year 3. If you can make it to that point, you can keep going, barring any unforeseen problems inside or outside the company. For example, you could be doing great, and then in year 5, your largest customer stumbles badly, creating a ripple effect in your company. If you've been astute enough to diversify, it should be no problem, but if not, you'll drown too. We'll talk more about the need for diversification and how to diversify your customer base in Chapter 4.

If you're choosing entrepreneurship as a response to a personal or professional transition, think through your motivations thoroughly. If you're starting a company because you were laid off from your last job, do you see it as a life-turning opportunity or are you treading water until a suitable full-time position becomes available? If a personal situation or crisis is motivating you to consider entrepreneurship as a way to balance your obligations, you may want to focus on being a sole proprietor for a while, as growing a company, of any size, is a very time- and energy-consuming endeavor.

Leaping from the Corporate World

As corporate life continues to offer less and less security and upside, more people are considering entrepreneurship. Some leave, taking their former corporate employer as their first customer. For others, it's an opportunity to enter an entirely new industry. For most of us, we're hoping to capitalize on our experience and know-how or on a new idea or market to fill a gap in our own industry.

Many entrepreneurs have actually discovered their vision and opportunity through a former employer. Karen See founded her first company, Abovo, by leaving her full-time job and taking her employer along as her first client. Success pounded down her door as she grew within three years to $15 million in service fees. Her Atlanta-based integrated marketing firm became the anointed local "diva" serving technology companies. Her leap, while successful, had some early starts and stops. Karen's motivation came from working for corporate managers who she felt lacked vision or work ethics, and sometimes both. She carefully planned her exit strategy, working on her business plan for three months with a colleague and partner-to-be and avoiding burning any bridges with her employer or clients. When her partner backed out at the last minute, she found herself questioning her ability to be an entrepreneur and reconsidered her decision to leave her job. Only after coaxing and commitments from two potential clients and the support of her husband did she finally decide to make the leap. The rest has been a wild ride of successes and challenges as she continues to grow her company. She's never looked back with any regret.

If you've spent your professional life in the corporate world, recognize that the early year or years of an entrepreneurial venture demand your very hands-on involvement. It's not a joke when I say that you should be ready to take out the garbage. Most of us have in the early days.

When you make the leap from corporate life to entrepreneurship, there are clearly some things to keep in mind. The biggest difference between being inside a large corporation and entrepreneurship is that entrepreneurs don't have a buffer between a mistake and total failure. When a large company makes a bad bet on a product or market, the damage gets absorbed, perhaps with a hit to earnings or the stock price at most. In an early-stage or growing company, a bad bet can destroy everything. There are no shock absorbers. This is one reason I don't buy into the concept of "intrapreneurship" that many large companies attempt to create inside their organizations. Sure, these internal groups may spur more innovation, but they're still far from the realities of entrepreneurship. They have far more resources than most new ventures. They are protected from feeling the immediate impact of failures and mistakes, and there's no immediate risk of losing a paycheck.

I'll talk much more about planning, budgeting, and funding in later chapters, but it's useful to note that large companies can often get away with making bad bets because the risk is less tangible to the person making the decision. An executive isn't going to lose his or her paycheck because of a bad deal, and spending too much is somewhat irrelevant because it isn't the professional's money to start with. The loss isn't personal. I had a controller whose wise response to me on every budget question was "It's your money." The entrepreneur has much more at stake with every step. If you're coming from a large institution, you need to be comfortable with this new reality.

In your own company, especially when it is in the early stages, a bad decision will probably result in a personal loss of money, whether it was paying an employee who didn't deliver or investing in a marketing or technology strategy that derailed. Even if you have outside investors, which we'll talk more about in Chapter 3, the loss of the company's money directly affects you. For example, you may have to raise more money, thereby diluting your equity stake.

I'm not pointing this out to scare people. Just the opposite. Entrepreneurship is one of most rewarding professional courses a person can take. I am not just referring to monetary gain, although that's certainly important for all of us. Entrepreneurship fulfills many of our unspoken dreams to create something lasting and real, to make a difference. Entrepreneurs who leave the corporate world are aware that entrepreneurship can offer an alternative to the corporate feeling that the company is going to keep plodding along no matter who is in each job. Further, entrepreneurship can remove the frustration of unspoken "corporate ceilings" and the difficulties of pursuing new ideas or taking on new challenges and opportunities.

By all means, I encourage all who are dissatisfied with corporate life and are considering entrepreneurship to make the leap. But do so with research, knowledge, and planning. It's essential to manage expectations and be prepared for new worlds.

Partnerships

As you think about what kind of entrepreneur you want to be, you may need to consider whether you want or need partners, either in terms of financing (which we'll talk about in Chapter 3) or strategy.

Family and Friends as Partners and Employees

You may be deciding whether you should be in business with your spouse, sibling, family member, or friend. If you are considering being in business with someone you know, you need to think about your compatibility and how the personal relationship will impact the business and vice versa.

My husband and I ended up working together in my second company, not by design but by circumstance. Because we hadn't anticipated his involvement, we didn't think about critical issues surrounding our working styles until much later, which is common for many entrepreneurs.

The following are some questions to ask yourselves up front. The answers are less relevant than going through the thought process and being comfortable with each of your answers.

1. Do you have similar work ethics? Do you both keep similar hours, or does one expect to put in substantially more or less, and is that acceptable to both of you?
2. Do you have similar approaches to quality and vision? Are you both committed in a complementary way to providing things like customer service or quality management?
3. What are your management styles, and are they complementary and suited to your industry? Is one of you a yeller? In some worlds, this is not only acceptable but required for effective management. In others, it's a huge taboo. Management and communication styles are particularly relevant if you come from varying industries that operate differently. Can that partner from the different industry make the transition?
4. How do you each handle challenges, stresses, and crises? Does one of you avoid challenges in the hopes that they will just go away? What's your mutual commitment level? Does one person expect others to take care of everything?
5. Is your personal relationship compatible with your professional roles? For example, if you are a parent and child, going into business together may mean that the relationship dynamics will continue. Is this suitable for your new venture?

There's no doubt more questions will arise as you begin to think about this. Spend time thinking about how the partnership or working relationship will function. Again, there are no right or wrong answers to the above questions. It's more important to be aware of some of the areas for both compatibility and incompatibility. Ideally, you're complementary in your approaches, and if you allocate roles and responsibilities early on, you're likely to go down the road to success. I'll discuss how partnerships impact new and growing ventures in relevant chapters.

As you consider entrepreneurship, don't let a fear of failure intimidate you. Believe in yourself and your idea. Of course, do your research and develop a thorough business plan. Be in touch with your personal philosophy, goals, and expectations. Many entrepreneurs are big on energy and enthusiasm, although not all have credentials in the exact industry they may be considering. Successful entrepreneurs follow a vision and pursue it with enthusiasm—believing in themselves the entire way.

CHAPTER 2

GETTING STARTED

W hen you decide to pursue your own company, getting started can seem either overwhelming or like an easy-to-manage linear process depending on your idea, your customer base, and your experience. From choosing a name and determining the right corporate structure to developing detailed business plans, all entrepreneurs have to take certain key steps.

What most entrepreneurs don't realize is that planning is a process, not just a checklist. It's the gradual and sometimes not-so-gradual evolution of your ideas and inspirations. Building a business into a sustainable organization takes time and planning.

As you start your venture, there are a number of issues you'll need to focus on. Planning is a catchall word that really encompasses many components, including the following:

- Choosing a company name
- Developing business plans
- Addressing personal and structural issues
- Managing legal and accounting issues
- Developing marketing and sales plans
- Developing contingency plans

For organizational purposes, I'll deal with the latter two in separate chapters, as both are more frequently dealt with during the course of a venture rather than at its outset. Having said that, you'll probably want to include components of a sales and marketing plan in your first draft, even though you may not be able to attend to them with the level of detail you will eventually give to it once you're up and running.

Choosing a Company Name

One of the first things you'll need to do is think of a name for your company. There are so many varying philosophies on naming companies that it's clear there is no right or wrong. Some people will tell you to make sure your name is clear and customers know what they are getting. Well, thank goodness Jeff Bezos didn't follow that line of thinking—Amazon turned out to be a great flexible name for a business that continues to evolve. Bezos' focus on finding a name that was at the beginning of the alphabet no longer matters in an Internet environment where listings are now "purchased" and are no longer just based on the alphabet.

Some people actually start the planning process before they finalize a name. Some change the name early in the life of their new venture when they have more information and market input. The name of your company should inspire you. If you like to get right to the point and clarity is very important to you, then make sure your name reflects that. If you prefer a vaguer name because you believe that you too will evolve over time, then go with that. Remember that good marketing can ensure your customers know who you are and what you can do for them. You don't have to rely on a name to communicate your mission to your customers.

Once you pick a name, do conduct a trademark search—you can do it for free yourself at www.pto.gov—and also see if the Web site is available. If you intend to get a lot of your business through the Web, you'll want to be sure that the Web site is easy to find and search for—in other words, it contains common search words through the engines; otherwise, you'll have to plan to spend both time and money optimizing it. Just remember that the Web is still evolving, and today's marketing and optimization strategies will not always be valid in just one year. It can become costly. On other hand, if your Web site simply supports your brick-and-mortar business, people will come directly to your site because of other promotions, and Web searches may not be as relevant or as critical. The real message here is that marketing strategies can change, but hopefully your very successful venture will be around for a long time—the name should be able to stand the test of time. Any changes in the name will require a budget for branding and marketing.

Do not bother spending any money on extensive market research. Informal research with advisors, potential customers, and colleagues is usually all you need. You can hire someone to design a logo and marketing materials but only after you have the basics of your marketing and sales strategy in place. More likely than not, you'll know your customer and market much better than a design firm.

Planning Process

Whether you're a first-time entrepreneur or a seasoned veteran, planning is something all entrepreneurs do; we just all do it differently. Think of it as a process and not as a checklist. All levels of planning require a sustained effort that evolves over time.

A business plan is an accumulation of the information and decisions made during the planning process, and it helps you articulate how you are going to seize and execute your great idea. There's great value in the exercise of going through the entire planning process and developing a business plan even if you never intend to use it for external purposes like fund-raising. It helps you organize your thoughts and strategies. It's important to include key management members in the planning process if you have them in place, as that will enable them to get a sense of ownership for their functional portion of the plan, budget, and areas of execution.

The process can help the entrepreneurial team ask key questions and challenge assumptions. It can help you identify potential risks and obstacles, many of which can be managed and overcome with advance planning. A plan is also a formal document that can be used to establish accounts and credit lines with your bank, as well as pursue investment options. It also provides a mechanism for you to monitor your progress and make modifications as needed.

Having said that, many great businesses were started by people who took a seat-of-their-pants approach. People like this will tell you that there was no formal plan at the start-up stage, although many probably created a plan later in the process. In most cases, however, the entrepreneurs were actively engaged in a planning process, even if a formal written plan was not prepared during the beginning stages.

People make many arguments against planning. It's out-of-date so quickly. You can't predict everything. It's time-consuming. It's tedious. The truth is that planning is something all entrepreneurs do—it's the level of the plan's formality that differs. A business plan is a written tool that helps increase the odds for success.

Developing a Business Plan

Let me start by clearly stating that I am not going to give you an overly theoretical overview of planning in this chapter. Rather, I have found it more useful to understand how different entrepreneurs have utilized the planning process. It's possible both to plan too much and to plan too little. The correct amount of planning really depends on your business and industry. Even the best business plan is not a guarantor of success. You need to pursue a combination of planning and actually operating in your market to guide your new venture to success.

Most successful entrepreneurs will tell you that they had distinct plans in their head, and many actually put those to paper. They may have not had a full plan pre-start-up, but somewhere in the early years they spent extensive time thinking about their goals and their time frame, which is in essence what useful planning is. Each business is likely to require a different level of planning. I have prepared business plans for all three of my companies, although the degree of polish and depth differed. You'll find that you'll need to modify your plan regularly as well to incorporate new information. A plan can actually be most helpful a year into your venture when you have tangible results and customer experiences.

The planning process really helps you avoid "talking to yourself" and hearing only what you want to hear. As you progress, you should share your plan with trusted and knowledgeable advisors and colleagues to get their input and suggestions. Advisors can help point out flaws in your logic, hopefully before it's too late. If you're using your plan for fund-raising, be sure to have your lawyer review the plan to be sure that the representations are appropriate and that there are no misleading statements.

There's usually a section in plans intended for prospective external investors that highlights the risk factors. To make your plan useful, you need to be honest with yourself at each stage of plan development in terms of what the risks and problems might be. Every business has some risks, although their severity differs significantly.

It's always helpful to find a successful entrepreneur to review your plan as well. He or she is more likely to identify operating challenges. A trusted industry expert can help review the marketing plan components. Don't hire a general reviewer or writer, unless he or she is functioning as a business consultant or investment banker in a broader capacity. A general reviewer or writer is likely to be a waste of your resources, as he or she is unlikely to know the business well enough.

You may not need a formal, colorful, and glossy plan, unless you expect to raise outside venture or strategic capital or to bring some angels on board. The most elaborate plans and budgets will not guarantee business success. As an entrepreneur, I know that it's what's in the plan that matters to you, not how good it looks. However, for the investment community, looks do matter, and a professional, glossy presentation will get you noticed faster, although substance will count far more after the initial glance.

If you're looking to raise capital, your plan will need to convince investors that you have a high-growth and leverageable opportunity, that you and your management team have identified a viable and realistic plan for success, and that you and your team are the right ones to execute the plan.

Going through the research, planning process, and actual writing of the plan can be incredibly time-consuming, even 100 to 200 or more hours over several months. As a result, some people consider hiring an outside consultant. Think and plan carefully before taking this step.

Going through the planning process allows you to carefully think through each aspect of your business. You need to intimately understand your market, customer, and opportunity. "Outsourcing" that planning work ensures that you miss critical information at key junctures. You may find that research challenges your original assumptions about your market, customers, or pricing model and presents you with different and better options. If you haven't done the research yourself, you may be wary of "trusting" any new strategies as a result of the information.

However, many entrepreneurs don't have the skills or experience to create a thorough business plan and financial projections. Most people actually lack the background to do the latter with enough understanding of how to build credible financial projections. Many entrepreneurs fail because they haven't focused enough on where the revenues will actually come from and when. Entrepreneurs often underestimate the costs required to get to certain revenue levels.

If you really need help, consider having an outside consultant prepare select sections of the business plan. Do not think that you can simply assign the full plan preparation to someone else and wait for that person to produce a useful business plan. You must be involved in the logic and reasoning. You still need to drive the research and talk to potential customers directly. If you are going to raise investment capital, a consultant or investment banker can enhance your draft, but you should prepare the first one. Determine where your strengths are and look for a consultant to supplement your weak areas. If like most entrepreneurs you need more help on the actual financial projections and assumptions, then look for a consultant who truly understands the numbers side of young ventures. Nevertheless, be sure you understand how the projections are developed and all of the logic and assumptions that are used to create them. After all, in a presentation or meeting, you'll be the one most likely "defending" your numbers, and you need to truly understand the building blocks of your business.

The best way to find qualified business consultants is to ask other entrepreneurs. Use referrals and ask to see what and how the consultant assisted with the company's planning process. You want someone who works alongside you and your team and strives to truly understand your market, your company, and its unique opportunity. Ideally, the consultant should have seasoned experience as an entrepreneur or with running a company as well as some industry experience.

A key part of the planning process is information gathering. Get out and talk to your likely customers and potential suppliers, as well as to other entrepreneurs and industry experts.

During the planning process, you'll need to consider a number of things, which at the macro level might include determining the best structure for your company (taking industry norms and personal preference into consideration), defining your market and customers, and determining the kind of staff you'll need and at which points.

Planning can seem somewhat insular as you try to anticipate everything, even with the best of contingency plans. For example, thousands of young and small businesses, as well as companies of all sizes, were deeply impacted by the 9/11 tragedy. Prior to 2001, it's unlikely that anyone could have anticipated or planned for such an event. Now, many of us think about how our businesses would be impacted in such national tragedy, whether in terms of our employees' well-being, our customers and sales, or our backup systems. We also spend time thinking about how our customers might be impacted in various scenarios. As we'll cover later, diversifying your customer base as early as possible is essential for long-term survival.

Your projections about marketing and sales should try to account for fluctuations in the general economy. How is your product or service impacted during recessions?

For companies at all different stages, business plans provide the broadest and most encompassing overview and road map. Business plans include sections on marketing and sales, but many companies also have a separate and more detailed marketing plan, which we'll cover more in Chapter 4. Contingency plans allow you to anticipate some of the obstacles and your reaction.

When you begin to put together a plan, know who your audience will be. Will you be using your plan primarily for yourself and for key employees or for external audiences, such as lenders and investors?

Initially, don't worry about how well your plan reads in terms of writing. You're not after a literary award; you're seeking to organize your goals and vision. Many people write a plan for outsiders only. While it's certainly likely that you may need to present your plan to a banker or to the investment community, you won't get much out of the exercise of developing a plan unless you write it primarily for yourself. These days, business plans often sound like they were written from the same "business plan factory." Forget about complex sentences, impressive words, or extravagant financials. Write to organize your vision and to create a tangible and realistic road map for yourself. Perhaps the most useful outcome of the planning process is the break-even set of projections and the milestones that need to be reached to get there.

Also, don't worry about writing too much. It's better to err on the side of including too much information in your draft, as this often helps you see your own logic and reasoning. You can always have a colleague or business copy editor edit your draft into a size and shape appropriate for the external audiences.

A good plan is to create a document that you will refer to over the course of the year. You should expect to refresh it, update it, and revise it based on results and new information. If it simply sits on your shelf gathering dust, it was a wasted exercise.

There are some very good industry resources already available on the technical aspects of writing good business plans, so I am not going to go through a detailed analysis of this exercise. Instead, I'll offer practical suggestions and advice to evaluate what kind of plan you need and the level of depth it should have based on the type of funding and involvement you anticipate. More resources are listed in Appendix B.

As you develop your plan, you're likely to have gaps in information, which is perfectly fine, but be sure to take note of the areas you would like to research more thoroughly in the future. For example, you may believe that there are global markets for your product or service, but in the beginning you lack the resources to assess and enter these markets. Your plan may simply state which countries you believe to be possible markets and then target a date when additional research will be conducted on these markets. You may even need to plan a budget to conduct that research, whether it's to travel or to hire a market consultant.

When you develop your plan, realize that it's the marketing and sales that are really critical. Most of us get enamored by our product and service and focus on them heavily. While understanding your product is essential, it's your unique selling proposition with regard to the product or service that's going to ensure you revenues, profitability, and viability.

Core Components of a Good Plan

So what really makes a good plan? There are, of course, standard ways of evaluating plans, but it's really the planning process that is most invaluable to the entrepreneur. The planning process allows you to test your assumptions about the business, industry, and market as well as the possible profitability scenarios. Most plans have the following sections.

Executive Summary

Executive summaries are really not intended for internal purposes, although you should be able to communicate the mission and purpose of your company in a few simple sentences.

In most cases, an executive summary is from one to three pages long and summarizes all of the key areas below. Companies that offer highly technical or complex products and services may find it difficult to keep their executive summaries brief. The goal of an executive summary is to hook your reader, who in many cases is a potential investor. In your first paragraph you should highlight the possible size of your market, especially if it is significant. A multibillion-dollar market will always catch a VC's (venture capitalist) eye, but your claim must be substantiated using the real data and research you will learn about in the "Market/Industry Research" section coming up in the chapter. Seasoned investors will quickly and easily challenge you if your facts and data are not in order.

A good executive summary is also a great way to hone your "elevator pitch"—that is, a convincing summary of your plan and opportunity that could be given in the one or two minutes it takes to ride an elevator. Even if you're not pursuing the investment community, it's an effective way to communicate your company's mission and focus to bankers, suppliers, and others.

Company and Product or Service Description

What are you selling? Describe your product. You don't need to have pages of technical detail, but clearly outline your product's or service's features and benefits. Use this section to highlight how your product or service will meet a critical market opportunity. Use photos or other visual representations if you can.

Indicate if your product has a unique methodology or patentable technology or architecture. You should not disclose any sensitive information in this section. Business plans are usually submitted to investors before a presentation. If an investor continues to express interest, you can provide confidential information at a later date, after having him or her sign a confidentiality agreement or provide similar protection.

This is the section where you can let your passion and vision shine through. You can discuss your growth strategy and the reason your company is best poised to leverage the perceived market opportunity.

Market/Industry Research

In this section, you'll need to describe the market or industry or industries that your products and services fit into. If there are multiple markets, that is even better. Size is usually a key factor for this section. How big is your potential market? When you define the size of your market, substantiate it with research.

You may want to look at the low-hanging fruit first, the markets you'll easily enter in the first one or two years. Make a note about potential markets that you will look at in years 2 to 4 after you've reached financial and other milestones. For example, there may be good markets in different countries. You might be able to repackage your product and sell into different channels. Get creative. Understanding the various market opportunities also ties directly into determining how you sell.

A point of caution: While you may see multiple markets or envision several product lines from the outset, realize that you can't pursue them all at the same time without spreading yourself too thin. Focus on the low-hanging fruit first, wait until your company breaks even, and then think about expansion opportunities.

Identify how much of the market you intend to capture and in what period of time. No one is expecting instant results or success, so substantiate this part by referencing the financials.

Competition

Do plenty of research as you develop this section, as it's one of the most critical factors. Who else does what you do? Why will people buy your product versus someone else's? What will be your unique selling proposition (USP)? How are you differentiating your product or service—by price, quality, features, service, and so on? And, quite importantly, does your customer care? That is, if you plan to compete on price, are your customers price-sensitive or are they brand-conscious and willing to pay for a perceived benefit?

Sales and Marketing

How will you sell to your likely customers? Will you go direct? What would be the costs of that? Would you sell through an intermediary? What would be the costs of that? How do your competitors sell?

As part of your sales and marketing efforts, you'll find that a detailed marketing plan is very useful. A good marketing plan includes not only the strategy and vision for taking your products or services to market, but also the required staffing, detailed pricing strategies, advertising, promotions, sales events, and other details, as well as the costs associated with each. You'll develop a marketing budget that is part of your overall planning budget. We'll talk more about developing a marketing plan in Chapter 4. If your plan is for internal purposes only, you may merge all of it in one document. If you intend to use the plan for external purposes, then the detailed marketing plan does not need to be included, but it should be summarized here. What you need in the plan is an overview of the marketing strategy, key factors you need to get to market, and your selling strategy.

Management Team

You're the most critical person on your management team. Instead of listing people involved in your company, first note positions that are required to start and operate your company. Identify the positions that are already filled. For those positions that are still vacant, list the skills that are needed to fill them. Bios of existing team members are essential. If you're raising investment capital, it's important to note if your investors will contribute key management members and, if so, which ones and when.

If you have a board of directors and/or an advisory board in place or in formation, list them in the plan. (Please refer to Chapter 5 for more suggestions on developing boards.) This part of the plan is most relevant to potential investors, and if your board has impressive industry credentials, you may consider listing this portion at the end of or directly after the executive summary. There's some flexibility in the order of the sections; while your summary ought to be logical in flow, you can manipulate the order to cast the best possible light on your project. Just be clear in the table of contents as to where each section is— don't make an investor or reader search. In general, each section should lead naturally into the next one.

Opportunities and Risks

This section is often intended for external investors, but you can consider summarizing the opportunities and risks for yourself, particularly if you're still deciding whether or not to pursue your idea.

Financial Offering

This section is only necessary if you are pursuing the investment community. Some may actually include a term sheet here or directly after the executive summary. If you use a term sheet, be sure to include the range of financing you're looking for, the investment that's being offered, and related terms. Plan to get external counsel on developing the term sheet. Many VCs will actually send you their own, but it can be an advantage to start with your "wished for" version, especially if you anticipate multiple investors.

Financial Projections

Putting together realistic projections is the most critical part of your plan. Your sales and marketing efforts may be sound, but if you're not sure what it will take to break even or become profitable, you're likely to run into challenges.

Financial projections can be either straightforward or complex depending on your audience. There are plenty of resources on developing step-by-step projections. For example, you can find sample projections in formats suitable for VCs online or in the books listed in Appendix B. One useful resource is *Business Plans That Work: A Guide for Small Business* by Timmons, Zacharakis, and Spinelli. Projections are always presented in a spreadsheet format, usually in Excel, but you'll also need supporting detailed text, not just a few footnotes. The supporting notes should detail your assumptions for all of the numbers. The core statements in the projections should include the basics:

- Income statement
- Cash flow
- Balance sheet

There are also additional supporting spreadsheets that will provide the basis for key numbers on these statements. The sales numbers will likely come from a customer-driven spreadsheet indicating how the number of customers and price points will result in various sales levels.

Your projected cash flow is critical, as it will really show when the venture will provide cash and what its uses will be and any projected shortfalls. It will help identify how much outside capital you'll need and when you will need it or when you will need to adjust expenses to reduce any shortfalls. You should include an additional statement that indicates the sources and uses of funds.

The balance sheet shows how a business is capitalized. You'll find that you need a balance sheet for your regular banker. To a potential investor, your balance sheet also indicates the strength of a company and who else is involved and through what kinds of structures.

Developing projections can be a tough exercise if you plan to raise external investment capital. You may be told that it's important to have impressive projections, and, indeed, for many VCs, a huge market combined with aggressive projections are important. However, I would caution against starting with potential external readers as the basis for creating your projections.

Draft your first set of projections for internal use with your team. Don't worry about impressing others. In fact, more conservative and internally generated projections can help you determine whether investment capital is necessary and right for you. Even if you need capital to start, well-thought-out projections can indicate what you really need and when. You can then survey the range of options that is highlighted in Chapter 3.

When you're doing financial projections, develop two or three scenarios. Your optimistic scenario should reflect your hopes, while your base case assumes that sales will be lower and slower than hoped for and expenses higher by 25 to 30 percent. Plan for things to go awry. If your plan necessitates that everything go exactly as planned, you're likely to face some challenges early on. Focus on cash flow and not booked revenues. Assume the timetable will be one and a half to two times longer than expected. The biggest mistake many first-time entrepreneurs make is assuming that a sale means cash. It can take customers weeks or months to pay, and some contracts may call for payments over the course of a year. If you can, try to get as much cash up front from customers as possible. It's in essence a source of funding, as I'll talk about in Chapter 3. Some companies have to give customers incentives to pay early by giving discounts. Make sure your projections account for this as well. Plan on having your likely customers enter into purchase orders or letters of commitment. Letters of intent are much more vague and really don't have any repercussions to customers by way of penalties or fees if they refuse to purchase later on. Incentivize the order. There are ways to finance a purchase order and/or invoice, but not a letter of intent.

Also, when you do your financial plans, keep the accounting simple. Large companies can fool themselves with creative accounting, but early-stage companies have no margin for error. The most important financial document for early-stage companies is the cash flow statement. For all of my companies, we have also used daily cash reconciliation so we always know exactly how much cash is in the bank at any given time. Plan for this process.

If you are not taking a paycheck or someone else is performing a function but not yet receiving compensation for it, put it in your plan. Expect to start paying the compensation somewhere in the first or second year. You can't go on indefinitely without a paycheck, so you need to plan for it early on. It should also be a part of any break-even projections.

We all hear that most early-stage companies fail because they don't have enough working capital. Honest assessments are critical here.

As part of your planning process, it's also useful to spend a bit of time developing milestones and benchmarks for you to achieve, by which you can judge your success. For example, "the company has to break even by X date, or I will need to reconsider my full-time involvement." Be clear with yourself about how much you're putting in and at what benchmark you'll stop putting in funds. It may not be a financial benchmark, but a customer one. Your planning process may require a certain number of customers averaging X revenues each. Your benchmark may focus on the schedule for securing customers with another set of benchmarks on the revenues and cash flows from those customers.

Structural and Personal Issues

Staffing

As you work on determining how best to staff your company and what kinds of people and skill sets you'll need and at which stages, you'll need to determine what kind of role you want and are happy with. Are you happiest running everything operationally and strategically, or is your time best spent staying close to the heart of the business, such as being the head of creative team or research and development. If you decide to take on a more functional role, you may need someone to function as a chief operating officer (COO) at some point in the growth stages.

Avoid hiring the "crack team." Don't hire big guns early on. You don't need them to sell your products or service. Most are rarely worth their big salaries and often come at a loss to young companies. Further, many lack the temperament to make it in an early-stage or growing company, which usually have less support staff and other resources.

Better yet, look for diamonds in the rough. People who have the right basic skills and experience and who can be trained. This group is likely to want to build their résumés and may eventually leave your firm, but not before providing significant value.

When it comes to creating an organizational structure, think again about your own style and philosophy. What environments are you most comfortable in and where would you prefer to work?

Roles, Responsibilities, and Other Issues in a Partnership

Most entrepreneurs who have a partner make the mistake of not delineating formally and in writing who has responsibility for what. While it's easy to generalize that one is sales or external and the other is internal, it's the day-to-day details that need to be clearly defined. It can also be confusing to employees who may not be clear as to which partner has final authority and over which matters. Vagueness may work in the very beginning when there are too few employees and far more work, so everyone does a little of everything. Clarity of roles is helpful to partners, employees, and outsiders—even if those roles evolve.

If you expect to co-run the company, ask yourself whether you have discussed roles and responsibilities, which, if not clearly defined, can present bumps along the way. Are you both absolutely comfortable with the give-and-take that will be required? Or, does one of you expect to be the "driver." Often, the person with the idea or vision will naturally be the driver, as employees, customers, and even investors will turn to that person for direction. Both partners need to be comfortable with this reality.

As you set up the company, you'll also need to consider the contribution of key players or partners. Is each of you putting in equal dollars, or is one bringing a tangible contribution and the other(s) an intangible? Also, just because you have joint ownership interests does not mean that you need to work together or that you both need to contribute the same amount of capital. Just because you plan to work together, you don't need to automatically have an equal ownership interest. In fact, most start-ups with family members or spouses involved do not always have equal ownership unless there is equal and required involvement. For example, as often happens in the early stages, if one spouse or family member is just going to manage the books and administrative and operational issues, then equal ownership is probably not needed. It can be misleading if you have not clearly identified roles and responsibilities.

In a situation in which you are dealing with friends and family, ownership issues are key. Always keep in mind the worst-case scenario. For example, if a marriage fails, you don't want to jeopardize your company because of a 50/50 stake. Over the years, I have heard of a good number of companies whose futures became hostage to a divorce process. If you retain all or a significant majority of your company's shares, your spouse cannot elect to close a business. At best, he or she can get a financial settlement, but your company continues to operate, much less affected.

It may sound harsh, but you don't need to show your commitment to someone by giving them 50 percent of your company. Actual ownership of equity percentages differs from control factors. One person or entity can own less than 50 percent of the shares and still have certain control capabilities. This is important, whether you're structuring a partnership, getting outside investors, or determining the right mix with family and friends. It's also relevant if you intend to apply to the SBA for minority- or woman-owned classification for both public- and private-sector opportunities. Determine which definitions and classifications work best for your company and market.

Another factor that's key with partnerships is exit strategies. After a few years, one of you may want out. How do you achieve getting out or exiting the business if the other partner doesn't want to sell or buy you out? Can you sell your share to someone else? While it won't address every scenario, put together a partnership agreement in the first year when you're both more likely to be rationale about some of these issues. Good agreements won't establish a price for a buyout but will establish a procedure to address these issues and formulas for determining the price. For example, the agreement may say that if one partner wants out, the other partner has one to three years to decide to sell or buy the partner out. The formula to determine the buyout price may be in the agreement, or the agreement may be to hire an investment bank to do a valuation and the buyout price is 80 percent of that valuation to be paid over x years. Since, in the first year, neither partner is likely to know which one of them might exercise such a provision, the agreement is likely to be moderate and acceptable to both. You should plan to use a good lawyer to help with this type of agreement. Even if you are just starting your venture, it's worth reading Chapter 9 on exit strategies now as well as later in your growth cycle.

Tales from the Trenches

In 1978, Gail Koff became the third partner in the legal business that became Jacoby & Meyers. She was based on the East Coast and offered the two California partners a chance to take their mission nationally, providing quality legal services to the general public, an unusual concept at the time. While the three had a basic partnership agreement from the early days, there was no provision for exit strategies or a buyout provision, a shortcoming that would come to haunt the partners 15 years later. In the early 1990s, because of strategic and operating differences as well as the changing nature of the business, Gail Koff and Stephen Meyers sought to buy out Leonard Jacoby.

The ensuing haggling consumed their attention and resources as they negotiated for several years. Finally, a buyout was achieved through mediation under the threat of expensive and messy litigation. The terms agreed to under the mediation were not in the best long-term interest of the firm and included a divided ownership of the name. It took Jacoby and Koff close to 10 years to redefine their relationship. In the interim, the firm lost many opportunities because of complications stemming from the prolonged and difficult process. Originally, to meet the needs of their investors, the three had not included a buyout formula or mechanism in the partnership agreement. In hindsight, Gail strongly recommends that entrepreneurs stipulate a mechanism for legal and financial issues in any partnership agreement.

Shortly after the agreement on a buyout, Gail's remaining partner, Meyers, was tragically killed in a car crash. Their partnership agreement had a provision on buying out a surviving spouse by maintaining life insurance on each partner, paid for by the company. Unfortunately, because of normal operating challenges and cash flow demands, the company had elected not to pay the key man insurance. This key man insurance would have been extremely useful in addressing outstanding financial obligations. Gail eventually worked out the financial situation, but not without liquidating her personal assets. Key man insurance is important for any venture. Most people involved with entrepreneurial firms just don't anticipate the premature death of a partner, entrepreneur, or key team member and the resulting financial obligations, many of which can be addressed with insurance.

Gail's personal commitment for social change and to the company's founding mission of growing a national law firm for the general public has remained high throughout the decades, and her experiences have helped her find creative solutions to meet the needs of the company's clients and employees. Her experiences highlight how essential partnership agreements are and how critical simple policies and procedures can be to the long-term viability of your company. Many entrepreneurs try to go without insurance or without fully clarifying partner issues. It's possible that they will never need to enter negotiations, but in many cases it takes extensive and disruptive litigation to resolve issues that planning and partnership agreements can help avoid.

As many people do, Gail sees partnerships like marriages, with stresses, issues, and resentments that can build over time. The critical issue is how to address and resolve these evolving challenges. It's hard to anticipate the wide range of things that can happen over the course of time, inside the company as well as in the market and industry. Carefully thought-out partnership agreements that provide mechanisms not only for financial and legal issues but also for resolving management differences through such things as mediators or consultants can go a long way toward ensuring the company's viability.

Accounting and Legal

Choosing the right type of person to oversee the books and make financial decisions is critical. When you're in the very early stages, you can probably use QuickBooks software and manage the books yourself. As you grow, you'll eventually need a bookkeeper to enter bills, as well as file and cut checks. If you need to set up the accounting system, you may opt for a more senior bookkeeper, finance manager, or accountant. Often, seasoned professionals are available on a part-time basis. At the early stages, make sure you're the only one with check-signing authority.

As you get larger, you may need to transition to a controller or chief financial officer (CFO) with experience in larger companies. If you're planning to seek investment funding, you'll find that a CFO with experience in dealing with the outside investment community can be very valuable.

A good CFO should be able to craft a financial vision for the company that complements your strategic plan and vision. He or she should be able to advise on how best to finance growth and expansion. The CFO should be able to offer insight on how to craft deals with customers and vendors. In many cases, he or she may have to deal and negotiate directly with the purchasing departments of your larger customers. The best CFOs are then those with business and finance backgrounds.

Now the reality. Depending on the size of your company, you may be looking for champagne on a beer budget. If you can't afford a seasoned CFO with VC experience but need to interact with the investment community, one option is to assemble a team of senior managers who will lend their names and résumés for the business plan stage for an agreed-upon compensation that includes equity and cash as well as other benefits. These agreements are important in your discussions with potential investors, as they want to know what their "investment" will buy—that is, what the uses of their investment will be. However, you should note that some VCs will actually expect to place their CFO in the company and will not want to hire yours. So be prepared to be flexible. An alternative option is to find the diamond in the rough: someone who is both presentable and knowledgeable on finance, and who may be willing to be the comptroller in the event the VC installs his or her own CFO.

Among the various controllers and bookkeepers I've hired, one stood out. He was not quite a CFO, since he lacked the business and VC experience to meet effectively with investors, as some were quick to inform me. But he was sharp in daily financial management and personable, which was important, since a controller or finance manager is likely to be your daily financial liaison with clients and vendors. Further, he was able to provide seasoned and useful advice in establishing processes and procedures, a critical factor when developing your senior team. Whoever you hire for this position needs to be able to encourage clients to pay faster, and sometimes even convince vendors to wait longer for their payments.

Finding the Right Advisors

You'll need to have different lawyers for different advisory functions. During your start-up and growth stages, you'll need advice on areas including corporate law, contracts, human resources (HR), and even collections. Law firms will tell you that they can do it all, but be very aware of how they bill and make sure you avoid overpaying. Over time, you'll see how much certain tasks cost, and you'll find out if you can get fixed rates. At the risk of annoying a few colleagues, I'll note that the larger firms tend to add extra items to their bills, even billing clients for coffee and snacks served at meetings. Large law firms are often used to working with large companies who are less likely to scrutinize bills. For example, they commonly bill you for internal conferences between lawyers who need to discuss matters relating to your business. You need to determine if this is valid and what is an acceptable time period. Look for consistencies and raise discrepancies early on. Most firms will make adjustments.

Like many entrepreneurs, I've used a large law firm and seen six-figure annual bills. I've also used small contract lawyers who charged flat fees by the agreement. It's important to remember that money doesn't always buy you the attention that your business needs. The best legal work came when I had a personal friendship as well as a professional relationship with the partner managing our business. We didn't get billed for every five-minute phone call. You need a lawyer for whom your business is relevant and important.

You need to be clear about what issue you need assistance with. If you have a more complex legal matter, you're better off paying more for a seasoned and knowledgeable lawyer. A good junior associate should be able to easily complete simple contracts, set up HR policies, or file basic trademark applications. Negotiate the rates for all work, especially these simpler matters. Don't assume that you need to give all of your legal work to one firm. Shop around.

If you're filing a patent, there are firms that specialize in patents and that often do flat rates for the bulk of the work. Even though it can take years to be approved, your patent is protected from the day of filing, assuming it is eventually approved. Use the trademark and copyright symbols on all materials and packaging even if you have not received final approval. Copyrights are the easiest to file, and you can usually do so yourself, although having a good lawyer to perform these services is usually worth the time and money, as you ought to be focused on running and growing your business.

Many lawyers are active in the VC industry as well and actively seek early-stage and growth companies in the hopes of increasing their business as you grow. If you access the investment market, your VC may be able to make suggestions on law firms. Just be sure that the VC does not give them other business; otherwise, your lawyers may have a conflict of interest, even if it is not directly related to your business. In challenging situations, they are less likely to get tough with the VC if the law firm generates significant revenues from the same VC.

Accountants are a bit more straightforward to find. There are many who focus on the early-stage and growth companies. For the first year or two, you'll really only need tax-related work. Once you have outside investors or when you get ready to sell your company, you'll need to consider having audited financials prepared at year-end. It is best to find both lawyers and accountants through referrals.

Choosing a Structure

Choosing a structure is important up front. Start with the most basic notion that a corporate structure will protect you. Unless you choose a corporate form of structure, the law assumes that you are your business—you're a sole proprietor. Even though you're taxed at the personal tax rates, you're personally liable for all business debts. If someone sues the business, that person can in essence go after your assets.

Each type of structure then provides different types of protections and benefits—at a cost since the tax basis is different for each. Deciding to incorporate is a decision that you'll need to make based on legal and accounting advice. Your company will be governed under the laws of the state in which you incorporate. If you are doing business primarily in a state other than the state of incorporation, you'll need a certificate for doing business in that state. There may also be tax ramifications.

Most companies choose Delaware for its straightforward legal code and low tax basis. Appendix A has a summary of the common forms of structure in Delaware. There are seven basic forms of structures, although four of them are the most popular. Some are more suited for certain industries and financial arrangements, so use this only as a guide and first resource. Get proper legal and tax advice before you make your final selection.

You should note that if you try to change the corporate structure later on, you may incur taxes or find that some options are not available for you. For example, you can choose to be an S corporation and later elect to be a C corporation, but you can't go the other way around. Choosing to be a corporation and then trying to elect limited liability corporation (LLC) or partnership status later may incur taxes, as the first entity will usually need to be sold to the new entity.

Also, if you are considering multiple shareholders, it's to their benefit to have founder's shares, as their cost basis will be higher if they "purchase" in later on, since, technically, the company will be deemed to have a value.

Structure is also important if you are not sure whether you are raising outside capital. Most VCs prefer to fund a C corp, which gives them the most flexibility on exit strategies, including the public markets. They also want to be sure that there's a plan for developing a board and possibly a team of advisors and that the structure will accommodate compensating and incentivizing them. Please see Chapter 5 for more on boards and advisors.

As you go through the planning process, keep in mind that everyone makes mistakes, even very serious ones. It's really how you deal with and manage these mistakes that defines you and your business. Plan to make frequent changes along the way and have a fluid process as your company grows.

CHAPTER 3

FUNDING

Deciding how to capitalize your company is one of the most critical decisions you can make in the early stage. Funding can be one of the biggest challenges for a start-up company as well as a growing company. Product companies typically require more start-up resources than companies in the service sector, although that can depend on the stage of development, customer requirements, and barriers to entry.

Deciding how to best fund your company can not only mean the difference between success and failure, but it can also significantly impact your personal situation if for any reason the company doesn't succeed as you planned or in the timetable originally envisioned—both very real possibilities for many entrepreneurs.

At the core of the funding issue is the fact that you need to fund your business with as much money as you are comfortable using and from the sources with which you're most at ease. I've started three companies, all of which varied significantly in their amount of start-up funding, from three figures to seven figures. There is no "right amount." You need to determine where your comfort level is and what your particular business really needs to either get your first few customers or to get to cash flow positive. You can have too much money as well as too little. Feeling a bit like Goldilocks, I must say that there's a perfect range in the middle that will enable you to execute your business plan without forgetting that you're in the early growth stages.

You also need to be mindful of not only how much you need but when you need it. Raising capital in any form and from any group is time-consuming. Obviously, some groups require more time than others. A lot of people waste time in the early years raising money rather than focusing on the business. Determine how far you can get your business with minimal external resources, and then focus on achieving that level of success. For some companies, achieving success is proof of concept; for most, it's proof of market with tangible sales results. Obviously, if you need capital for initial R&D, you should choose from the options outlined in this chapter. But as a rule, try to get as far as you can before raising capital. Not only will your time be well spent, but when you do need to raise capital, it will likely be cheaper, as your valuation will be higher.

In this chapter, I'll cover funding for both start-ups and expansion. Many options are similar for both, although the cost will obviously differ depending on the stage of your company. In each of the sections, I try to highlight the risks associated with each type of capital and fundraising. Far from being a pessimist, I believe it's all too easy to minimize risks, particularly when you're focused on the upside. It's managing risks and expectations as well as understanding the capital options that is critical for start-up and growth companies. Remember, start-ups are high risk. Even sales contracts are not guarantees, as your customers' financial conditions can change.

Yours

As you decide how to finance your company, you'll have to determine whether you'll use *your* personal access to capital, debt, or equity, or *theirs*—outside sources, lenders or investors—to meet your company's funding needs. It can deeply impact how you run your company.

Personal Assets

Your own assets. How much are you willing to lose? Some people are willing to sell their homes, investments, and any other personal assets to help fund a business. I did. However, more often, people don't *start* by selling the bulk of their assets or some such grandiose but usually foolish gesture. Usually there is a sum of money, obtained from a home equity line of credit, personal loan, savings, or loans against insurance or retirement assets. The challenge for entrepreneurs is to know when to say "enough" in terms of putting in their own money. It's a bit like being in Vegas and saying "My maximum pot to gamble from is x dollars. When I hit that, I'll stop no matter what." It's usually easier said than done, as most casual gamblers can attest to.

Like most entrepreneurs, I've misjudged how much of my capital my company will require and found myself putting in more and more over time. Businesses almost always require more money and time than anticipated to reach profitability and sustainability. Typically, the golden rule is that sales take twice as long to materialize and expenses are usually double what entrepreneurs anticipate. Using your own assets, while free of some of the pressures associated with outside funding (see below), can be a deceptively slow IV drip into your company. Before you know it, you've used far more than you had ever anticipated.

The lesson here is that it's perfectly fine to use your own assets if you've put some thought into the planning and budgeting phase, but expect to put in more than twice what your plan calls for. You should also be prepared to lose some or all of it and be able to support yourself until your company is revenue-generating, breakeven, and, eventually, profitable.

Credit Cards

Credit cards have funded many businesses, some successful and some not. Again, think through the repayment strategy. Make sure that you can make payments for at least the first year or two without sales. Many have high interest rates, and falling behind on payments will affect your credit rating, which will in turn impact your ability to get more credit, rent an apartment, or buy a home and other basic assets.

If you decide to use credit cards to either fund your business or to pay for expenses, look for ones with the best marketing programs, especially for frequent flyer miles. These added benefits can help you save cash for other critical expenses.

Credit cards typically provide only a small amount of funding that is usually inadequate for most growing companies. However, if you decide that's all you need, then credit cards may work for you, as they did for Liz Elting of TransPerfect/Translations.com, who started her business with $5,000 on a credit card and managed to grow in 12 years to become a $50 million global translation company.

Loans

Plan ahead and get some type of loan in place. Lines of credit are usually the most flexible types of loans, and you should set one up as early as possible, even if you never intend to use it. These are, in essence, loans you can borrow from, repay, and then borrow from again from time to time. With a line of credit, you do not need to take the money up front, and there are usually no conditions on how and when you can access the funds as long as you make the minimum monthly payment, which is usually interest and a small principal payment. You may pay a small annual fee for having the line available to you. It's worth it, even if you don't use it. It's peace of mind, which will allow you on a second's notice to respond to a capital need.

With a term loan, you get all of the money up front and start to pay interest on day one. Term loans may be cheaper than revolving loans if you need the money immediately or if it's for a capital purchase like equipment. Lines of credit are good ways to finance your receivables, as you may need to make payroll and other operational payments while waiting for a receivable to come in. A line is usually better than a term loan, unless you expect to use all of the cash up front for buying product or equipment.

Both types of loans can be secured and unsecured. A loan is "secured" when something or someone (usually you) is guaranteeing payment. It can also be secured by an asset like your house or an investment account. Be very wary of securing a business loan with personal accounts. No one likes to think of the downside in life, possibly even bankruptcy, but it happens to hundreds of thousands of businesses, and it could happen to yours.

Many banks and commercial finance companies, like GE or American Express, offer lines of credit of $20,000 to $50,000 that are personally guaranteed. There are commercial finance companies that can offer lines up to $1.5 million and sometimes even more, but the terms can be expensive. The size of the loan usually depends on the creditworthiness of the entrepreneur or signer. While these may not be secured by an asset, you'll need to personally guarantee them, so be sure you can make the monthly payments and can handle the personal obligation. Pay attention to fees and be sure to compare interest rates. While those that offer lower-interest-only payments for the first two years or so are appealing from a cash flow perspective, remember that you're paying more for the loan over its entire life. Also, make sure that there are no prepayment penalties. Once sales kick in, these are the types of expenses you'll want to repay quickly, especially if you have personally guaranteed them.

Some people will take out a home equity loan to finance a venture or expansion. While you won't have to give up any equity to an outside investor, remember that this is your home and you need to be able to make sure the payments will be made in a timely manner every month or you may risk a default and problems on the home front.

Theirs

Debt or Equity

When you're first setting up your company and even as you grow, you'll often have to decide between funding your company with debt or equity. Very simply, *debt* is money that's borrowed and must be repaid. *Equity* is money that is invested in return for a percentage of ownership, but is not guaranteed in terms of repayment.

As such, debt requires repayment with a fixed return in the form of interest, although certain types of debt allow the lender to benefit if all goes well. The previous section talked about basic loans and lines of credit, which are the simplest forms of debt. Investment funds and VCs can also provide funding in the form of debt or convertible debt, which simply gives them the right to convert their debt to equity through a predetermined formula or price.

Equity as an investment does not guarantee repayment, but it provides for a higher upside. Equity equals ownership, and understand that, if you choose this route, you'll share ownership of your company with one or more investors. All types of funding sources can provide you with capital in the form of debt or equity or sometimes a combination. However, there are some basic principles to keep in mind.

Debt can be *senior, senior secured*, or *subordinated*, depending on its priority in the capital structure. Priority is most relevant in the event a company is liquidated. Debt that is senior or senior secured enables those lenders to get their money out first, with the latter usually having the highest preferred position. Subordinated debt takes lower priority but is higher than equity. As a result, most lenders prefer their debt to be senior and usually secured by the assets of the company, if possible. Many lenders may seek to secure the debt with your personal guaranty. Again, think very carefully before you take this step.

Some investors look to invest as convertible debt, which allows them the best of both features. In the negative scenario, the convertible debt gets out first, especially if it's senior and secured. In a sale or merger, the convertible debt can benefit from the upside by converting to equity. It's easy to negotiate good scenarios. It's the negative cases that are harder. Lenders and investors like to have liquidation preference. The higher the preference, the better for many.

A key factor of equity is a concept called *valuation*, which refers, in essence, to how much your company is worth. Most start-ups have very little value. Early-stage companies that have a proven product or market, as indicated by a customer commitment, have a higher value, although the exact number is often debated and an assortment of complex formulas and approaches considered. There is no golden number. Entrepreneurs love to jack up the value of their companies, and as I'll note below, investors and VCs will make relentless efforts to bring down the valuation as much as possible before their investment. Accordingly, the approach for determining valuation differs for each.

The following sections cover some of the sources for your capital, whether it's debt or equity or a combination. The first two sources of early capital are from family and friends and angels.

Friends and Family

Friends and family are often the toughest category. In some instances, friends and family may function like angels and are included in the same round of financing as early angels.

Every entrepreneur will most likely warn you about the dangers of taking money from friends and family. Every VC will tell you to get your first money there. The reality is that it may be your only option early on.

It's important to recognize that while investors invest in a deal, family and friends are likely to invest in you. This means that they are likely to see their contribution as a "loan" (regardless of the technical structure) and not as an at-risk investment, unless of course all goes fabulously well, and then the higher returns of an investment are expected. Putting aside any legalities for a moment, should things not work out as expected, you'll probably feel the need to make good on any investments that go south somehow in the long run; otherwise, you'll suffer through many awkward family holidays.

Treat your friends and family much as you would an angel investor. Make a formal presentation, and give them a business plan. Make sure they understand that their investment is at risk, although keep in mind the reality noted previously. You're not their stockbroker, and they aren't investing in Coca-Cola. This is not a sure thing, and it is far from secure. You certainly expect it to do well. Point out how you have invested your money, time, or skills and are deeply committed to the success of the venture. The reality is that most friends and family, as do many angels and VCs, invest in you, the entrepreneur. Their confidence in you may make them blind to the realities of the risk level. Hopefully, you'll spend more holidays toasting to your mutual success together, but you need to be mindful of the relationship risks if things do not go as planned.

Angels

Angels are typically people who invest in the very early stages of companies, including start-ups. The more supportive and valuable angels tend to be those with extensive senior experience in your industry. They can bring not only early financing, but access to customers, partners, and possibly venture capital or secondary financing.

Finding Angels

You can find angels in several ways. The first is by networking in your own industry. Look for those who have been successful. Consider former colleagues, customers, industry experts, and even unrelated service professionals who have personal wealth like doctors and dentists.

There are individuals who help early-stage companies find capital either from angels or VCs. The more successful and experienced intermediaries require a success fee and may actually prescreen you and your firm and only take candidates they are confident of finding funding for. Some may ask for a retainer. Be wary. A retainer or fee is only warranted if they are doing significant work like writing or fine-tuning the business plan and presentation. Opening their Rolodex, while valuable, warrants a success fee, not a retainer. You can, however, agree to reimburse all mutually agreed-upon expenses incurred on behalf of your fund-raising efforts.

Another way is through the many angel groups. This can be a bit trickier. Some angel groups are organized by industry, others are geographic, and still others are more random. There are online sites, but you're better off networking with other entrepreneurs and advisors in your area or industry to find credible angel forums.

Some Web sites advertise angel lists, and even the SBA has tried to facilitate the process; but the reality is that these produce few results. Remember, unlike an institution, bank, or VC, as we'll cover later, this is the angel's money. The angel is likely to be very protective about who and what he or she will give it to—as would any of us. People really only give money to people they know, so don't waste your time on generic and public databases or Web sites. Angel forums give angels slightly more comfort in that the entrepreneur has been vetted by another angel in the group and also, in many cases, by a steering committee.

Some angel groups require entrepreneurs to pay a fee in order to obtain access to their forum. Be wary of paying fees to participate in any forum, angel, or VC. Small fees to cover administrative costs are reasonable, but anything over $500 is too high and likely to be unnecessary and not produce results. The forum is making money from you rather than helping you access capital. Some enterprising individuals have made it a business to "help" entrepreneurs find angels. Functioning somewhat like investment bankers, these intermediaries may ask for up-front and/or success fees.

Angel groups that organize entrepreneur forums require companies to submit an application including an executive summary in order to be considered to present to the angel group. Angel groups tend to have already prescreened the angels as accredited investors as defined by securities law. Also, you often have to be recommended by other angels to be eligible for angel membership. However, don't assume that someone is credible just because he or she is in an angel group. While some groups require at least one investment over a certain period of time, not all groups are as diligent about enforcing guidelines and rules for their angels.

The more established angel groups ask the angels to pay a small annual fee to have access to company mailings and to attend monthly or periodic meetings, where select companies make a 15- to 20-minute pitch. They're usually managed by a steering committee, which decides, among other things, which companies can present at the monthly meeting. The group also helps set investment parameters, with $25,000 as the typical minimum investment. On occasion, some angel groups will try to invest as a group for a series A funding. This usually enables them to secure more rights as a group. Understand that there are no hard-and-fast rules. Much of this is always up for negotiation.

Contacting Angels

When approaching angels, you'll usually need to submit a business plan. Angel groups often have committees to review plans and meet with prospective entrepreneurs. These steering committees prefer executive summaries profiling the company, industry, opportunity, and investment sought. Some groups use their own format to gather this information, online or offline. It's important to remember that while many of these people are personally successful on a financial level, they usually lack the experience and know-how to properly evaluate a wide range of business opportunities. Try not to get stuck in the "process," and be sure to find an angel to introduce you to the group and ensure that you'll get a chance to present.

If you're selected to present to the full angel group, you need to focus on your 20-minute presentation. You have a relatively short amount of time to capture someone's interest and convince him or her that there is a sizable market and that your solution or product can meet market demand. Often, angel forums provide time for the angels to informally meet the companies for longer periods of time. But if you didn't catch their interest in the presentation, they will probably not come looking for you during the "cocktail hour."

Most companies use a PowerPoint presentation. Spend some time to make yours stand out from a marketing perspective. Rehearse your pitch extensively. Get colleagues to coach you so you sound assured and confident of your opportunity. The more complicated your product or service, the more you need to think about how to make it real. For example, if you have a really complex tech, medical, or engineering product and your audience is less likely to be savvy about the complexities, don't focus on dry details. Instead, focus on the market size, opportunity, and application. Make it real to your audience. If the angel forum is industry-specific, you may want to consider focusing on how you are different from the competition and why your company is likely to succeed. Most forums will allow you to distribute some literature or information.

Angel Forums as Intermediaries

Many angel forums will also specify that the group will receive a finder's fee, often around 1 percent to 2 percent at closing. This fee helps to defray any legal and other expenses of the angel forum. You shouldn't need to pay for the legal expenses of the angel investor, but again you may need to negotiate if a particular angel is important to you. The finder's fee for the angel forum can be in addition to a broker's fee if you are working with one, so be careful, as it can add up. Better to negotiate different rates for these types of forums. A broker can be useful in getting access to an angel forum, but you can negotiate for the broker to pay part of the fee, half or more, to the angel group. Law and accounting firms are often good entrées to angel groups. In fact, many are angels themselves, seeing it as a way to generate business from promising up-and-coming companies.

Angel Deals

Most angel deals are for equity, often with warrants attached. Some may ask for the option to buy in at the next round of financing. Many will want some sort of dilution protection. Some angels may ask for board representation. If you have done a group of angels as a series A, you can provide one board seat for the group as is standard. For individual investments, you'll need to determine the value someone brings and decide if it warrants a board seat. You may also consider creating a board of advisors as opposed to a board of directors. (Please see Chapter 5 for a more detailed discussion.) Industry experts are usually better placed on the board of advisors, as they are more likely to help with business and do not necessarily need to have a fiduciary role. All of these are terms for negotiation.

Managing the Angel Relationship

You should treat angels as seriously as you'd treat a larger investor. In recent years, most have become more sophisticated investors and can provide valuable strategic input and advice. Many are often successful entrepreneurs, so in addition to industry advice, they can assist in steering the early growth. Having said that, be clear with your angels from the outset as to your expectations of their role, and make sure that you understand their expectations as well.

Angels bring in relatively small amounts of money, usually averaging from $25,000 to $100,000. However, they can become very time-consuming to manage. Angels may expect to be briefed on the business often, and some may act like senior executives of the firm rather than board advisors or members.

I've heard of many an awkward situation where the angel perceived his or her investment as an entrée to a management role. I've also known VC investors to make the same assumption. Once I had a VC representative try to get on the payroll as a part-time, paid senior executive. This seemed to be representative of his standard operating mode with his portfolio companies. While a nice guy, he did not have any useful or relevant industry experience for my company.

Having an angel or VC representative on the payroll can present a conflict of interest, and you need to think very carefully before considering such an option. If you feel as though one of your VCs or investors can provide significant value, better to reward the person with equity or warrants than cash compensation. You'll find that most will prefer this option, as they usually expect to offer their expertise as part of their investment.

Venture Capital

VC money: the most talked about capital-raising source. A bit of reality: Most venture capitalists do *not* fund start-ups (i.e., defined as non-revenue-generating companies). The aberration of the late 1990s continues to fool many who think that VCs will just give money to great ideas.

VC money comes in two forms, the good kind and the bad kind, much like cholesterol. You need to learn the difference, as the latter will most likely lead to an early crisis, if not demise. Venture capital is an industry, and the VC is your "customer." You need to understand how the industry operates, how to get your "product" (i.e., your company) noticed, and how to close the sale (i.e., get your funding). While there are certainly nuances, treat it like a sales process from start to finish.

Understanding the Business of a VC

If you're thinking about going the VC route, learn more about the industry and community. VCs are basically fund managers who are looking for high returns for their investors. It's very simple.

VCs are not altruistic and hoping to fund the cure to cancer, although for many that would certainly be an added benefit. At the end of the day, the money is what matters—it's business for them. I make this point, perhaps a bit harshly, because most entrepreneurs are quite emotional about their product or service. They're passionate in believing that they have found the equivalent to the "cure for cancer" for their industry or market. Entrepreneurs are supposed to be zealous. You can't very well get others to invest in your grand idea if you're not singularly passionate about it. An entrepreneur who thinks that a VC has the same perspective is likely in for a rude awakening at some point in the process.

VCs run a business, one that they are held accountable to by their investors. More often than not, the people you meet at a VC firm are not the actual investors (although the senior principals may have some of their own money in the fund); they just work for the VC firm.

VC investment focus often follows market trends, whether it's biotech, the Internet, or the current perceived "hot" industry. While it's still possible to get funding if you are not the current trend, it's certainly harder.

VCs typically look at groups of investments and in theory like to have 3 or 4 companies out of 10 in each fund that are likely to provide exceptional returns. They expect the rest of the businesses in the portfolio to either be low performers or to fail. Sounds harsh, perhaps, but this is purely statistical to the VC industry.

It's important to ask VCs about the expected returns for their fund. When VCs market their fund to potential institutional and wealthy investors, they have to indicate a vision, strategy, and target range for returns to these potential "buyers"—that is, investors. If you're beginning to think that a VC sounds suspiciously like an entrepreneur, you're correct. I've heard many senior partners at VCs say they are indeed owners and operators of growing businesses.

You need to realize that in the same way you're raising dollars from a VC, the VC is raising dollars from someone else. They are simply a sophisticated, value-added (or so you hope) middle person.

For those of you hoping to raise VC money, be aware that VCs expect a hefty return on their money. As mentioned, only 3 in 10 companies in a portfolio are usually considered likely to bring in a return. Remember too that VCs are held accountable to their projections by their investors—hence, the "money circle of life."

A key issue for most investors and VCs is exit strategy. It's great if a company does well, but they want to know how they're going to get their money out and when. Experienced VCs usually have a time horizon of three to seven years. The entire life of their fund may be only 10 to 13 years, after which time their investors expect to receive their monies, the original investment plus all the returns, back.

While an initial public offering (IPO) is certainly a sexy exit strategy, it's not for every company. If you do business with the companies who are likely to buy your firm, then be sure to highlight this early on. Many VCs also like to see a list of possible strategic acquirers. I'll highlight Rosalind Resnick's, founder of NetCreations, successful IPO ride and subsequent strategic sale in Chapter 6.

Many VCs will look at varying stages of development, although they rarely look at start-ups. They often consider a variety of investment structures, including equity; convertible debt, which allows them to convert debt to equity; short-term bridge loans with the option to convert to equity; and hybrids of these and other structures. Understanding what options may work for your firm may actually increase the range of possible investment firms.

Remember that when you're talking to a VC, you're entitled to "interview" the VC as well. Understand the VC's portfolio's mission and goals. Most have multiple funds in their portfolio each with different investment parameters based in part on the various investors. For example, a fund with public institutional funds may be more favorable to minority-owned-and-operated companies or firms that operate in urban development zones. There are many funds that receive monies from state agencies to promote entrepreneurship in their state or geographic area. You need to understand the investment parameters clearly. Not every VC is right for you and, of course, vice versa.

Additionally, learn about their investment style. Do they prefer to be heavily involved? Or are they hands-off? Is their investment style consistent with both your operating style and stage of business? Experienced and well-connected VCs can be very useful for an early-stage company. I once made the mistake of not entirely appreciating the additional value VCs can bring, and so, while my core investors were nice guys, the kind of guys you might enjoy having a cocktail with, they knew nothing about my industry and couldn't contribute any contacts, networks, or customers.

Understand that there is a certain amount of groupthink to the VC industry as well. VCs move in herds like sheep. Few can distinguish themselves from the herd. My personal theory for this phenomena is the blame factor, the logic being that since VCs need to prove themselves to their investors, it's better for them to stumble in a group so they can blame many different factors. There's nothing worse than being the only one to stumble while all the others seem to prosper, hence the motivation for groupthink. Of course, the reverse is obvious. If other funds seem to be doing well, then they emulate the same strategy, sometimes even if it seems unsound.

Many wise and experienced people understood that the dot-com period was not based on sound business principles, and yet most felt compelled to "follow the herd blindly" in order to provide their ever-demanding investors with astronomical returns. When the bubble burst, there was no shortage of blame including that placed on the analysts, which was a bit like blaming McDonald's for getting burned by their hot coffee. No sophisticated investor ever relies on the sole advice of a single and, in many cases, young analyst. Individual analysts usually provide just one perspective to be considered prior to making a decision. However, groupthink can enable the avoidance of responsibility.

What Makes a Good VC

Most entrepreneurs would agree that what makes a good investor is a financial and strategic partner who works toward mutually beneficial success. The key areas to think about include the following:

- **Network.** What is their network? Are they in your industry? Do they know clients or partners or both and at what decision-making level? Are they willing to assist with networking on an active basis? Look at their portfolio companies closely to see if there's an overall synergy. It's helpful if the VC is willing to facilitate interaction with key strategic investors in the fund as well as other complementary portfolio companies.

- **Check-writing ability.** What is their process for obtaining more funding if warranted? VCs fund companies from one of their portfolio funds. If monies in those funds run out, then there's limited ability to find more funding. Most experienced VCs save a portion of each fund for follow-on funding for their portfolio companies (which are companies they have already invested in). Remember that VCs have an interest in making sure your company succeeds, so long as the business parameters warrant it. They are not likely to keep funding a venture with minimal life left in it.

- **Mutual respect.** Is there a mutual acknowledgement of respect and that you both need each other to succeed? Sure, you need money. But, the VC needs to also be aware that they need good companies with solid ideas in order to be successful and profitable. Many VC's appear to operate as if this fact didn't exist. Just as you will likely turn to your VC for creative financing and exit strategies, they should respect your industry and management experiences. Success can only be achieved if there's mutual respect and a focus on creating a win for all involved.

- **Level of involvement.** How involved do the VCs want to be, and are their expectations in line with yours? Do you and your management team perceive it as helpful involvement or intrusion? Negotiating a VC's level of involvement can be really challenging, as expectations may change over time. Some VCs who take a hands-off approach in the beginning may increase their involvement at the first hint of difficulties or problems. Overall, most VCs oversee investments in multiple companies, so they don't always want to be heavily involved. Just be sure that the level of involvement meets both of your needs and expectations.

- **Fit.** Are your professional styles compatible? Is there a cultural fit between your firm and the operating mode of the VC? Some VCs view their role as partners and others more as seasoned directors who offer guidance and directives early on. There can even be differences in operating and communication styles based on a factor like geography. An East Coast firm in the United States may sound and act different than one on the West Coast. Many have commented that VCs from the two coasts operate differently and have a different focus. West Coast firms are more likely to be hands-on and involved in the company's growth, whereas some say that an East Coast firm is more singularly focused on deal terms and finances. Stereotypes are at times limiting, but they can help you make sure you're sensitive to possible differences.

What Entrepreneurs Should Watch Out For

It's harder to identify exact issues that make less-than-desirable VCs, but following are a few issues to be wary of. In general, an unsuitable VC is someone whose interests are not in line with yours to grow an early-stage company to long-term viability and profitability. (I'll talk about what VCs don't like in the next section.)

- **Unreasonable terms and demands**. Here, the VC is not motivated by a mutual win and seeks to extract terms from you that are potentially dangerous to the long-term health of the company. For example, the VC may try to extract personal terms from you, such as a deferred salary or personal guarantees. Even if you are independently wealthy, terms that may make your personal financial survival more difficult only distract you and make you less focused on the business, which should be your and the VC's priority. In such cases, the VC is less interested in your well-being; after all, everyone needs to pay their bills. These terms are never in anyone's best interest, let alone the company, and will undoubtedly come back to haunt both you and the VC. The entrepreneur should also be wary of having unreasonably high compensation demands.
- **No real management experience.** VCs predominantly still tend to come from the worlds of consulting and investment banking. Most have never worked for a company. As a result, their knowledge base of a corporation tends to be academic and theoretical and doesn't stem from any tangible experiences. They tend to be unfamiliar with corporate operating practices as well as general line management. Despite some efforts to hire

entrepreneurs on their teams, most VCs still hire people who are just like themselves, a practice that drastically limits the range of experiences and perspectives of their team. Look at the individual backgrounds to assess any diversity of experience and perspective.

- **Questionable integrity and greed.** Be wary of the VC who shows interest in doing your deal and suggests he or she receive a fee personally for doing so or wants to go on your payroll as an "advisor." Kickbacks are not legally standard in the VC world, although they occur in varied forms more often than not. The only person who may be entitled to fees are those you have "retained" as investment bankers, advisors, or intermediaries. Additionally, a VC who operates this way is likely to have a pattern of doing so and is not likely to provide the kind of professional support needed during the challenging periods. Know the Security and Exchange Commission (SEC) rules for your stage of firm and type of investment. It's just not worth engaging in unscrupulous business practices. Even if in the short term, it helps to fund your company, the long-term repercussions could be disastrous. Find another source, and above all, strive to keep your integrity in all your business dealings.

- **Personality, egos, and power trips.** VCs who are undeservedly full of themselves may be more interested in satisfying their egos than partnering to grow strong companies. Some VCs will show such characteristics by playing mind games at early meetings. Others may try to intimidate you or be unconstructively condescending—for example, demanding very aggressively and rudely that you close your PowerPoint presentation and answer obtuse questions in a hostile environment. You may find yourself the target of a barrage of foul language. While every industry has its share of egomaniacs, what you really need to focus on is, can you build a level of professional trust that will enable you and the VC to work together during challenging periods? Some VCs can forget that it's a partnership with the entrepreneur, who is likely to have an equity interest in the company as well. The VC may seek to treat the entrepreneur as a subordinate or employee only, and not a co-owner. Without a sense of cooperative teamwork, you may not have the VC and board support you need at critical junctures.

Interestingly enough, the code of conduct that most professionals are expected to follow in the corporate world is not always standard in the VC world. Stay above it and stay professional. Despite the allure of money, you probably wouldn't want to do business with these types of people in any circumstance.

If I sound a bit strong on being wary of certain kinds of VCs, I am just trying to create some balance. Most entrepreneurs see the VCs in an incredibly elevated sense, a fact that's not lost on most VCs, as many use it to their advantage. As a result, many entrepreneurs fail to question the practices and approach of their VCs until it is often too late.

What VCs Watch Out For

I've spent some time talking about what to look for from a VC. The following are a few things that VCs do and don't like in entrepreneurs:

- **Be prepared.** Come to any VC meeting with a clear presentation and detailed business plan. If you can't answer a specific question, say so and promise to get back to them within a specified time frame with further information. Even if you don't have an answer, be sure to get back to them later with a follow up that indicates you are still researching the answer.
- **Be professional.** Conduct yourself professionally at all times. Dress and act like you're going to a job interview. It's quite similar.
- **Don't act like you're "entitled" to funding for any reason.** You may think your idea is great, but VCs see many "great" ideas. Support your request for funding with clear business rationale and facts. Lose any attitude.
- **Don't name-drop or imply things you can't do or deliver.** Everyone can see through such ploys, and you'll just lose

credibility. Only mention names of people who you have access to and will actually help you and your company. Also, don't make claims about your product or service that can't be substantiated. Again, your credibility will suffer even if you actually have a solid product or service.

Finding a Good VC

There are a number of ways to find VCs. If you have angel investors, they can often help lead you to VCs, as can lawyers, accountants, and sometimes even bankers. Law firms actually often provide good access to VCs. The more ideal law firm is one that has a group dedicated to providing services to early-stage companies. They have likely developed extensive relationships with certain VCs, either in a specific industry or geographic region.

There are people who act as intermediaries in exchange for a finder's fee, usually success-based. If you choose to retain an intermediary, be sure the person is credible and experienced. Most are simply just introducing you to potential VCs or investors by e-mail, letter, or phone. You will need to do all of the work. These finder's fees can range from 1 percent to 3 percent, depending on the extent of their involvement. Higher rates are associated with investment banking firms, and the involvement is much different and more extensive.

Many intermediaries will call themselves investment bankers, while they are really not. An experienced investment banker will take over more of the capital-raising-process functions, including preparing the business plan, fine-tuning the presentation, and coaching management, as well as identifying and contacting VCs, strategic capital, and other suitable investors. Some may need to prepare an offering memorandum if you are doing a new series of financing. Investment bankers will accompany you to presentations and assist you through the entire due diligence process, the term sheet, and usually the deal negotiations.

For all this, most bankers can charge a success fee of between 7 percent to 10 percent, sometimes on a graded scale depending on the size of the funding. Some will charge you an up-front monthly retainer as well as expenses. Any up-front fees should be deducted from the final success fee. With investment banks, it's somewhat justifiable to receive monthly retainers to cover ongoing expenses; however, the success fee should compensate for the labor expenses more than adequately. I have always preferred to give a higher success fee, but a small or no monthly retainer. On occasion, some mutually agreed upon expenses, for example, travel-related, can be paid on an ongoing basis rather than at the end.

There are many credible investment banks, some small and industry-focused. As your company gets established, you'll often receive unsolicited marketing materials from investment banks that help small and midsize companies merge, acquire, or be acquired. Try to establish relationships with the investment banks that service your industry, even if you are not looking for capital. Many of these firms are often retained by the very large companies when they are looking to acquire products, customers, or a market. It's helpful if the bankers are aware of your firm and can bring your company into consideration. You never know when an acquisition may seem right to you.

If you decide to seek out the VCs directly, you can find many lists, usually online and for a nominal fee. Unlike angels, VCs are more open to unsolicited business plans, and many indicate clearly on their Web sites how to submit yours. VCs want to be sure they get access to a range of great companies as well.

If you have a dedicated person to assist with the capital-raising process, online searches might be a viable option. Just remember that the process can consume all of your time. The sites continue to evolve, with no one site standing out from the rest. You may want to start with an online search. Some of these sites also provide access to templates of business plans, term sheets, agreements, and even presentation materials. These are useful as guidelines, but don't assume that any of these materials can replace appropriate legal or accounting advice.

You'll find that having an experienced chief financial officer (CFO) is valuable, even if the person is part-time. When looking for someone to fill a CFO role, look for experience in fund-raising and making presentations. If you take this person with you to a presentation, he or she has to be credible, convincing, and capable. Don't use a comptroller or senior bookkeeper for this role. These roles are very different (please see Chapter 2 for more discussion on planning your team).

There are also many venture forums that select firms to present to VCs. Selection criteria differs widely, but it is usually based on a business plan and the anticipated interests of attending VCs. Some are just forums for presentations, a few may operate "boot camps," which can be an invaluable way to hone your plan, sharpen your presentation skills, and meet potential investors. The better boot camps tend to be targeted to certain kinds of entrepreneurs and ventures (please see later in this chapter for more information for women and minority firms and boot camps).

Some VCs may look for investment opportunities before they close a fund. This can be acceptable, assuming the timetable works for both of you and the VC has a track record of closing funds. Otherwise, make sure not to put all your eggs in one basket and continue to shop your deal. Closing a fund refers to whether the VC has been successful in raising money for a fund and has met at least the minimum requirements to stop fund-raising for that fund and start investing. If the VC does not close their fund, he or she cannot invest, and you're out of luck and will have to start your fund-raising process all over again.

You can also use a VC's Web site to find more VCs with similar industry and investment focus. Under the About Us section, many VCs list their advisors and boards of directors. In their brief bios, you can see each VC or company affiliation. Similarly, if you know of companies in your industry that have received investment funding, you can access their board of directors online to see which VCs did the deal. The backgrounds of the people listed on Web sites can often provide you with information on investors, key partners, and customers.

Another way to find a VC is through existing investors, especially when you are doing additional funding rounds. As you look to add more VCs, be sure to find out if there's a work or personal history between the VCs and perhaps even between the VC and your angel investors. If another deal soured between them and there's remaining bad blood, you don't want the investors and VCs using your company as a battleground to settle old scores. I didn't realize the possible impact and initially didn't know that two of my three largest investors had an awkward personal and professional history. This impacted how each viewed the other's investment and related terms in my company. If they do have a history, be sure that one party didn't benefit from another deal at the expense of the other investor. Entrepreneurship is enough of a ride without trying to manage competing VCs, unless, of course, it's to your advantage.

Business Plan Screening

Business plans are a critical step in the fund-raising and planning stages. However, you need to understand how VCs are likely to assess plans.

Most VCs will rely on the plan for initial screening. If the market opportunity seems convincing and if the product or service has some unique fit, they are likely to consider additional review. VCs are most interested in proof of concept, product, and market. If you can get letters of intent or actual purchase orders, you'll find more VCs willing to review your plan.

More often than not, it really takes an introduction or intermediary to get a VC to review your plan. If you send a plan in without an introduction, try to get creative in order to be noticed. Think of your plan as a marketing tool. Package and present not just the information but also the plan, in a tasteful, professional, and unique way.

Other factors that impact a VC's decision to review a plan in detail may be unrelated to your company, including their internal deal flow and how many people are already assigned to potential deals, as well as how much money they have available for investment. You should try to get information regarding these factors when you interview a potential VC.

Every VC has his or her own approach to analyzing business plans. Most tend to be conservative and often will assume that the projections are too aggressive and cut them in half. In meetings with VCs, I have often experienced varying views of the same business plan. One would tell me that my growth projections were too conservative and small and that they needed to see a bigger "hockey stick" (a term that refers to the shape of the sport equipment, which plotted on a graph indicates quick and steep upward growth). I would go back and revise the numbers, only to be told by the next VC that he didn't think my projections had a chance in hell of being achieved. And, sometimes, they weren't even that kind in informing me of their opinions!

Yes, another typical mistake of early-stage entrepreneurs—allowing a VC or investor to sway business logic and planning. You need to be comfortable with your projections regarding market size and opportunity. Not every VC will be the right partner. You may also find after talking to many VCs that while the size of a market sounds great to you, it may be too "small" for most VCs. Remember that they too have performance goals, including investment returns and a clear exit strategy. In such cases, strategic capital may be a better option, and I'll discuss it later in this chapter.

Meeting with a VC

The first meeting is likely to be a short presentation, perhaps up to an hour or two. Be clear about how much time you have and what they want to focus on in addition to your general presentation. You're not likely to have been given a meeting unless something in your executive summary or business plan struck their interest. The key to attracting VCs' attention is differentiation. Use more than just words to communicate your opportunity. Visuals are a powerful tool.

Like a good salesperson, prepare in advance. Find out what they liked about your idea and if they have any immediate concerns. Plan to raise them proactively in advance. Also, these days many VCs have a Web site and some even list their portfolio companies on their public site, as well as on the password protected areas. Research their existing investments. Find out if any have been in your industry, and find out how the companies are doing. If their previous investments in your industry have not been doing well, you'll need to address their specific concerns. As noted previously, VCs also try to gain strength by specializing in an industry. Having portfolio companies that are complementary by way of products, industry, or customers is a plus. It's a good idea to highlight the ways your company may complement their current portfolio.

Some VCs like to think big and may look for opportunities to merge portfolio companies and then sell the firm for an even higher valuation or take it public. Your best bet is to be open to everything. No VC likes to hear that you have a singular path for your company. Remember, they need an exit strategy, and it needs to be broad with some clearly defined options. Multiple exit strategies are the best—IPO, mergers and acquisitions (M&A), strategic acquisition, and so on.

When interacting with VCs, manage your confidence. Again, it's a good idea to veer to the middle ground—you can be either too confident or not confident enough. Don't let their questions or tone or manner intimidate you. Some use these psychological strategies to test you and your vision and perhaps even commitment. Some just get a power thrill. Keep in mind that seasoned VCs think they have seen all types of entrepreneurs, and some may indeed have. They can be quick to stereotype or label you or your company based on previous experiences, for good or for bad.

Due Diligence

If a VC expresses interest in your firm, he or she is likely to conduct a research phase that can last from one to six months, although the average is about three months. During this phase, the VC will literally take your business plan apart, number by number, assumption by assumption. The VC will assess your market expectations and usually cut your projections in half and then some, while doubling your expenses—all along testing to see how the business is likely to fare under various conditions. VCs are likely to want to talk to key customers, partners, or others to assess both your product and capabilities. They will go through much the same research as you did in compiling your plan. They will also want to learn more about you as the entrepreneur and CEO of the company. They need to be comfortable that you can execute the plan.

Negotiating and Structuring the Deal

If a VC is interested in making an investment in your company, he or she will likely start by sending you a term sheet that outlines the terms and structure of the investment. Term sheets are usually only a few pages long but cover the critical terms. Term sheets are then followed by complete documentation as is legally appropriate for the type of deal. Some prefer to negotiate term sheets and then move to documentation, which also entails negotiations. Others prefer to negotiate everything at once. The term sheet is negotiable, and you should spend time sorting through it to make sure the structure and terms make sense for your company.

This book is not intended to be a comprehensive source on each and every funding variation. It's an evolving market, and new structures and hybrids come in and out of popularity based on market conditions. You're well advised to find a lawyer or financial advisor who stays current on these structures or, more importantly, knows how to ask the right questions and analyze any proposed term sheet with experience. Some terms can also be impacted by changes in tax and investment rules, so again, understanding the VC industry is critical.

There are some concepts to focus on in any deal. The valuation of a company and resulting equity percentage are critical factors. As a result, many structures and terms seek to increase or decrease an investment interest. Antidilution terms seek to protect earlier investors from the reduction of their investment interest with additional rounds of funding. The challenge is often that even with these terms in place, later VCs can force a restructuring of select terms as a condition for their investment. The following are some key issues to focus on.

Equity, Valuation, Structure, and Liquidation Preferences

In many cases, the fundamental challenge is that the entrepreneur and the VC are fighting over a finite item: equity. Sure, 100 percent of nothing is still nothing, but most companies will have a value in time. If your investors think that they are putting in that value by way of cash, they will try to get the lion's share of equity. At the same time, you, the entrepreneur, need to be sure that you are left with an equity stake that will motivate and incentivize you.

When you're doing your projections, realize that VC expectations are toward higher returns. They get that by investing early at a low value and selling eventually at a high value of the company. Value is usually a multiple of revenues or earnings, usually the latter, although the former created the huge monetary successes that were characteristic of the late 1990s Internet economy. It's unlikely that those kinds of multiples will return anytime soon, if ever again—although this *is* the United States, where optimism and groupthink can run amuck at least once in every century.

This is one of those business scenarios where it can be a "zero-sum" game, unless the VC is experienced and intends to create a mutual win. Seasoned VCs know well that too little equity can be disincentivizing to an entrepreneur. The trick is to find the right balance, and again, there are no hard-and-fast rules. Some may allow entrepreneurs to gain back equity by achieving financial or other milestones. Each deal is different, as are the motivations of the participants—entrepreneur and VC alike. Make sure you have a seasoned attorney to advise in this process, although it's likely you'll be doing the bulk of the actual negotiations. Ask questions and educate yourself.

The term sheet may propose an investment structure of, for example, debt or equity and combinations thereof. Depending on the stage of your company, you need to choose an investment structure that is conducive to growth and expansion. For example, don't fund a start-up with debt. Your balance sheet will be heavy with liabilities, and it will be hard to raise equity capital. However, if you are a revenue-generating company and can pay interest, a debt structure may be a way to fund your expansion without giving up equity.

Based on the final terms, it's also likely that they will get out ahead of you depending on the structure. Liquidation preferences are important for the distribution of assets in the event a company is liquidated. In essence, this refers to the order in which investors; lenders, if applicable; and entrepreneurs get their money. Some VCs like to use debt-like structures because as creditors they would get their money out first whether it's a liquidation or a merger or sale of the company.

Control

Determining the right amount of board seats to give your VCs is critical, and you should spend some time thinking about it. As board members, they'll help steer the company, but they can also provide critical votes for and against issues that are important to you. The challenge is that most VCs are like consultants and investment bankers—well-educated and well-intentioned, but more often than not, with little or no experience in actually starting, growing, and running a company. Sure, some may have run a large company or unit, but running is step 3 in starting, growing, and running. Without hands-on experience in starting and growing, running is useless. It's just maintaining with respectable increases, not being "the little engine that could" up steep mountains and against tough odds.

Many VC firms have realized this and often bring experienced entrepreneurs on board to help make funding decisions as well as act as advisors to companies. Seek out the experienced entrepreneur on a VC team; he or she is likely to be your best source of day-to-day advice. This person knows how to grow a company with limited resources—money, talent, and so on. They are expert at entrepreneurship on the fly.

Preferred, Participating Preferred, Double Participating Preferred, and Other Mind-Numbing Structures

Preferred stock is basically stock that has preferences over common stock, which is usually what you'll have as the entrepreneur. Many VCs will invest by way of preferred stock, which usually gives them dividends, preferential voting rights, redemption rights, and the right to convert to common stock on terms most beneficial to the VC.

Participating preferred stock is preferred stock with the additional benefit to the holder—that is, the VC—of getting more liquidating distributions at the common stock level. Many VCs will try to get participating preferred stock during the negotiation process.

Double participating preferred, while not common, is found in some deals and gives the VC the right to not only get all of his or her money back first, but the right to get dividends and distributions at the common stock level.

When you're structuring your deal, if you are putting in money, look to put it in on the same terms as the VC. This will help to align your mutual interests. Many entrepreneurs, myself included, usually just put their money in as periodic cash infusions as needed with little thought to the structure and terms. If you have outside investors, it's important that they value your investment, in terms of time and energy as well as cash.

As I noted earlier, some VCs may look to structure their investment as convertible debt. This gives them the protection of debt with the benefits given to equity. Obviously, you can see that this is likely to be more beneficial to the VC than the company. In my second company, the investment was structured as debt and convertible debt. This made it more challenging to get additional equity funding, as no equity investor wants to be behind large amounts of debt. We had an inverted balance sheet, which means that the debt was greater than the equity on the balance sheet. While it's not uncommon for all of the earlier investors to restructure with new rounds of funding, it's never easy, and in our case, with conflicting objectives, it became impossible.

As with any negotiation, time is an important factor. If the VC knows you're running out of cash, the VC is more likely to be more aggressive in asking for terms that most benefit him or her. Expect the VC process to average between 9 and 18 months to actual closing of a deal and funding—assuming that your company's plan warrants funding. Give yourself time to find the right deal and negotiate it well.

These structures and terms can indeed be mind-numbing, and you're not alone if your eyes start to glaze over in the negotiation process. Just keep in mind that most of these terms focus on getting the maximum monetary value and legal protection for the VC, and you need to work toward keeping it a win-win. There's an old Wall Street saying that can be a guiding principle here as well: *Bears and bulls make money, pigs don't.*

Rejections

Don't get attached to anything. This is incredibly hard for most entrepreneurs, who are usually driven by passion and emotion as much as hard critical analysis. However, it's important to stay objective. If you find that you are being rejected by the VC community, try to objectively assess why. Is it the company, the product or service, the market or the timing? Again, your market opportunity may be too small for a VC but just fine for you individually. In that case, look at other ways to grow.

Just because a VC isn't interested in your business, product, or market does not mean it's not good. VCs are looking for the companies with the strongest hockey-stick growth opportunities. Steady, moderate, and profitable growth doesn't really excite most VCs, unless it's in a huge market. They need to satisfy their investment parameters, and most are

Tales from the Trenches

I'll reference my own experience to illustrate the importance of qualifying your VC, choosing the right ones for your stage of company, and structuring a mutually beneficial deal.

My second company was funded by a couple of funds, which were not quite seasoned VC firms, although one was led by a guy who thought he was. They were all really nice guys, and yes, it's still very much a guys' world, no matter what you read or think . . . but that's another book unto itself.

Unfortunately for both of us, we were mismatched. My investors did not fully understand the role that VCs of start-ups need to play, nor did they have the skills or experience necessary in our industry. I was relatively naïve in the world of capital raising and agreed to structures and terms that weren't productive for the company or myself. I was also unsuccessful in persuading them of the need to restructure before it was too late.

It took me a long time to determine that while my concepts, ideas, and market were feasible, despite any temporary economic setbacks triggered by 9/11, the corporate structure stunk. I had an inverted balance sheet (more debt than equity), the funding markets were dried up, and my investors felt no imperative to restructure. Further, I was in a very disincentivizing structure where I finally saw no upside for myself. I had relegated myself to the back of the line in terms of every right and, having made just about every financing structural mistake known to early entrepreneurs, I couldn't have possibly been at a greater disadvantage. Still, despite the obvious problems, it took me a long while to part with the company.

In the end, we had a company with a good product, a decent and respectable market, but a lousy capital structure, nonsupportive investors, and a completely burned-out and disincentivized entrepreneur. It couldn't move forward, and it didn't. I recount my experience only because having outside investors does not guarantee success even if your product or service meets market demands. Further, focus on the issues I've highlighted in this chapter from the beginning. Don't assume that you can "fix" things once the company is operational, profitable, and successful.

looking for 20 to 50 percent growth with the opportunity to at least double or triple their money in four to seven years. That takes us back to valuation. But another thing to keep in mind is that the due diligence—in other words, the research, legal, and documentation stage will cost just as much for a $1 million investment as a $10 million investment. So guess which one looks better from a return on investment (ROI) point of view? The $10 million investment, even if it's more likely to come in stages of $3 to $5 million per stage as certain product, sales, market milestones are achieved. The challenge is that not every company warrants the higher investment.

The key is to move on and look at other ways to pursue your vision. There is no one sure path to successful entrepreneurship.

Funding Options for Women-Owned and Minority-Owned Firms

The world of investments relies somewhat on trust, interpersonal interaction, and intuition, as well as on detailed and concrete business analysis. As a result, as in much of the business world, VCs, who tend to be men, seem to intuitively "connect" with male-run companies more than with women- and minority-run companies. There's a cultural fit of management and professional styles. For almost 15 years, I have made my living providing insight and products that help people understand the cultural fit among people from different countries, yet it's easy to forget that each industry has its own distinct culture as well.

This is no doubt fodder for another book, but it supports the emerging efforts of funds and forums designed to assist women- and minority-owned companies. The reality is that more than 90 percent of VC money still goes to male-owned-and-operated companies.

There are forums designed specifically to give minority- and women-owned companies the opportunity to present to VCs. Two national ones are the Emerging Venture Network (EVN) (www.evn.org) and Springboard (www.springboardenterprises.org). Both operate as not-for-profit organizations that seek to assist early-stage companies in getting access to capital. EVN focuses on a broader category of minority as well as women entrepreneurs, while Springboard is focused on women. A key value that both can provide is that selected entrepreneurs go through a relatively rigorous boot camp. Not all entrepreneurial forums offer boot camps, but those that do are worth seeking out. Some may charge fees, and you'll need to evaluate the cost-benefit to your firm.

These boot camps include training on the entire funding process, on enhancing the business plan, and most importantly, on presenting to and interacting with VCs. Even for talented entrepreneurs with great presentation skills, there is much to be gained from these boot camps. The advisors are usually a combination of legal, accounting, and marketing professionals, as well as VCs themselves. I participated in the EVN boot camp, which was very useful. Having also presented at regional VC events, I can attest that the boot-camp process is valuable and clearly a market differentiator between forums that do not offer this service.

The VCs that attend these targeted forums may not be the largest or most high profile VCs, but they are more likely to be open to companies owned and operated by women and minorities. The reality is that people do business with those they are most comfortable with. The VCs participate in these boot camps without necessarily expecting to make any investments. As a result of the diminished pressure, they are often more likely to candidly discuss the funding market and make useful suggestions and introductions.

Some VCs focus on women-owned-and-operated companies. They can be a bit harder to find, but EVN and Springboard can assist you in finding them. VCs like Fund Isabella (www.fundisabella.com), which looks for women-owned-and-operated companies, will invest in early-stage companies, starting with smaller amounts such as $250,000. Each VC's Web site tells you more about targeted industries and investment parameters.

One thing to note about many of these women- and minority-focused VCs is that they usually have an active board of directors and advisors, many of whom work with the larger VCs. Exposure to these people obviously increases your chances of finding larger pools of capital should you want and need it for expansion as you grow.

Small Business Administration
and Related Government Entities

The SBA is a relatively staid organization that provides capital for established businesses, usually with two or more years of revenues and profitability. Hence, don't bother if you're a start-up or are not yet profitable. If you're not yet profitable, you may want to reconsider your decision to borrow money rather than raise equity anyhow.

It's also important to remember that the SBA doesn't give you money directly; rather, it guarantees your loan, but a local bank actually provides the funds. In most cases, your local bank will handle the entire process, and you don't always need to go to the SBA first. However, as for any loan, you will need a good business plan, a clear and reasonable (for the bank, the SBA, and the company) repayment schedule, and good personal credit.

For those who are eligible, the rates can be reasonable, but understand that it's debt and not equity, so you have to pay it back. Usually it comes with a personal guaranty, which, as noted earlier, you should do your best to avoid. It's not uncommon for early-stage companies to have to reorganize at some early point even if they go on to become huge successes. FedEx and AOL are just two of many big-name companies that restructured in their first decade of operations. The SBA has also opted to support affiliate programs, Small Business Investment Companies (SBIC) and New Markets Venture Capital (NMVC), to help early-stage and small businesses gain access to capital. Both of these programs are discussed in more detail a little later in the chapter.

The SBA offers minority-owned and disadvantaged early-stage businesses an opportunity to participate in a program, commonly known as 8a. Basically, if you qualify for certification, you can get federal contracts on a noncompetitive basis up to a certain dollar amount, $3 million or $5 million depending on your industry. Far from being an easy or guaranteed source of sales, the certification process can be cumbersome and lengthy and requires an operating history of two years. Also, you need to be sure the government is actively buying your product or service. The program can assist with developing government contracts, but you're going to have to spend a great deal of time cultivating those over a multiyear period.

I point this out because selling to the government, while profitable for some, usually entails a longer sales cycle than the private sector and with much thinner margins. Nevertheless, 8a can be a valuable program for those who qualify and are successful in understanding how to best manage the program.

Tales from the Trenches

In five years of participation in the 8a program, Martha Daniels, founder of Information Management Resources (IMRI), successfully became a $7 million California-based software developer. Her firm eventually "graduated" from the program once sales and her net worth reached milestones. Nevertheless, she had made valuable contacts, had proven the company's ability to deliver successfully, and had developed a pipeline of both public and private contracts. She used 8a to become a viable, successful, and profitable company.

Martha's experience highlights the evolution as well as the personal restrictions for participating in this program. The 8a program is no longer the program that, once in place, would make business owners "very wealthy, very quickly." The current program is no longer even technically limited to minorities and now embraces anyone who can prove that he or she has been restricted in his or her progress as a result of socioeconomic causes. The government has also streamlined the application process, which originally deterred many qualified entrepreneurs from applying. Still, it's not a cheap, quick, or easy process. If an early-stage business seeks consulting help to complete the voluminous application, they can still expect to pay between $10,000 to $15,000, and the process can take 6 to 12 months.

Martha was eventually in the program for nine years, due to an extension to complete outstanding government contracts. During the entire term, she keenly felt a loss of personal privacy as a result of participation in the 8a. Any entrepreneur who participates in the program cannot have a net worth that exceeds $1 million. This includes the assets of a spouse and continues throughout the entire term. The government calculation doesn't include your primary residence or assets that are held in the business. However, vacation homes, rental properties, boats, art, stocks, and other businesses are all part of this valuation. The annual 8a paperwork requires a full disclosure for both the entrepreneur and spouse, all of which can seem very intrusive. Martha has seen people circumvent this restriction in many permissible ways. For example, some entrepreneurs use their business to guarantee a bank loan on an investment property. As a result of the guarantee, the property is considerate a corporate asset and falls outside of the net worth calculation. For Martha, the benefits of the 8a ultimately outweighed the discomfort with this intense analysis of her private life.

There are other government options that are more innovative and come in the form of grants rather than debt. Small Business Innovation Research Program (SBIR) (www.sba.gov/sbir) provides grant money totaling up to $750,000 in three phases for feasibility, development, and commercialization over the course of 18 to 24 months. SBIR tends be very competitive and focuses on technology solutions, but it can differ by government agency.

All the SBIR information is online. You'll have to check for annual schedules for Phase 1 grants. Usually the Department of Defense (DoD) and the National Institutes of Health (NIH) have the most funds to give away. Keep in mind that if you receive the second- or third-phase money, the government may have some rights or preferences to use your product. Usually for the third phase, the government prefers VC, strategic partner, or private-sector capital involvement to ensure commercialization. However, you're past proof of concept, and any fund-raising should be at better terms for you.

SBICs

SBICs are privately held investment companies who invest their own capital as well as borrowed capital from the SBA. They are designed to provide capital to small businesses. Some SBICs target women- and minority-owned companies, while others are just focused on the size of the company. By definition, SBICs can invest in eligible firms, which are defined as having a net worth of $18 million or less and average net income after taxes of less than $6 million. There are some exceptions, and you can find more information at the SBA Web site (www.sba.gov). The site also lists SBICs by state.

Treat a SBIC like a VC, and approach them with the same strategy. Because their options are more narrow, SBICs are more likely to review unsolicited business plans and grant a meeting more easily. However, SBIC funds tend to be smaller, as they may have fewer private investors involved and have less money to invest. When you contact an SBIC, make sure to ask early on if they have funds and are making investments.

Unlike the SBA, which tends to only provide loans to profitable companies, SBICs will invest with equity in early-stage and even preprofit companies.

NMVC (New Markets Venture Capital)

The NMVC (www.sba.gov/INV/NMVC/index.html) is a relatively new program from the SBA designed to provide capital to companies operating in lower-income areas. Signed by President Clinton in 2000, it received its first funding in 2001 and only a handful of New Market Venture Capital companies were created. The program is still in its infancy stages and really only appropriate for the small number of companies that operate in lower-income neighborhoods.

Alternative Options

Strategic Capital

Strategic capital is a valuable way to finance your company as well as expand your business and ensure long-term viability. It usually comes from a larger company in your industry that's interested in getting access to your product or service to expand its market.

The most challenging thing about using strategic capital is usually that it involves an exclusivity clause. As might be expected, many strategic partners don't want others in their industry to get access to your product, technology, or service before they can fully capitalize on the market. Only you can decide if what you get more than compensates for what you leave on the table. Having said that, strategic capital is often perceived as a relatively safer way to grow a company, particularly as the strategic partner provides one of hopefully several exit strategies. Be sure that any deal includes revenue-generating opportunities. Otherwise, you'll be at the mercy of the strategic partner for capital, and they may use that as a way to buy you on the cheap or get access to your product or service.

Strategic capital can come in many forms, including an actual equity investment, loans, presales, bartering, and letters of commitment that may be able to be funded by investment banks or VCs depending on how strong they are. Some may look to barter services for equity. This can be useful, but be careful with the valuation, as it normally works to the benefit of the strategic capital. For example, in exchange for equity, a consulting firm may give you advisory services to help put together the business or marketing plan. They are likely to value these services at full retail cost, even though you'd never pay that amount in cash. Sure, there's a benefit, since you need the service and don't have cash, but you're also going to give up more equity.

With strategic capital, the mutual interest is not financing, but usually a product, service, or market, which will enable you to be more creative than you would be with a traditional VC. Some of the larger companies that are likely strategic partners have VCs arms that oversee these types of investments. Approach them as you would any VC with the added provision that they are interested in both how you can benefit them in terms or products, service, or customers and the long-term financial upside.

Sales, Retainers, and Bartering

These options can provide much-needed capital and can be some of the cheapest forms of funding. Getting your customers to "fund" you with orders that they pay for in advance is a cheap option. At most, they will impact your profitability and income statement and less likely your balance sheet, although you may be carrying a short-term liability if a customer has prepaid and you have yet to deliver the goods or services. Many companies also seek to have their customers commit to a monthly sales minimum, which can function like a retainer. This is enormously helpful in planning and managing your monthly cash flow needs.

These are every entrepreneur's favorite forms of funding. While I raised a lot of money for my second company, I am also a big fan of bootstrapping it in the early days. It helps you use what little resources you have very wisely and minimize mistakes and expenses, since you just don't have money to throw around. Customer-oriented funding approaches allow you to focus on quality product and the first set of customers, which means you'll more likely be moving toward building a lasting business.

Bartering is an effective way to do business without using cash directly. Find companies of any size who need your products or services and from whom you also need something, and then exchange those products or services. For example, a tech firm may swap services for a logo and marketing design with a marketing firm. Companies often swap advertising space for content, for customer databases, and for technology. As you get creative, you'll uncover more opportunities.

Accounts Receivable Financing and Factoring

Factoring or accounts receivable financing is a good but expensive way to generate cash flow to meet short-term obligations, without taking on any long-term obligations or giving up equity. The basic difference is that in accounts receivable financing, you're borrowing against an invoice. The customer continues to deal with you. Usually the structure is a line of credit, and your bank or finance company will set up an address for customers to send the payment in the name of your company.

In factoring, you're actually selling the invoice. This means that the customer must authorize that the invoice is valid, that they have received the goods or services, and that they commit to paying it to the factor directly. Factoring is widely used in the garment industry where retailers often pay 120 days after receipt of shipment. Factoring is not cheap; in fact, it's probably one of the more expensive forms of lending. However, it's short term and only when you need it. If you have a line of credit, you'll find it's cheaper to use that for cash flow needs till your receivables come in. I have successfully used factors, and it works best if you have large invoices of at least six figures each and need cash to pay for working capital needs. The larger your invoices, the better you can negotiate your rates with a factor.

You need to know a couple of things about factors, however. Choose your factor wisely. Many factoring companies are a bit rough around the edges in terms of customer relations. Remember that they will be interacting with your key customers and "representing" your firm. In our case, it became awkward, as we had Fortune 1000 companies who were not accustomed to the typical brusqueness of a factor. It can impact your business relationships. We prefer to use good customer relationships and get them to pay faster rather than factor invoices.

Some banks and groups will finance purchase orders, but usually through an established line that is secured by you personally. It can take up to two to four weeks to set up a factoring or receivables financing line, so plan ahead if you are considering this option. Your banker, lawyer, accountant, or a fellow entrepreneur is often the best place to look for reputable factors. Your bank may also have products that will allow you to finance receivables or factor invoices.

There are many options to finance a start-up or expansion of a company. Do your research thoroughly, and understand the motivations and expectations of all of the funding sources.

CHAPTER 4

MARKETING AND SALES

Marketing and sales are the life source of your company. You can make the best product or provide the optimal service, but it's irrelevant if you can't sell or your customer won't buy. Like business plans, marketing plans evolve with an organization. In this chapter, I'll review the core components of marketing and sales and give you things to think about as your company grows.

Marketing and sales are often mistakenly considered one and the same, even at the largest and oldest of companies. Marketing designs strategy and sales implements, but in reality, salespeople gather very valuable information that helps fine-tune the strategy, forming a delicate balance between the two departments. In many organizations, there's a struggle between marketing and sales as to which directs which. If you work to coordinate these areas in a complementary way, you're likely to have a more successful strategy, and more importantly, you'll be able to adjust your strategy quickly in response to market conditions.

Many entrepreneurs are actually quite good at some aspects of marketing and sales, usually as early promoters of the venture, as it takes a bit of sales to get a company off the ground. It's the sales vocabulary that sometimes confuses people. As with most industries, the marketing, sales, and advertising world has its own lingo. Don't let the lingo trip you up. Focus instead on the concepts' objectives.

Many companies err because they don't fine-tune their marketing strategy enough. Plan to revisit your strategy at least quarterly. Monitor sales, customer feedback, and industry trends. If you do this frequently enough, you're less likely to be surprised by any industry changes and more likely to be able to incorporate new information steadily.

Integrated Growth Strategies

Before you develop your marketing and sales plan, you need to be sure there really is a market for what you are making and selling. Companies of all sizes routinely forget to verify the market before they launch marketing campaigns. When sales are below expectations, then they reassess the plan, not whether their product or service actually has a market. Once you have market verification, you can begin to develop an appropriate marketing and sales plan.

The most fundamental question to answer is "what problem am I solving with this service/product?" If you cannot answer that question in a way that compels customers to say "I'll buy it," friends to say "cool," or investors to say "tell me more," then perhaps rethinking the concept is in order.

Assuming you have studied the opportunity and believe you have something unique, market size becomes another consideration. Are there enough buyers in your market? How big is your industry category, and how much potential overall money is available to buy products/services like yours? If you're offering a very niche product, you may need to take into account that you will only be able to grow to a certain size, even if all the stars and moons line up.

Market Research

Today, the Internet provides a rich and free source of market research. It should be one of the first places you go to find industry data, competitive information, corporate name availability, and marketing opportunities such as trade show listings.

An essential part of any marketing or sales plan is the research phase. A lot of entrepreneurs use the media to follow trends. The media can be a useful source—to an extent. Don't let your use of the media replace more specialized research. Try to find out as much as possible about the writer or lead researcher. Most are professional writers and might not necessarily have enough experience in your industry to interpret market-specific information accurately. Further, there are very few writers or reporters who have formal business training or experience. This doesn't mean that you should dismiss traditional business publications and newspapers, but rather that you should utilize the facts to make your own conclusions rather than blindly adopt the reasoning of the published word.

Gathering information from these types of sources is called *secondary research*. It's critical to take the time to find out about the competitive landscape and market potential before spending a lot of time, energy, and money chasing the wrong idea. You can access a wide base of resources, publications, and potential customers. Verify and evaluate the credibility of lesser-known sources. Otherwise, you may get incorrect information. It helps if you can verify information obtained online with an offline source, such as an industry expert. If you're researching global markets, there are a number of options, which I'll cover in Chapter 7.

Despite the utility of secondary research, you will still need primary research to help build out your offering and to set the course for how you're going to market your product. Primary research's fundamental role is to provide feedback specific to your product/service. It can be as informal as interviewing people familiar with the industry or as formal as hiring a professional research firm to conduct sophisticated studies with quantifiable results.

More structured interviews with potential customers can also be useful. It's amazing how many companies do not take this critical step. Understanding the pain, buying preference, and motivational behavior of this audience makes all the difference in knowing whether your product meets their needs.

Companies that need direct customer input find focus groups useful. Utilizing focus groups is part of an overall marketing strategy, and you need to be clear on the profile of the participants as well as the objectives for each group. You should use experienced focus groups to facilitate these meetings.

Developing a Marketing and Sales Plan

Going through the marketing and sales planning process enables you to focus on how you'll reach your customer and complete the sale. If appropriate, you'll be able to prepare for a repeat sale—preparation that is critical for ongoing sustainability.

The plan is simply the document that will state the strategy and allow you to track it. In the business plan, as discussed in Chapter 2, you include macro-level parts of your marketing and sales strategy. In the marketing plan, you add the details. Both marketing and sales have several key factors to focus on. We'll start by looking at marketing first.

Marketing

There are several key areas that you'll need to focus on as you plan your marketing strategy:

- Product or service
- Target market
- Pricing
- Distribution
- Building a brand
- Advertising and promotions

Product or Service

Your business plan will include an in-depth description of your product or service. Use your marketing plan to expand the description to include uniqueness, service options, warranties, and other features and benefits. By understanding your core target market, you'll be able to refine your description even further.

What's Your USP?

It's essential to have a USP, or unique selling proposition. For some companies, it's the uniqueness of their product. For others, it's their low price, and for others, it might be their distribution. By distribution, I am referring to how a customer can obtain the product or service. Where or how can they buy it? Is it exclusively or readily available? Often a USP is a combination of factors, as markets do not remain static but are constantly changing. A product that is new and unique today may have many competitors within 6 to 24 months, especially if it's successful. Its USP may initially be that it is new and unique. Over time, the USP may evolve to be new product versions or price or both.

The importance of articulating a USP *cannot* be understated. It is **THE** most important sentence you say about your company. As mentioned in an earlier chapter, some call it the "elevator pitch," based on the concept that if someone on an elevator asks you what your company does, you have only the time between the 10th floor and ground floor to say something compelling, so that by the time you get off, the rider is saying "tell me more."

Putting your pitch down on paper is critical to the process of developing a compelling USP. Your pitch should be no more than two sentences and should capture the imagination of the listener while explaining the need you are meeting in your particular market. Working with your team on this can be a very enlightening experience. Don't be surprised to find it a very difficult task. However, once you have reached consensus, you'll find you've created a clear vision for the company that others can now execute.

Features and Benefits

You'll need to be clear not only about how your product will work or how a service will be delivered, but if you intend to provide additional features and benefits. There's an added cost to such things as providing warranties and customer service, and you'll need to account for those in your budget.

You'll also need to think about when you need to have a new product version, based on industry standards. Your product or service will continue to evolve over time, particularly as you respond to competitive pressures and market demand. You may offer new features or service features, like warranties and customer support. All of these help determine the value for your product or service.

If your core offering is based on price value, you need to be confident that your competitors can't (not just won't, but actually *can't*) match you while you grow to critical mass. Your competitors won't be able to match you if you have a new technology that allows you to build more cheaply. You need to plan for how much time it will take to build that critical market share. You're best off if you can add to the lowest cost feature by adding a nonmonetary value such as a service feature.

Target Market

Knowing your target market is critical. Many businesspeople confuse buyers with users and market to the user and not the buyer. Who is your customer and who's your user? In some cases, they are one and the same, but other times they're different. You'll need to know the demographics of both of them.

Understand how your buyers decide to "buy." What influences their decision? Are they motivated by low cost, high quality, easy access, or the prestige of a brand? Often, they are motivated by a combination of these factors. It's important to monitor all these influences, because they are likely to change over time in order of importance.

Talk to your customer and your potential customer as early as you can. Create informal focus groups to test and use your products. If you can, reach out to potential competitors, partners, industry experts, and so on. Their input is essential in growing a company. It's also helpful to talk to potential advisors and even VCs, as everyone has a piece of wisdom to share, much of which could be quite valuable.

Trade Shows

A trade show offers a great opportunity to learn more about your target market as well as the market in general. You'll be able to see how your likely competition "speaks" to your target customer. You can also learn a great deal about the nuances of the industry. You do not need to exhibit to attend a trade show. Many offer a day's pass for a fee and occasionally require some proof of industry activity. In many cases, that proof is as simple as a business card with the company name, address, and Web site.

Industry association Web sites are a great way to find potential competitors. Lists of trade show exhibitors can also direct you to the same type of information.

In these days of trade show overkill, the best way to find the most productive trade shows is to find out which ones competitors and customers attend. One or two key shows are all that you need. You can search online by your market or industry association. You can also find trade shows by searching on the Web site of your city's or another major city's convention center. The bigger the trade show, the more expansive its range of exhibitors and customers. However, keep in mind that trade shows are an industry and business in themselves. Be wary of hard sells to exhibit or attend.

Many trade shows also provide a forum for continuing education or training for professionals. If you're looking to influence doctors, then attending a conference or trade show on medicine will likely put you near your target market. If you're interested in selling companywide solutions, you need to be sure that decision makers attend the show and not just junior staff who may be doing course work.

Price

Pricing your product or service is always tricky. If you have established competitors, then there are some industry benchmarks. But your USP may suggest that there is the opportunity to challenge the industry pricing, either at higher or lower levels. Make sure to account for customer service and related expenses when determining your price. Many entrepreneurs don't realize the cost of these features and then are faced with cash flow challenges.

There are many books and articles on how to approach pricing—some theoretical and some practical. While pricing is industry and market-specific, there are two basic ways to approach pricing. You may want to read a marketing reference book or access resources, particularly if you don't have a business background. Business educations, no matter how stellar, are rarely enough to navigate the world of entrepreneurship—you need the real-world experience to completely understand how to apply your education.

The first pricing approach is based on cost plus a margin. This basically determines your cost per unit and then adds a margin that is appropriate for your industry. Obviously, you want to maximize sales revenue, but you should focus on profitability or margins, which refers to the revenues or sales minus the actual or direct cost of making your product or providing your service. For your reference, indirect costs are all of the expenses you incur that are not directly related to actually making the product or providing the service. Indirect expenses include all overhead costs such as office rent, office administrative costs, and professional expenses for lawyers and accountants.

The risk for new companies in using cost-based pricing is underestimating their costs. Just about *all* entrepreneurial ventures underestimate their costs. Even the most established and largest companies routinely under budget for product development. One option is to provide a margin for unanticipated costs, but realistically, your figures may not take everything into account. It's not uncommon to be over budget by more than 50 percent.

The second approach prices according to what the market will pay for your product or service. Take a look at competitors' pricing. If you believe that your product's USP puts it in a new pricing category, take a look at some possible comparables and estimate what mark up you think the market will pay for the unique new features.

The first step in the market-based pricing approach is to make sure you can profitably make the product for that price. You need to not just break even, but to be *profitable* with a clear and healthy margin. This is where it's important to understand industry benchmarks. Some industries have margins less than 50 percent, and others have margins around 90 percent. Larger margins provide more room for indirect costs and a solid net income. Service-related businesses where labor costs are high tend to have lower margins.

Your customers will not pay more for a product or service unless they clearly understand the perceived benefit or extra feature. Also, pricing yourself too far below the market may call into question issues of quality or service. If a lower price is part of your USP, you need to clearly communicate that in your marketing efforts. When you do your budgeting, look at your margins to make sure they are competitive with your industry. Your long-term viability depends on this factor, especially if your competitors are more profitable and will have more to invest in marketing or product development.

If your product or service is completely new to market, you may want to look at similar products or services, although not necessarily competitors. For example, for a new drink with no perceived direct competitors, you will do well to research pricing and margins of other soft drinks and fruit drinks. You may be able to charge more, as Starbucks has demonstrated, but your customer must clearly understand and value the perceived features and benefits. In Starbucks' case, the taste and variety of the coffee, along with the comfortable ambiance, allowed the company to charge more for a cup of coffee and led the company to success.

In practice, most companies will use both approaches, cost plus a margin and market-based pricing, to come up with one or more price points. You can then use industry benchmarks and market feedback to finalize the price. Always aim for the highest price the market can bear. It's relatively easier to lower your price than to increase it for the same product or service. Companies that are able to increase their pricing beyond the basic inflation percentages usually have to offer new features or benefits. You don't usually have to justify a price decrease.

Some companies also conduct price tests before finalizing a particular price. You may want to use this option if the industry benchmarks and market demand are not clear. You can do a "limited run" and offer your product at select price points. You can even try different price points to test small market samples. This test-pricing approach has been used successfully for products offered through catalogs or direct mail. Companies print limited catalogs or direct mailers with different prices and mail them to different target audiences. This method is increasingly less common as a result of the Internet, where it's much harder to control which target audiences have access to which price points.

If you decide to test pricing, have a clear strategy in place and be in direct communication with your customers. This is, of course, easier to do with smaller groups of customers. Sales may vary for a variety of reasons aside from pricing, and you need to be in touch with your customers to understand what is impacting their buying decisions.

For service firms or custom projects, many firms use a cost multiple to determine the price they should charge a customer. To obtain the multiple, companies look at the indirect costs and spread them over the projected revenues for the year. Many firms use cost multiples of between two and three times.

For example, if a project will cost $1,000 in direct costs, most likely labor-related, it would be multiplied by a cost factor of, say, 2.5 to determine the final fee that the customer should be charged; $2,500 in this case. The cost multiple ensures that the indirect costs are spread over all of the projects. Some service industries can get away with higher multiples by increasing the gross margin. If you're faced with lower multiples, you may want to assess the pricing and analyze your venture and the industry overall, as you're in a low-margin business.

Distribution

Determining the optimal distribution strategy will help you determine your sales strategy. Will you sell to your customer directly or through resellers or both? Learning what is typical for your industry will help you understand your customers' expectations. You don't want to spend unnecessary and extra marketing expense to educate your customers on how to find your products or service if they already know where to look for your competitors.

You may also have more than one market for your product or service, and each market may be accessed by a different distribution channel. For example, you may sell through retail stores and/or through value-added resellers who will sell your products along with their other products.

How your customers obtain your product or service is a critical issue. You can have a great product, but if your customers can't find it or you can't get it in front of your customers, there's no sale. This is particularly relevant in the retail industry. Retail distribution is challenging because shelf space is often controlled by large companies. In the retail world, you're "selling and marketing" to the distributor and/or retail buyer as well as to your end user and store customers. Communicating with all of these groups may require several different communication strategies. You'll need to determine how best to forge essential partnerships.

For example, let's say that you have a great new take on an old classic: chocolate chip cookies. Your product's USP is that it's chewier and tastier than other store-bought cookies. You'd love to be on the shelves of giant national supermarkets like those found in Wal-Mart, but those shelves are often controlled by large product companies, many of which are likely to see you as a tiny competitor. It could take quite a while to get on the shelves of Wal-Mart or a major grocery chain. Your better option in the early stages of your company may be to focus on gourmet food stores where new high-quality products may find earlier and easier reception from both the store and customers.

Companies also consider direct mail or catalogs. Both options have been successful and there are pros and cons to each. More recently, the Internet enabled many companies to reach potential customers directly. In each of these three options there is a cost to acquiring each customer. "Acquisition cost" refers to the money it takes to get each customer. It includes purchasing names from a database, mailing costs if it's direct mail or a catalog, and Web advertising or similar promotional costs. You'll need to assess these costs as you evaluate the optimal distribution channels.

Remember that each channel does have a cost, even if it may not be readily evident. For example, if you act as a wholesaler and sell to resellers or buyers, your costs will include sales support staff, marketing materials, and trade shows. We'll cover developing sales teams later in this chapter.

Some businesses sell into channels at a low margin because the volume of their sale compensates for the margin or because the exposure enhances their overall brand. This is often the case for product companies that sell through Wal-Mart. The mass retailer has a reputation and history of squeezing manufacturers' margins. Some have even claimed that they sell at a loss in this channel. However, for most the benefit is clear. The potential volume is one of the largest and provides exposure to the widest customer base. This is an example of the types of pros and cons of pricing in different channels that you'll need to review. There is no correct way to arrive at a price for your product. The strategy you decide to employ depends on your company, the stage of your company, and your overall marketing and sales strategy.

Building a Brand

Many people share the misconception that a brand is a company's logo. While the logo is a visual "expression" of the brand, it is not THE brand.

A brand is the entire package. It is everything about your company. It is how people perceive your offering and the experience they would have if they should choose to select your product or service.

If you are Apple, your brand represents youthful, cool, and cutting-edge technologies and consumer electronics products. And yes, the Apple logo reflects that image as well. If you are Starbucks, your brand represents community, comfort, and enlightenment while enjoying unusual (and expensive) coffee or tea drinks.

On the other hand, if you are the *Wall Street Journal*, you are serious, astute, and rich with knowledge, connections, and quality business news coverage. You are THE source for savvy businesspeople who want to be in the know about important business events and experiences.

One of the first exercises a good marketing firm should do is help you define your brand personality. This definition should then drive how you market yourself, how you create your business environment, the kinds of personalities you hire, and the way you interact with your customers and partners.

One of the first expressions you'll develop from this base is your corporate name and logo. Think about what would have happened if Google had named itself Knowledge Vault. The name Knowledge Vault conveys a very different feeling, doesn't it? Next imagine how the logo would have looked if it was designed around the name and brand personality of Knowledge Vault. Of course, the name Knowledge Vault conveys the company's purpose a lot faster than the name Google. Remember that anytime you do something different and bold like this, you must be prepared to invest heavily in its initial marketing.

Advertising and Promotion

There are many ways to promote your company and products. To decide which medium is best, talk with your market and find out how your potential customers tend to receive information. Do they read magazines? If so, which ones? Do they use the Web to find resources? What sites do they like? Do they go to trade shows? Which ones? Is direct mail or telemarketing more effective?

Determining the best course of promotional investment will depend on many variables such as

- Is this a business-to-consumer offering or a business-to-business offering?
- How big is the target market, and how dispersed are they? In other words, is this a nationwide market or a zip code market?
- How long is a typical sales cycle? One week? One year?
- What's the average price tab? $100 or $1 million?

These types of questions drive the type of promotion you will need and the dollar amount required to penetrate and motivate your target market. The bigger the ticket, the longer the sales cycle, and the more complex the offering, the more expensive and complex the marketing campaigns will need to be.

As you grow and expand, you're likely to consider different types of creative strategies to get your customers to buy your products. Advertising and promotions strategy is a core part of your marketing plan. This section should include the general strategy as well as the detailed action items used, for example, if your strategy is to use trade publications to advertise and promote. For each targeted publication, the specifics may include

- Core message for the publication.
- Timetable for each advertisement and/or editorial—issue release date as well as deadline for the ad or editorial submission.
- Copy for advertisement and creative elements.
- Evaluation for publication—what are the expectations for the publication, and how will you determine if it is successful in reaching your target buyer or influencer? For example, you may measure the hits to your site or phone calls for information.

Using Professional Resources

There are as many types of marketing service firms as there are mediums to use. There are strategic marketing consultants, independent graphic design and writing freelancers, integrated marketing firms, advertising agencies, public relations (PR) agencies, direct-marketing firms, telemarketing firms, event planners, and specialty advertising/promotion firms. It can get quite overwhelming when you are trying to figure out how best to take your offering to market.

Let's discuss the roles as well as pros and cons of each type of organization.

- **Strategic marketing consultants.** These resources can take the form of independent contractors, boutique firms, or large, top-tier firms like the McKinsey or Boston Consulting groups. Their role is to help the executive management team determine the best course of action to obtain optimum growth potential. They may be engaged to validate a strategy, determine M&A prospects, build pricing models, determine product viability, or create the one- and five-year strategic plans, either for fund-raising or for organic growth. You can usually work with these types of firms on either a project basis or a retainer.
- **Independent contractors or boutique firms**. These companies usually charge on a day-rate basis of anywhere between $1,200 and $3,000. Large firms can often have a minimum-size engagement of around $50,000 to $100,000 per month.
- **Freelancers.** On the other side of the spectrum are freelance graphic designers and writers. These people are a wonderful resource if you have already established your strategic plan and developed your value proposition. They are looking for very specific instructions as to what you want, so the more vague you are, the more likely you will be to have several rounds before you are satisfied. These people tend to work out of their homes and can be extremely creative, but not necessarily fabulous business thinkers. Their rates will be somewhere between $45 and $150 per hour.
- **Integrated marketing firms.** These firms have a holistic approach to marketing. They have built in-house teams and/or

strategic alliances with people who have experience delivering all aspects of the marketing mix. They tend to look at the market challenge through a more collaborative, cohesive lens, understanding the functions and timing of each medium. These firms tend to be smaller in size with a more boutique feel. You may find they have certain areas of expertise such as B2B (business to business) versus B2C (business to consumer) or are industry-specific with a focus on technology, law firms, health care, and so on. You can usually work with these types of firms on either a project basis or a retainer.

- **Specialty firms (advertising, PR, direct marketing, etc.).** These firms contain experts in their fields. They have built a business doing their "thing" very well and can apply a wealth of experience in their particular medium to your business challenge. They can charge based on a project or retainer basis. (More on advertising and PR firms coming up in the chapter.)

   For companies whose products are best sold via direct-marketing, finding this type of expertise is also important. True direct-marketing firms know all the postal rules, have fulfillment warehouses established, and use sophisticated software systems to personalize and distribute the information, whether in a letter form or in a three-dimensional kit. They should also own or have resources for list procurement, one of the most fundamental aspects to a successful direct-marketing campaign.

The pro of using any of these types of specialty firms should be obvious. If you pick the right one, they should produce fabulous results. The con is that it will take more money and more management to oversee a diverse group of providers. It can be done quite effectively, but you will probably need to assign a full-time marketing executive to manage these resources and to make sure they are all on the same message and brand strategy.

Project Basis Versus Retainer

Unless you provide services on these models, it is often confusing and intimidating to discuss the best type of payment program with a potential marketing partner. Here's how a project basis works within the firm: All work is tracked on a time basis, usually captured in 15-minute increments, like law and accounting firms. Projects are estimated based on the detailed specs established, and time is factored by individuals required to complete the task. If the specs change, expect the price to change as well. The pros to this type of arrangement are that you only pay for the work you have authorized and that the work has a beginning and an end. The con is that the firm does not function as a strategic partner but only as a vendor, as they are not compensated to play any other role.

Retainers, on the other hand, are fixed monthly fees spread across a 12-month period. These fees are mutually established and should be assigned to specific tasks and individuals. The pros of this type of arrangement are that it gives you total flexibility to change priorities and allows the firm's leaders to fully engage in helping market your company. The con is that if you are not working with an ethical firm, time can be padded and wasted, putting more pressure on you to manage the details.

Advertising Firms

Knowing when to hire an outside ad firm can be a tricky decision. The right time could depend on your marketing and sales experience as well as your overall entrepreneurial experience launching new companies, products, and services.

In the early days, it's highly unlikely that you will need a large ad budget, let alone an ad firm. Your advertising and promotions need to be targeted and results-driven. Given that most start-ups and early-stage companies have modest budgets, you may get better results by hiring a part-time advertising consultant to come in-house and develop and implement initiatives. Most ad firms use a retainer-based business model and assume advertising budgets that far exceed those of most young companies. You'll end up spending more money to train a junior person in the ad firm and are likely to find that many of the best ad strategies come from your own employees, who are closer to both the products and the customers.

As you grow, you'll need to consider advertising and promotions a core part of your strategy. Most companies start with limited print or radio advertising or with direct promotions such as coupons, discounts, and other incentives, as these advertising strategies tend to be the most cost-effective. You should plan to use an advertising consultant or a smaller ad firm to develop and implement this phase of your strategy. Your network and colleagues can help you find credible professionals. Additionally, take a look to see which agencies are creating campaigns that you feel are effective. Just keep in mind that any advertising and promotions strategy will need to be constantly reassessed and revised to meet changes in your marketing and overall business strategy.

Hiring an advertising firm makes sense when you are ready to conduct a major launch, whether on a local or a national basis. These firms' expertise is coming up with campaign "concepts" that best articulate your value proposition while motivating your audience to take some sort of action. You should have multiple concepts to choose from, each a distinct representation of your brand strategy. Traditional ad agencies get compensated in two ways: creative concepting and production, and media planning and buying. Depending on the size of an ad budget, some firms will bundle the creative campaign work into the 15 percent commission fee they get for placing the spots. For this, we're probably talking media buys in the millions of dollars. The smaller the firm and the buy, the more likely you are to work on a project basis.

Public Relations

Public relations efforts can be a very cost-effective way to communicate with your target market. While it's often lumped in with advertising, it's a separate strategy and requires dedicated effort to be effective. In essence, PR is when you can get media attention for your product, service, or company through nonpaid opportunities. There are many publicists in the market, some with firms and others who operate independently.

If you believe you would be best served conducting an aggressive PR campaign, then hiring a specialist in this area makes great sense. He or she should have a Rolodex full of media contacts that cover your industry. A great PR person has built his or her reputation over years of cultivating relationships. This greatly enhances their value and effectiveness and should be appropriately compensated. If you can afford it, be sure to request senior-level talent on your account. Some firms will delegate media "pitching" to junior staff, which can damage your company's image. PR firms almost always only work on retainers, as they are providing a pure service that cannot be taken back or held up if a client doesn't pay its invoice. Therefore, these firms will usually expect to be paid up front for the services they are providing.

PR is a great way for a young company with a unique new product to make the news on TV, radio, or in print. This is in essence free advertising, although you may not always be able to control the message. Large companies routinely focus on promoting their image by supporting worthy charities and other causes. This in turn reinforces their brand and indirectly encourages customers to buy the company's products and services.

Finding a Good Firm

Whether you are looking for a strategic marketing consultant, an ad agency, a PR agency, or a direct-mail house, the best way to find a resource is to ask others who they recommend. Talk to other business owners, call the chamber of commerce, research companies you admire and call them, use search engines, and read marketing magazines.

Before you call any of them, determine your business objective and establish your budget. If you want to learn how to work with different types of firms, ask to meet with a principal, and tell him or her what you are trying to accomplish.

Once you've established the direction you want to go, get a list of no more than eight firms to send a request for proposal (RFP). Provide them with a high-level background on your company and your business goals. Come up with a list of questions that are important to you. For example, you might want to know

- The firm's background
- Types of clients and examples of work/results
- Bios of account members

- In-house or alliance relationships
- Average size of engagement

Review the responses and look for sloppy work, typos, and unanswered questions. Toss those immediately. Narrow your list to four contenders, and ask them to give a formal presentation. Set up two days of presentations in which you'll have two presentations per day: one in the morning and one in the afternoon. Make sure the executives and decision makers are all available. Ask them to give a capabilities presentation and to provide some initial thoughts on how they may approach your engagement.

Do not ask for or be swayed by "spec" creative work. If you are seeing ad concepts before there's been any kind of strategic dialogue or knowledge transfer, you are getting pretty pictures, not business-building and thoughtful marketing.

After you have seen your four presentations, narrow the field to two and go visit their offices. Ask to meet the team that will be assigned to your account. Take a tour. Does it look like a creative, organized environment or a sloppy, disheveled heap of stuff? Do the people have the appropriate appearance and "bright eyes"?

Call references and determine how the firm plans to kick off the relationship. Be prepared to tell the firms your budget early in the process. Don't do the "you tell me" routine. Any firm worth its reputation will give you everything it can for the dollars you have to spend. If they know what you have available, you won't get ideas you can't afford. If they don't think you've budgeted enough to accomplish your business goals, you should be told and a win-win solution established.

Guerilla Marketing

Guerilla marketing is a popular concept often associated with low-budget, early-stage companies. It can be quite successful depending on your product or service. There isn't one clear set of guerilla strategies. Rather, the term "guerilla marketing" refers to any low-cost approach. PR, for example, can be an effective guerilla marketing strategy if you manage to get noted in a magazine or on the news.

Companies are increasingly using the Internet to market their products and services. For example, we sell our products through resellers. On a regular basis (weekly, monthly, or quarterly) depending on the reseller, we create an e-mail that has some interesting information (for value) as well as limited product information. It's usually in an engaging format with graphics and links to more resources on our site. We customize our e-mail for each reseller by adding their logo and contact information. In essence, we have created a marketing tool that is turnkey. We send it to our primary marketing contact at each reseller, who in turn sends it to their entire e-mail customer distribution.

Just remember that guerilla marketing is a catchall phrase that encourages entrepreneurs and their teams to get creative on a cost-effective basis.

Developing a Sales Strategy

One of the first things you'll need to focus on in your planning is determining what kind of sales organization you'll need to develop. Different products and services require different selling solutions.

Identifying your optimal distribution strategy will help determine the type of sales organization you use. How and where do customers find and purchase your products and services? Your sales strategy will need to be suited for your distribution strategy. In my first company we sold directly to corporations. As a result, our efforts were limited by the number of calls and meetings we could do on a daily basis. My second and third companies operated in multiple industries. We determined that the optimal selling strategy was to align with partners and distributors in each market. Our products were complementary and provided a new revenue source for our partners, who didn't incur any product development costs. The advantage to this strategy is that you have many more salespeople "selling your products," but you don't incur the cost of building a sales organization. The challenge is that your partners are likely to be selling multiple products: theirs, yours, and others. As a result, selling your products may not always be their priority. One option is to partner with your resellers and distributors to incentivize their sales team with contests, bonuses, and promotions.

Every sale strategy has its pros and cons, and you'll need to analyze them thoroughly before deciding on one. Competitor structures and strategies can also provide insight on what's likely to be successful for a specific industry.

As you develop your sales strategy, you'll need to focus on the following key areas:

- Building the optimal sales organization
- Developing sales forecasts and pipelines
- Managing your customers and your customer diversification

Building the Optimal Sales Organization

Building a sales organization takes time, and your strategy will need to account for the evolving structure. In the beginning, you're likely to have a key role in sales, and most successful entrepreneurs maintain an active involvement in the sales process even when they hire a senior team. This is one of the best ways to monitor issues and trends within your market and with your clients and sales team.

Hiring Salespeople

Most entrepreneurs will candidly tell you that it is difficult to hire good salespeople. Lots of people will tell you they are great salespeople, and most will be quite convincing, as they should be. But the key issue is whether or not they can sell your product or service. Do they understand your buyer? Do they know potential buyers and have an industry network? This is particularly useful for corporate sales. Do they have experience with similar sales and cycles? Someone who sells office products is probably not going to be able to transition easily to selling complex software on a corporate-wide solution. The size of the sale, the length of the cycle, and ability to deal with the level of decision makers are all different.

One strategy that's used by many companies is hiring salespeople from their likely competitors. These candidates understand the industry, know the buyers and influencers, and are likely to produce results more quickly. Having said that, they are also likely to be more expensive and may have signed noncompete contracts with former employers. In any interview process, be sure to ask if the candidate has signed a noncompete with his or her current or former employers. If so, ask for a copy so you can properly determine the person's ability to be effective in your organization.

Monitor your sales team's results daily. There's no substitute for knowing what's going on with your market and customers. Daily monitoring helps you evaluate your team's performance better and also track changes in customer preferences. Use daily call sheets that note how many calls a salesperson made and to whom and the status of the call. Be prepared to spot-check names and numbers, as there are unscrupulous salespeople who list friends or fake contacts in order to fill their sheet. Review phone bills as well to make sure calls are really being made.

When you sell to corporations and institutions, you'll need to understand how decisions are made and the budget cycles. In many cases, when you're selling to large companies, your user is often different than the final person who says yea or nay. However, you may have to first market to the user and get acceptance and the sale before selling the "value" all over again to a purchasing department. Again, the size of the sale will dictate the height of the hurdles.

Developing Sales Forecasts and Customer Pipeline

There are essentially two ways to develop sales projections for a new venture. The first is to use industry comparables, and the second is to estimate based on market size and share.

Industry comparables are most useful if you can successfully adjust for critical variables including the age and size of the firm, size of the sales team, and marketing budget. For example, a company that projects that it can sell the same number of units in its first year of operations as its competitor, which has more than two decades in the marketplace, is likely to fall short.

Tales from the Trenches:
Building a Direct Sales Force

Liz Elting, president and founder of TransPerfect/Translations.com, built a sales organization from scratch. She and her partner, the company's first salespeople, determined early on that they needed to have their own in-house sales team to be most successful. Rather than hiring seasoned and expensive salespeople, she opted to hire young graduates who showed promise. By investing in sales training and coaching over the course of the hire's first year, she was able to groom a successful sales team. The sales training enabled the company to make sure that each new salesperson understood the company's products, capabilities, and unique entrepreneurial culture, as well as position in the marketplace.

Early on, the company's low starting salaries resulted in turnover, which was a challenge, although a manageable one. In this case, Liz saw the benefits of the lower cost and the ability to train new candidates directly as outweighing the turnover challenge. Additionally, over time, Liz realized that much of the turnover came from young hires who came to TransPerfect directly out of college with no other corporate work experience. As a result, the company now seeks to balance its new hires to ensure that more have previous work experience. Further, as the company grew and earned an industry reputation as the fourth largest translation company, it has become easier to hire more qualified and experienced candidates.

In the early days, all new sales hires received a draw against their commission for a year or more as appropriate for their sales territory. This draw was intentionally low and has remained around $25,000 to $40,000 based on the new hire's experience. The commissions are paid at 9 percent of the sale. As a result, the intent is to motivate the salesperson to quickly exceed their draw. Of course, there's frequent oversight to see if goals are being met and to assess any shortfalls. If a salesperson is unable to exceed his or her draw over time, then it's likely they are not a good fit with the firm. However, if someone is doing all the right things, the company will continue to work with him or her with a continued focus on results. In addition to high commissions, salespeople are incentivized by bonuses, vacations, and other perks. For example, in the early days when she had only 26 employees and a banner year, Liz took the entire team to the Bahamas as a reward for the year's growth and profitability.

Managers are also incentivized with a bonus based on the revenues and profitability of his or her team. Additionally, as a market differentiator, even project and quality managers on the production side receive bonuses based on similar models. This strategy helps align everyone in delivering the best-quality services to the customer in the most cost-effective manner.

In training and motivating the sales team, Liz's company has preferred to promote from within, a strategy that has worked well. The company works hard to develop its team and twice a year holds training sessions, one in the company's New York offices and one at an off-site location. The overall sales strategy has clearly worked, as TransPerfect/Translations.com reached more than $50 million in sales in its twelfth year of operations and has offices in 27 cities worldwide.

The market share approach is similar and focuses on achieving gradual market share over three to five years. For example, if the total market for the product is $1 billion and you target achieving a market share of 1 percent in three to five years, then your projections would gradually build to those levels.

The challenge with these forecasting approaches is that while the revenue projections may seem doable, most entrepreneurs underestimate the cost it requires to achieve those sales. If you have 2 salespeople and your closest competitor has 10 salespeople, as well as a healthy marketing budget, you can easily begin to see why achieving the same results would be very difficult if not impossible.

In developing your forecasts and sales strategy, it's very helpful to determine the sales revenue per employee or per salesperson. It should be consistent with the industry, and your goal should be to increase it. As a general rule, if your firm tends to have higher-paid employees, it should have higher revenue per employee number. Achieving $100,000 to $200,000 in revenues per employee is common. Well-run and very profitable companies may have even more than $500,000 in revenues per employee. This number is important to monitor because it will help you realize when you have too many people on staff, with diminishing returns to revenues and possibly the bottom line. If the number decreases and revenues increase, then your team may not be as productive as you think, and you need to look at everyone's functions more closely. Your goal is for both revenues and the number to increase, although the latter may be more incremental in growth rate.

Managing Your Customers and Diversification

Plan early on how you will diversify your customer base, whether by adjusting the ratio of large and small customers or by reaching out to new industries. Be careful to ensure that one company or industry's problems won't adversely affect your firm. This customer diversification should be a core part of your early sales and marketing strategy.

Do a periodic credit check on all major customers, vendors, or suppliers. This will help you adjust your policies—particularly your payment policies—if their ratings are poor or change over time. If your business relies on several large customers, or if you sell through a few large distributors or retailers, keep abreast of how their businesses are performing and talk to their employees if you can. Their financial health will directly impact yours.

Many young companies are so happy to have customers that they don't bother to see how much each customer is costing them. Managing your customers requires customer service and marketing. Some customers can become so time-consuming that you may be spending a disproportionate amount of resources servicing just one or two. Monitor how much time and money it takes to maintain a customer relationship. If you're spending 70 percent of your time tending to the business demands and needs of a customer who accounts for only 5 percent of revenues, you get the picture—something is wrong. You don't necessarily need to get rid of the customer, although some companies choose to do so, but rather you may discreetly shift resources and diplomatically realign the customer's expectations of what level of customer attention is acceptable for both.

Effective marketing and sales strategies evolve throughout the growth of your company. Paying close and frequent attention to these evolving strategies will help to ensure your long-term success.

CHAPTER 5

MANAGING, GOVERNANCE, AND ADVISORY

There's no shortage of books, people, and advisors who will tell you that good people are one of a company's most important assets. In working with employees, board members, or advisors, make an effort to manage them well and channel their passion and talents in the same direction as yours.

Managing People

Hiring employees is one of the biggest challenges for many young companies. Issues arise from deciding which types of people you may need to hire to managing expectations as you grow. The following are some key issues to think about along the way.

Hiring: From One to Many, Many More

As you expand and begin to hire employees, take extra care before bringing on new people. Some growing companies can be in such need for people that they will hire too quickly, without a thorough hiring process in place. Having guidelines from the beginning will help avoid wrong hires. Many seasoned entrepreneurs have candidates meet with all of the senior management and many of the team members that they will work with.

Your review process should include the following:

- **Résumé check.** You may want to spot-check facts on the candidate's résumé to ensure accuracy. Before you start checking, get the candidate's written permission to check on his or her résumé, background, and references. You may need to fax this statement of permission before some organizations will release verification of employment or school attendance. Most companies will only formally verify or not verify employment dates. Some may release salary information, but most will not. To get more detailed information, your best bet is to talk to references—see below. Also, check the résumé timetable for gaps. Most people have good personal reasons for gaps on their résumés, but be sure to ask. You can often tell a lot about a person by the way he or she answers. For example, some may be defensive about a time gap, while others may happily tell you they took time off to travel and find themselves. I am often happier if someone has already done their intense soul-searching—he or she is less likely to need to do it while in my company's employment.
- **Multiple interviews.** Have a prospective candidate meet with several other team members. Additionally, meet with the candidate at least twice on separate occasions. Sometimes first impressions can change for the better or worse.
- **Skills check.** If you are hiring for a specific skill, you may want to test the person. Give him or her a brief marketing or technical project to complete before the next interview. Ask him or her to consider a hypothetical problem during the interview to evaluate the candidate's thinking process and/or ability to think on his or her feet. You can also ask to see samples of previous work or writing samples if communications are a key part of the job. Be sure that the candidate has the skill set you need and not just on the paper résumé. For fairness and accurate evaluations, be sure to ask candidates the same or very similar questions.
- **Reference check.** Always check references. A lot of people correctly assume that references will always be good. That's true—who would give the name for a bad reference? However, if you ask questions in different ways, you can glean a lot of information by how things are said or not said. Always ask if the

candidate would be eligible for rehire at the old firm and if they would hire that person again. Most people are candid in their responses. Also call references; don't send letters or e-mail. People are always more candid by phone, as they perceive written responses to be more legally liable.

- **Background checks.** Depending on what the employee's function will be in your company, you many want to consider some type of background check. Note that many states have guidelines about what kinds of background checks are legally permissible. Know the rules for your state and check periodically, as they can change from year to year. If someone is going to be handling money, you may want to conduct a credit or criminal check. However, many states have guidelines on how you can use the information and whether or not you can keep it in the employee files.

- **Probation or trial period.** It sounds more ominous than it is, and almost all companies have a provision for a trial employment period. For most companies it is three months, which is usually adequate time to know if the hire is right for your firm. Most companies actually have benefits begin after this probation period. Make sure to schedule a review at the end of the three-month period, so that both you and the employee can be sure that the position is right for both of you. This probation or trial period policy should be stated in your employee manual, a copy of which should be provided to all hires.

Successful hires are dependent not only on getting the right skills, but also the right personality fit. Consider a candidate based on his or her suitability for the company, not just a specific job. Does the candidate have the right work attitude and ethic to fit in with your firm? If people work in close quarters or need to be flexible and work on different teams, it's essential that they get along. Sometimes, it can just be a case of a personality fit. If you hire someone who quickly seems to not fit the organization, you may need to take immediate action. Use the trial employment period to meet to discuss the employee's style and the company culture. If a couple of meetings over the first month or two do not seem to be working, you may need to terminate the employee rather than let discontent grow and widen. The productivity of the rest of your team may be negatively impacted if a new hire can't and won't fit in.

With new employees, use both a new hire letter and a confidentiality/noncompete letter. The new hire letter should state the person's employment is "at will" and while employed the new hire has a salary and other basic benefits. The following is a good template for an offer letter. Don't add too much detail or make binding promises. While this provision has been standard for all companies, many firms find that their ability to exercise their "at-will" provision is increasingly limited.

After you have a couple of employees, it's worth implementing an employee manual. A lawyer should be able to provide the basic form of one that you can customize if needed. Your employee manual should state the details of any benefits. Remember that you don't need to provide overly generous benefits and privileges. A basic manual will state working hours, dress code, if applicable, policy toward discrimination and harassment, and any procedures for addressing office issues. Manuals can and should be updated annually or once every two years to reflect changes in the company.

The employment at will provision is simply to provide you flexibility in case you need to fire someone for cause or not for cause. Remember, you can't ever fire an employee for discriminatory or retaliatory reasons. If you need to terminate an employee—and almost every entrepreneur will have to at some point in his or her company's growth—conduct a professional and tactful termination meeting. Always have at least one other senior manager present, preferably from human resources (HR).

If the issues are skills-based, you should have already conducted one or more performance reviews in which you met with the employee to discuss the problem areas. Document the meeting and action items that need improvement. Once an employee fails to improve, you'll have cause and be able to terminate employment without facing legal actions.

Your employee manual should outline the specifics regarding what is and isn't "cause" for terminating an employee as well as standard benefits relating to days off, and so on. You should have a lawyer review or create your manual for you, as it is the official set of guidelines for

SAMPLE TEMPLATE
FOR OFFER LETTER

DATE

Dear _____:

It is with great pleasure that we extend to you the following offer:

        Position:

    Annual Salary:

        Vacation: _____ vacation days

                        All federal holidays (this is optional)

  Effective Date:

     Start Date:

These compensation terms are conditioned upon your continued employment with XYZ Company. In accordance with XYZ Company's policy, your employment is "at will" and may be terminated, with or without cause, at any time at the option of XYZ Company or you.

You will be receiving, under separate cover; information related to health insurance and benefits and will be eligible for health insurance coverage effective _____.

Regards,

_____

employees. It will also obviously contain language about not discriminating and equal opportunity. Most lawyers will tell you that less is best and that you should provide clear guidelines for both the company and the employee on the terms of employment. Spend some time giving the manual the right tone. You will probably need to modify it from time to time.

If you have proprietary products or technology, you should implement a confidentiality agreement. Many companies also opt to have salespeople sign confidentiality and noncompete agreements. I'll talk more about this in Chapter 6.

Corporate Culture

Pay particular attention early on to establishing a corporate culture that is both complementary to your management style and to the needs of your company and employees. Different industries and talents require distinct cultures in which to flourish. Don't wait until things get sour to think about culture. Nurture it from the beginning.

I'll talk more about culture in Chapter 7, particularly as it relates to doing business globally and marketing. In building a corporate culture, there are many similarities. Culture is a set of shared values and attitudes. Corporate cultures are really the company's personality and include everything from determining the dress code and physical ambiance of the office to the ways employees interact and relate to one another and to you and other senior managers.

Think about what kind of corporate culture you want to promote. How do employees perceive you? What kind of environment do you work in best? Manage in best? The answers to these questions are likely to greatly influence the culture. If you have one or more partners, it's particularly important to have a consistent culture. If your management styles and business values are very different, it can be confusing for your employees, who may get mixed messages. Invariably one of you is likely to have a stronger influence on the corporate culture, for better or worse, and hopefully for better. Make the effort to discuss these issues early on as you add employees to the office.

Never underestimate the impact of the outside world on your workforce. It shapes their expectations of themselves as an employee and of you as the employer. In good economic times, obviously the demands increase, and in recessions, while the demands decrease so too does overall morale. The outside world impacts productivity, customer service, and overall enthusiasm. This should not be news to you. Considering all factors that impact your workforce is basic management.

Unfortunately, many entrepreneurs forget to incorporate basic management practices and thinking into their daily management style. It's always more relevant to younger companies, as these issues can become more magnified and disrupt the bottom line much more quickly in a small company than in a larger company where groups of employees are more segregated from each other.

Corporate culture is also impacted by the structure of the organization. In the early days, you're likely to be very lean, and everyone will need to multitask nimbly. As you grow and add people, specific job responsibilities will become more defined. You'll find that some employees may thrive better in one type of environment versus another, and others are able to transition. Employees who love the freshness of multitasking may become bored and lose work performance if their job becomes narrowly defined. On the other hand, some people do best when they know the specific tasks associated with their job and like to remain within well-defined parameters. You will need both types of people. Be aware of who on your growing team fits in which category and who fits in the shades between.

As part of defining and communicating your corporate culture, most companies find it useful to write down the company's values and mission. Make sure as you go through this process that your mission statement reflects principles that you (and any partners) sincerely embrace. If it's just a paper exercise, your employees will not pay it much attention. It's helpful to have these principles noted not only in public areas, like a poster in the common area or, if appropriate for public access, on the Web site, but also in the employee manual.

Access

In the beginning, you're likely to have a more junior or more technical team. You'll probably spend a great deal of time with each person, often working in close quarters, as space is usually limited. These people are essential to your early growth, and most will take great pride in knowing that they were the "ground crew," so to speak.

The challenge occurs when you begin to add more people to the team and have less time and attention to give to people who have come to expect it. You may also hire more senior people, creating management layers that will limit the ground crew's access to you. This will occur even if you maintain an open-door style of management. It's just simply an inevitable aspect of growing. The key is to manage the expectations of this group of people. Find ways to communicate regularly, either through e-mails or newsletters. Often people who enjoyed "being in the know" resent no longer being first in line for communication. Make it a point to recognize their work and efforts, publicly if possible. During the dot-com boom, many early-stage companies gave each hire a number based on the order of when he or she started working. This sense of historical hierarchy helped to mitigate the angst that many felt from the natural and inevitable corporate changes.

Expectations

Managing employee expectations as you grow can be both rewarding and challenging.

The weekly Friday pizza party that was just fine for 5 employees is going to start eating into your budget at 50 employees and be financially unreasonable for 100 employees. In my second company, in the beginning, we used to celebrate every person's birthday with an office cake. It worked fine while we were at an inexpensive 8-inch cake from our local grocery store, which happened to taste pretty good. Once we passed about 10 people and the cake size changed, we realized that celebrating *every* birthday was too costly. We opted to celebrate birthdays once a month, and instead of getting one big custom bakery cake, which would have become very expensive, we chose several of the 8-inch options.

Your perks will need to be adjusted as you grow, and you may get some resistance on some of them. The cake example worked out fine in the end. On the other end, it's possible that people will get annoyed as some benefits are reduced or modified as the employee population grows. I know many colleagues who have experienced what I call the "hot cocoa and coffee variety challenge." It starts when, in the early days, you may offer a variety of benefits like beverages, snack foods, and Kleenex boxes for each desk. Companies usually do this to keep break times quick and employees focused on the work at hand. Some companies that expect late nights from their employees may also keep well-stocked kitchens to keep people at their desks. Over time, you'll realize that instead of five or six varieties of coffee, two should suffice. One type of tea will do instead of stocking a full assortment. Many entrepreneurs face this type of situation and find that when they try cutting nonessential expenses, there can be employee dissatisfaction.

This is not an unusual scenario. It happens even to the largest and most established of companies, who have to reduce some perks in times of cost cutting. I point it out here because most entrepreneurs are unprepared for the backlash. Entrepreneurs who provide these benefits in the early days are more used to the positive feedback and are unaware that changing times may require adjustments, even of the smaller and less significant items. Some entrepreneurs prefer to not provide these items as daily benefits but as exceptions so that no one takes them for granted.

Employee Benefits

There is a wide range of federal and state guidelines in the United States that govern benefits regarding parental leave, jury duty, military leave, and so on. You'll need to consult with a labor lawyer to identify the guidelines that apply to your size of company. Also project out at least 12 to 24 months, and make a note of the types of guidelines that may apply once you have reached certain benchmarks on the number of full-time and part-time employees.

It may help you plan your staffing needs more efficiently to hire more part-time or project workers, for whom many of the guidelines may not apply. Early-stage companies often prefer to use "temporary" or "project workers" instead of hiring them as employees. In general, most companies do not pay taxes for temporary or project workers, often called consultants. Instead, companies give a gross payment, based on a negotiated hourly, weekly, or monthly rate. The IRS has guidelines that define a full-time employee and that state when payroll processing and taxes are required. Your accountant can help you understand the way taxes may impact your staffing plan.

Many young companies find that they can acquire senior skill sets by hiring skilled individuals as part-timers. For example, they may hire a part-time CFO or human resource manager. Many of these jobs are essential for building strong, long-term viable organizations; however, there's rarely enough full-time work for these professionals. Many Web sites can help you find this senior level of part-time professional.

Medical, Dental, and Life

Most growing companies find it advantageous to offer some type of medical benefits, often because the entrepreneur needs these personally. You will also find that having some sort of medical coverage is an important recruitment tool. You may lose valuable potential employees who need coverage, and who may even be willing to pay for it themselves. In the United States, insurance companies will provide medical plans for young companies with at least two employees being covered.

You can decide what constitutes an eligible employee based on his or her employment start date and the number of hours the employee works per week. Most companies choose to offer medical benefits to employees who work at least 30 hours per week and have been employed with the company for a minimum of three months, although some may wait till six months. Part of this decision depends on whether your company pays for a portion of the expense or if the employee pays for all of it, although on a pretax basis. If you are in your early years and not certain of your profitability, your best bet is to offer medical coverage but let the cost be 100 percent covered by the employee. It may not be a well-liked policy, but it helps to manage expectations as you grow and need flexibility with costs. As you grow and become more financially stable, you may opt to cover up to 50 percent of the expense, which is pretty standard. It's rare these days, but some companies do cover 100 percent of the expense. This is often industry-specific, and further, if you have union employees, there may be additional considerations that you need to be aware of.

Some companies choose to provide additional employee benefits in the form of life insurance, disability, and travel accident insurance. In general, remember it's always easier to give more coverage as you grow and much harder to reduce benefits. Most employees are aware of the financial limitations of young companies and will be more tolerant of fewer benefits earlier on.

As you grow, you may want to consider using the services of employee benefits administrators and consulting firms to determine which benefits fit your company's budget and make you competitive from a hiring perspective. Many of these firms will manage the benefits for you for a fee.

Vacation, Sick Leave, and Holidays

In the United States, depending on the number of employees you have, you may be required to provide unpaid sick leave for medical or family leave. Most professionals coming from the corporate world are accustomed to a number of paid sick days. You'll need to determine what works best for your growing company.

Over the years, from talking with many entrepreneurs and owners of young firms, I have found that combining personal and sick days allows employees the most flexibility and does not penalize those who tend not to get sick or stay home for minor ailments. For example, we give five combined paid personal or sick days for each employee. These days do not include maternity or disability leaves. On the off chance that an employee is sick for more than five days, then he or she begins to use up vacation days. Some companies prefer to have illness periods instead of days. For example, three illnesses a year, whether it is one day or five days. This way someone who has the flu for a week does not use up vacation days. All of these benefits incur costs, so determine the mix that makes best sense for your company, employees, and industry.

When determining your company's vacation and sick leave, you should always retain the option and right under your employee manual to make exceptions at the company's discretion. However, if this becomes an ongoing issue, modify your leave policy, as you do not want to make exceptions a habit.

Vacation days are usually based on seniority and range from 10 to 20 days per year. Most young companies find it costly and cumbersome to let vacation, personal, and sick days accrue to the next year. Accordingly, "use it or lose it" policies are standard for young companies, just as they are for many established larger firms. You may want to see what is standard for each position in your industry, and award vacation and sick days accordingly.

A perk that is often very well appreciated by many employees is the opportunity to take their birthday as a holiday. Some companies offer a rotating birthday holiday so that the employee can choose to take their own birthday or that of another immediate family member. This can be a great way to build good will with your team.

Most companies give major holidays as paid time off to their employees. You'll need to see what works best for your company and industry. For example, if your customers expect 24/7 service, who will manage issues on holidays? Young companies often manage this by having a more general policy in place providing e-mail customer response within a set time frame, such as two business days, not including holidays. You'll still need to assign coverage, but it will be less onerous. You may also consider staggering the holidays employees can take or make it volunteer-based for the popular ones like Thanksgiving, Christmas, and New Year's.

Bonuses

Bonuses can come in many forms: cash, stock (which I'll discuss in the next section), vacation days, company and group events and outings, and so on. The first step is to determine what you want bonuses to mean to your employees. Is it recognition of outstanding achievement and, therefore, an award for few, but not for all? Or is a bonus an annual "thank-you" to all employees for jobs well done. In countries like Japan, which focus on the collective spirit of a company, traditionally every employee gets a year-end and a midyear bonus that is based on a predetermined multiple of his or her weekly salary. In some industries, like finance and investment banking, bonuses represent a form of profit sharing, and each employee's take is based on a predetermined formula of his or her contribution to the revenues and bottom line.

You may want to take a look at your competitors to see what their policies and benefits are. At the minimum, you want to be competitive in your ability to hire the best candidates. At best, an innovative approach might help you stand apart if you compete heavily in the market for the best employees. As with other employee programs and benefits, consistency is key. You can always add more in later years, but don't be overly generous one year only to have to completely pull back from any bonuses in the next down year.

You can use a bonus as a way to motivate everyone to repeat the year's successes. Be sure that you set aside a good portion of the year's profits to grow the company rather than distribute it to employees entirely.

Cash is one of the more traditional bonus rewards. Some companies give gifts at key holidays—for example, a turkey for every employee at Thanksgiving or Christmas. Remember that every form of bonus has a cost, and you'll need to think about not only how it impacts your bottom line, but if it meets the expectations of your employees and is in line with your industry. Some may love the holiday turkey, and others would prefer a significant cash gift. Another option used by many companies is gift cards, for example, from Visa, MasterCard, American Express, Borders, or Starbucks. Some can be purchased in bulk and at a discount. Again, you'll need to understand what your employees will value.

Recent studies have shown that most employees prefer bonuses in the form of extra vacation days. This is usually one of the most economical ways for entrepreneurs to reward valued employees. While there is still a technical cost—the actual wages and benefits for the day or days the employee receives—it is not an additional new cost. The employee's wages and benefits are already part of your firm's budget. Chances are that valued and conscientious workers, for whom you'd be considering bonus time off, are also likely to be sure to complete all of their work, so there are no loose ends or unmet customer needs. Many employees may just relish being awarded the extra bonus time off and may not take it for months.

Additional incentives are vacations, meals, and trip vouchers. Company events and outings are a great way to reward the team as well as to encourage employees to get to know one another and to build loyalty. Some companies have an annual holiday party in December. Some invite families and others limit it to employees. Part of your decision will be based on budget considerations and whether you can host the event at your office or if you need to rent outside space. If you are having a holiday event for clients, plan a separate one for employees.

Stock

Stock is an additional form of compensation for employees. It can be used to reward valuable employees as well as to encourage loyalty from early employees who may be making less than market salaries or have to put in significantly more work time. There are three forms of stock compensation. The most commonly known is the stock option. Lesser known but quite useful are stock appreciation rights and actual outright stock purchases. I'll discuss all three.

Many companies, particularly those that are funded by private investment from angels or venture capitalists, establish stock ownership plans. Stock ownership has become a very common incentive tool, particularly for senior hires. Stock options actually give the employee the right to buy the stock at a specified price for a certain period of time. These options can also be exercised if the company is acquired. Once purchased, this stock represents actual ownership in the company.

For many employees of public companies, this can be a lucrative form of compensation. For employees of young, nonpublic companies, the issue is the time it may take for this benefit to have actual financial value. Further, the value of options can disappear quickly and can take years to reacquire value. Unless you have a growth company with very strong potential either in the stock market or for being acquired, your employees may not all value receiving stock options.

On average, most companies reserve around 15 percent of the company's stock for employees. There are no hard-and-fast rules, and obviously you should not give up the whole 15 percent early on. This number may get diluted by future rounds of fund-raising, depending on the terms of each round and your negotiating ability. Dilution means that the stocks held by any investor or employee represents a smaller percentage of the equity as new shares are given to new investors. In this case, in the early days you may reserve 15 percent of the shares for employees, but with your next round of funding, this may go down to less than 15 percent.

As an employee of the company, you can choose to participate in the employee plan. Some entrepreneurs and VCs see stock options as a way to get some equity back to the entrepreneur for a job well done. Options are usually priced higher than the current value or are triggered in the event of an acquisition.

Stock appreciation rights enable employees to receive financial payment if a stock appreciates, but they don't have to actually exercise the option. Some companies choose to give stock directly, but this is less commonly used than options.

If you are the sole owner of your company, you can incent your team with similar concepts without giving up equity. Some entrepreneurs implement a form of profit sharing or financial benefit if the company is sold. This enables employees to benefit in the upside without the entrepreneur giving up equity. This is a more realistic option if you're not intending to go public or be acquired in the next five years. You can always add a new stock plan as you grow and an IPO or acquisition become more realistic exit strategies. Remember, the goal is to provide incentive and reward for your employees. They should perceive value in a reasonable time horizon.

Governance and Advisory

There are two types of groups that provide governance and advice: a board of directors and an advisory board, sometimes called an advisory council or group. The operative word is "advisory." Everyone tells you to set up a board and advisory council, but many entrepreneurs don't pay enough attention to establishing truly useful boards. Board and advisory members can be enormously beneficial if they are selected, cultivated, and utilized wisely.

Board of Directors

Legally, most types of companies must have a board of directors. However, many young companies do not necessarily institute one until they receive external funding—usually venture capital. Boards of directors primarily have a fiduciary duty. With the increased threat of litigation from many angles, many potential board members may be initially reluctant to take on this role, as it brings on legal obligations.

Your first set of board members is likely to be your investors, whether friends and family, angels, or venture capitalists. When you get to the venture capital or "institutional" stage of investors, you may find that your new members would prefer not to be on a board filled with friends and family and will help start the process of finding more professional board members to fill key slots. This can be quite helpful in getting people with access and experience involved with your firm. However, be aware that some of them may have allegiances to your venture capitalist, often as a result of other deals, and that some may not be able to retain objectivity in challenging scenarios. Board members can have their own agendas that may not be in your interest (as you'll read in the example at the end of this chapter).

Boards of directors should provide expertise and outreach, particularly VC board members, to customers, vendors, and key industry members. They can provide references for accessing lawyers, accountants, investors, and investment bankers.

To recruit board members, you'll need to get board liability insurance, usually called D&O insurance (for directors and officers). This has become even more relevant in the past decade, as seasoned professionals are well aware of the potential liabilities if they serve on a corporate board. Many professionals may prefer to serve on an advisory board that has no fiduciary responsibilities. Once they are comfortable with a company's operations, they may agree to serve on the board. Be clear in such situations on what you expect from members of either type of board and whether you will need them to switch eventually.

Use the process outlined below to identify a plan for each board member to bring in sales or know how to help grow the company.

Advisory Boards

Many companies use advisory boards as a way to gain insight, expertise, and contacts. In some industries, the advisory board may be a technical advisory board providing scientific or technical expertise. While less common, some companies may have both a general advisory board and a technical advisory board. For example, a biotech firm might have two distinct needs: one on the scientific side and the other on the sales and marketing side.

Be wary of just assembling a list of names, no matter how credible. Just as there is for your board of directors, there should be a clear mission for the group and a plan for each member. Educate board members thoroughly on your firm, and establish mutual expectations. People serve on advisory boards more for the industry outreach rather than for a monetary compensation. You can give advisory members warrants or other equity incentives.

Tales from the Trenches

As CEO of a hot growing branding firm in Atlanta, Karen See of Abovo Group successfully built an advisory board without giving up any equity. Members found value in networking with others on the board as well as with Karen, who often introduced members to others in the local business community. Advisory board members were also likely intrigued by Abovo because it was a hot growth company, and it had been named the fourth fastest growing female-owned business in Atlanta in 2000.

Deciding whom to ask to be board members required some strategic planning, however. Karen made a list of the people she wanted and put a sales plan together for getting them. It started with her former boss and mentor, Larry Ferguson, who was the former CEO of First Data Corporation, Health Systems Division. Even though Larry lived in Charlotte, he was willing to travel to Atlanta once a quarter to help because he had been the one to encourage her to start the business in 1997 and had been her first client. In Atlanta, Karen focused on getting Tom McNeight, CEO of GuardedNet. Tom was one of the city's top technology executives, and people were always trying to find a way to be introduced to him. Karen used Larry to get Tom, and Tom was used to get the remaining board members. Once these people knew who else was on board, they quickly agreed.

Karen made an effort to make meetings engaging, strategic, and focused. She'd fax or e-mail agendas and detailed strategic information a few days in advance. She openly solicited and encouraged members to offer innovative suggestions for all parts of her fast-growing company. Having grown to almost 100 employees in just three years, she wanted input on management issues as well as overall strategy. She shared everything with her board, from the financials to HR issues to sales opportunities to strategic growth plans. But she never forgot that these board members were also a sales channel, so dwelling on the negative was not good for getting new business.

Her board gave her candid feedback on her strategic plans as well as helped interview new executive applicants. As CEOs often find, getting useful and positive feedback can be rare. Her board provided the positive reinforcement and encouragement executives need. They not only helped her manage the growth up, but they helped her successfully manage her way through the economic downturn that hurt so many marketing firms . . . particularly those with a heavy technology client base.

Compensating a board of advisors of this caliber can be daunting. Karen realized that most of the members were financially well-off, so she decided to compensate them with creative rather than financial incentives. She gave quarterly gift cards for things like fine dining and a yearlong subscription to a business book-of-the-month club as a way to say thank you.

While the roles of boards of directors and advisory boards differ in some areas, many factors are actually quite similar. Issues relating to recruitment, plan development, education, compensation, and evaluation overlap. I'll cover these below and highlight any differences. Boards are only useful if you plan and utilize them strategically.

Recruiting

The optimal candidates for boards depend in large part on your industry and the stage of your company. Focus on an advisory board first, as it will eliminate the need to address the candidate's fiduciary responsibilities, and, accordingly, the compensation component may be less.

An industry expert brings credibility to young companies. You may also want to consider people with industry sales, marketing, and distribution expertise. Many companies also seek out professionals in law, finance, and accounting to provide valuable expertise at critical junctures. You may also want to add one or more entrepreneurs. Look for people with not only industry expertise but experience in successful and unsuccessful ventures. We live in a culture where successes are valued more, but it's the failures that can provide essential lessons. Don't underestimate this group of people, especially if they have other complementary skills in addition to raising capital and industry experience.

To attract credible candidates, you'll need to have a formal business plan and perhaps even a PowerPoint presentation. Advisory board member candidates may even be suitable angel investors, but be clear in defining both of their roles to avoid confusion and frustrations. If they do invest, be clear that the advisory board role is for a finite time period and the investment did not buy them a lifetime seat. This is where a clear manual can be very helpful. Term limits are a useful management tool. As one of my lawyers once reminded me: You can always make exceptions to a term limit, but it's at your discretion and is not their automatic expectation.

As you build your boards, you will often find it easier to attract new people. Seasoned professionals often see boards as a way to meet and network with other industry experts. If you have some strong members, use this as a recruiting tool.

Set a Plan

As you begin to develop your board, outline your strengths and weaknesses. You need board members who can help fill in gaps in terms of networks, experience, and expertise. The plan should highlight the kinds of board members who could provide value and at what stages of the company's growth. This will help you time your recruiting efforts for the right stage of the company. Board and advisory members need to feel useful, and bringing them on too soon could frustrate both of you and limit their involvement when you need it most.

When you begin to recruit potential members, outline a plan for each candidate. Be specific and realistic in the action items. Start by stating modest expectations for what you want the member to do. For example, you may need introductions to one or more specific key customers. You may also want a monthly coffee hour with that person for general advice and strategy planning. This can be more useful if your company is still young and you need senior guidance in several areas, for example, internal management, financial, and sales and marketing. Specific action items and goals will actually help your board member feel useful and begin to provide value quickly.

Include expectations such as attending meetings in your plan. Indicate whether board members will receive compensation or expense reimbursement. Also, you may want to clearly state the term for serving on either type of board. Clarity will avoid any misunderstandings.

Educate

As you approach and recruit board members, you're likely to focus on people who know your industry, but remember that they probably don't know much about your company.

You may find it helpful to prepare a binder of information that includes the following:

- Summary of the company's mission and executive summary
- Business plan (including financial projections as well as recent historical financial statements)
- Marketing and sales plan (include key target customers)
- General board plan and guidelines—include information on board meetings and terms for members
- List of other board members with contact information and a brief background paragraph on each
- Brief, one-page plan for the specific board member
- Information on options, if applicable
- Samples of marketing materials and products

Some companies also provide each board member with a business card. It's a great way to expand your company's reach and enable board members to more easily network on the company's behalf.

As your overall strategy and plan evolve, be sure to communicate it to board members. They can only be useful if they are up-to-date on strategy, new clients, products, and corporate successes.

Compensation

Initially, board and advisory members are compensated with small amounts of equity, usually in the form of warrants. If and when you establish an employee stock option, you'll want to have some guidelines for this group of people as well. Be careful not to give away too much equity in the early days. You need to pace yourself and make sure everyone is impacted evenly. Any dilution from raising more equity should occur later on.

Additionally, you'll probably want to consider some compensation or reimbursement for attending meetings. Karen See of the Abovo Group used gift cards from popular retail establishments like Starbucks and Borders. Her advisory board consisted of very successful professionals, and as a result, they were not motivated by financial compensation, but rather by the thrill of helping to guide a very fast growing and publicly visible company. The gifts usually were in the $100 range and were meant to be more of a token of appreciation for the time and expertise the board was providing.

Evaluation

As part of your board plan, you should consider how you'll evaluate the role of each member to ensure that it's mutually beneficial. I've heard countless stories of board members who, rather than contributing to the company, ended up asking favors of the entrepreneur and the company's employees. Whether the board member asks for introductions, a job, or help creating a Web site, you'll have to determine if they are continuing to provide value or are becoming a drain and distraction.

As you build your boards, you'll need to pay close and discreet attention to each member's personal motivations and how these may evolve over time.

Overall, there are many good and bad stories of boards' impact on entrepreneurs. Most entrepreneurs are reluctant to publicly disclose the details of this private business forum, but if you can ask someone to privately tell you about his or her board, the stories can be illuminating. It's important to know your board members well—not just their professional experience, but also how effective they have been on other boards and in previous executive roles as well as their personal ambitions.

One team of entrepreneurs learned the importance of such fact finding the hard way when one of their trusted board members of five years used his knowledge of the company and customers to their detriment. When the company came upon challenging economic times, he quietly used his relationships with other board members to tip the company into Chapter 7 bankruptcy and purchase the assets for a deep discount. He reestablished the company under a new name and his ownership and installed himself as the CEO. He could have just demanded a restructuring before investing more money, but his personal motivations inspired him to use a different tactic. Sound farfetched? Perhaps, but also a true and bitter experience for many entrepreneurs, although not always with the board member themselves as the new corporate head; it can also be another board member, an outside professional, or sometimes a family member.

Venture capitalists have been known to carry out maneuvers like this one without the semblance of any personal motivation. Usually VCs will do this if the company is in trouble and the VC is unwilling to put in new money without this type of restructuring. The entrepreneur is often aware of the process, even if they are not part of the new company.

Board members and employees are all valuable assets that need to be well managed. Make an effort from the early days to draft a plan for how you will grow both your employee base and your boards of directors and advisors.

CHAPTER 6

ENTREPRENEURSHIP ON THE FLY

As your company becomes established and grows, you will have to establish processes, procedures, and plans, all of which will need to be modified many times due to external as well as internal changes. How you manage and what kinds of processes and structures you implement will depend in large part on your firm, its stage of growth, your industry, and the state of the economy. In this chapter, I'll highlight the kinds of issues you should be aware of as you navigate bumps in the road and experience different stages of growth. Even with the best of planning, you'll need to be able to think fast—effectively and efficiently—and respond to challenges and opportunities with creativity, flexibility, and speed. It's what I call "entrepreneurship on the fly."

Navigating the Bumps in the Road

The key for most entrepreneurs is to know that they are not alone. Most entrepreneurs worry at least once in their journey that no one else has made the mistakes or faced the challenges that they face. The reality is that no matter what kind of mistake you made or what kind of scenario you're facing, you're probably in good company. Lots of businesses have their ups and downs, and lots of businesses go through growth cycles. Good entrepreneurship is all about navigating the bumps and restructuring or redirecting.

Many people don't realize that even AOL was once a fledgling technology firm in search of a mission and profits. Emerging from restructuring in the early 1980s under the guidance of Steve Case, the company gradually found its way to new heights, but only after more than a decade long process to find its mission and market. Case navigated through many bumps along the way.

As you grow, continuously assess your policies, products, and procedures and even people. Be willing to let go of whatever is no longer working or effective. It's often most difficult to get rid of people and products. We get attached to both—usually because they have a face and personality and spirit. And, yes, I am not just talking about the people, but the products too.

Understand that you *will* encounter several cycles—business cycles, sales, economic, and product cycles—and be ready for them as best you can.

Business and Sales Cycles

Every business experiences cycles. No business is ever in an up cycle all of the time. In fact, the longer you've been around, the more likely you are to experience higher peaks and lower valleys. While you can't always avoid a market downturn, you can monitor your market well enough to anticipate challenges before they become crises.

Toward this end, you should find a key number in your business that tells you if your sales are on track or off. Some people monitor shipments, while others monitor days of inventory. In my business, we monitor the inventory of our resellers. We initially tracked the dollar volume of sales but found that the number of units in their inventory was far more telling. For example, one reseller booked revenues because products were sold, but the products were not actually distributed to the customer. As a result, we experienced sales slowdowns because they didn't need to reorder the product quickly enough. By focusing on units instead of revenues booked, we could pinpoint distribution problems as well as anticipate sales slowdowns and work with our resellers and partners accordingly.

Also, if you do use resellers, pay close attention to their profitability and how their salespeople are incentivized to sell your products versus others that they carry. If the salespeople make more money from selling other products, guess which ones they will push harder—even if the products are not competitive. Pay close attention to your reseller or distributor's sales structure and process.

Make the effort to focus on existing customers. They're likely to generate your most cost-effective new sales. It's common to hear that it costs five times as much to get a new customer than to keep an existing one and grow them. Focus on your most profitable customers with the best margins. At the same time, there's a delicate balancing act of focusing on both managing your current customers while filling your sales pipeline and diversifying your customer base.

Focusing on diversifying your customer base from day one is essential. A downturn in sales to one major client often tips young companies into failure. Even the government can't remain a reliable majority customer. Strive to have no single customer account for more than 10 percent of your total revenues. This will help minimize your pain when your clients stumble. Many career entrepreneurs take the idea of diversification one step further and get involved with or fund another company once their first company is growing and stable.

As you grow, treat all of your customers and potential customers with kindness and respect. Sometimes fast-growing companies turn away business for varying reasons. For example, the customer is too small or is not profitable enough. When you experience your bumps in the road, you may want to take on some of these customers. Make sure they still want to do business with you.

Product Cycles: Diversify and Innovate

This may sound basic, but many companies enjoying the success of their new product or service forget to think about what's next. You need new products or new versions of your products to keep customers interested in your company. The frequency with which you develop new products or services depends on your customer and industry. But whether you innovate every year or once every five years, always remember to plan for the next success.

It's also important to differentiate between product and corporate loyalty. One of the secrets of truly successful and enduring companies is the ability to not get attached to their "products or service." Your business should be based on satisfying a customer need. When your customers need a change in your product or service, you'll be able to act proactively rather than reactively. Your passion should be directed toward building a long-lasting company focused on meeting customers' needs, not a long-lasting product.

Managing

If you worked for a company before you started your own venture, think back to how you viewed corporate life and management when you weren't in a management position. Fast-forward to the days that you were a manager or executive and think of how you viewed business processes. Then speed ahead to the present where you're now an owner. Business can look very different from all three perspectives, and it's important to keep this in mind. When you're an employee, it's easy to blame "management" for everything. When you're a manager, the board, CEO, owners, and even employees can seem like good targets. When you're an owner, well, you get the picture; it's the others that lack the loyalty and commitment and who demand too much from a young, growing company.

The biggest difference in perspectives comes down to loyalty and ownership. Entrepreneurs tend to think of their companies as their "children" and to think that those "children" need undivided attention and nurturing. Career entrepreneurs may be slightly more experienced in keeping a Chinese wall between their ventures and their personal emotions and world, but even then their companies are still their passion. For many employees, let's face it, it's just a job. Even if they love their jobs, as many do, it's still just a job, and they can leave and will do so if they need to. Even investors are likely to regard your business as just one of a number of deals. Balancing these varying perspectives between the different stakeholders is critical. Strive to see issues from all perspectives so that you keep a balanced approach to management and are more likely to make the fair and best decisions for all.

Employee Issues

Most entrepreneurs will tell you that as they ramp up and progress, the people issues increasingly dominate their time. Every company has a workforce diverse not only in race and gender, but in terms of skills, commitment, loyalty, and personality. Finding, keeping, and motivating the best people is perhaps one of the hardest tasks for entrepreneurs. Keeping different perspectives in mind, think about the kind of company you would like to work in, and then attempt to create the culture, the processes, and the compensation systems that reflect that kind of work environment. Young companies operate best when their culture is based on a meritocracy, a culture that prizes capabilities and results. Integrity drives most people to do the best that they can. Understand the difference between intent and outcome.

As you start to grow, you'll need to pay close attention to how employees manage the growth process. Some get used to the perks of being part of a small company—for example, having close proximity and easy access to you, the founder and president. Managing employee expectations is critical, and it's a daily process. People, especially the ground crew, will expect the same perks, treatment, and access as you grow. It's not likely that you can maintain the same level of perks, and it may not even be desirable to do so. Pay attention to the human resources (HR) component. Have weekly meetings with your employees to help them understand what is going on or what to expect. If meetings aren't doable or efficient, sending e-mail updates at regular intervals helps. Sometimes you need to go out of your way to provide some personal attention to valued employees to help them along the way. I should note that providing personal attention does not mean becoming close friends with employees. If you become friends with your employees, it may be very hard to address tough business issues like poor performance. You may even need to fire them at some point. Keep a professional distance, at least for a few years, until you're sure that performance will not be an issue.

With senior hires, it's important to recognize that growth companies tend to have strong entrepreneurial cultures and are usually led by strong entrepreneurs. It can be hard for senior outside managers to fit into companies with strong entrepreneurs and distinct operating cultures. Additionally, they may not always understand how best to manage others in this type of environment. Outline clear roles and responsibilities, and monitor them often in the first year to ensure there's a good fit.

Focus on helping your employees understand the culture of a young, growing, entrepreneurial company. Review customers, revenues, and expenses with the entire team. Start early on, and teach your team to watch expenses so that, as you grow, everyone is paying attention to cost control and doesn't become complacent. Often, there's more wasted expenses when companies grow quickly, as everyone tends to be more focused on revenues than on expenses. Help your employees understand how businesses become sustainable and the relationship between revenues, expenses, and profits. You may find that your employees even generate ideas over time to increase profits as well keep costs down.

Sometimes people are reluctant to be innovative, not because they don't have good ideas but because they're afraid of failure or of offering dumb ideas. Encourage your team to make suggestions, no matter how wild. You may want to consider incentives for new ideas. These incentives may include small bonuses of a couple hundred dollars. Often what employees really want is public recognition for their contributions. You may have an employee of the week or month award or a "Great Idea" certificate the employee can display when he or she has contributed to the company. Ideas that get implemented may warrant additional congratulatory attention depending on the corporate impact. Small but meaningful gestures go a long way to make everyone feel as if they are a critical member of the entrepreneurial team.

Institutionalize Decisions and Processes

Expect to experience turnover. Have people learn multiple functions wherever possible. Also work to institutionalize decisions and processes as much as possible. Many young companies fail to do this in the early days, and then when a key employee leaves, there's often a gap in institutional knowledge.

Keep detailed files on how a decision is made and what analysis and process was used to create things like pricing, marketing campaigns, and product designs. If your new hires are going to be effective, they need to know the company's history so they can challenge assumptions and decisions as appropriate.

The reality is that everyone can be replaced. Even presidents come and go. As a result, your focus should be on institutionalizing a function or job and not making it fit a particular person. Even in the best of circumstances, employees may leave your company, often for personal reasons, not just financial. If you have crafted job descriptions and spent some time putting policies and procedures in place, then replacing even talented people should be more straightforward. When you're growing quickly, it's too easy to not spend time institutionalizing roles and procedures, and then when a key employee leaves, you feel the impact far more deeply than you expect.

Also rotate senior managers periodically. People who have these jobs for a long time run them like fiefdoms and don't always look for new solutions or ways to cut costs or improve efficiencies. Most entrepreneurs stay close to their customers. Be sure that key customers have relationships with more than one salesperson on your team. Otherwise, you may risk that customer's business if your key salesperson leaves. Worse, your salesperson may try to take the customer. Confidentiality agreements are essential and are covered later in the chapter in the "Legal" section.

Management Tips

This section includes some lessons and tips that are worth remembering as you navigate the bumps in the road.

Complement Don't Duplicate

Many entrepreneurs don't take the time early on to figure out where their personal knowledge or skills gaps are. They're too busy doing a little of everything and don't accurately assess their strengths and weaknesses. With too much to do and anxious to delegate some of their work, entrepreneurs tend to hire people who look like them on paper, thereby duplicating skills and knowledge. Take the time to figure out what you don't know or aren't very good at. Hire to complement your skills and knowledge gaps. If you're great in sales and marketing but aren't as good with numbers, plan to hire a strong financial manager as soon as possible, perhaps even before you staff all of your sales and marketing functions. You'll probably continue to perform the tasks you're good at for several years in your company's growth.

Taking the Unpopular but Needed Action

It's common knowledge that managers sometimes have to make unpopular decisions. As you grow into your managerial role, you must be prepared to do the same. You must be prepared to find yourself the target of displaced anger, hostility, and accusations—sometimes these are deserved, but more often they are not. Accept that you're growing a business, not competing in a popularity contest.

Having character is doing what is right when no one else is looking. Do what you think is right, even if it's not popular. In hard times, make sacrifices before you require them of others. No one likes a paycut or delayed paycheck, but they can be slightly more bearable if your employees know that you are feeling the pain first. And be sure that if you share the pain during tough times, you also spread the gain during good times.

During bumpy economic times, you may find that you need to downsize. Communicate frequently with your employees through company or group meetings. People often know that times are tough, so layoffs don't always come as a surprise, although it's always painful for an employee to be out of a job.

If your firm can afford to pay severance, it will always be well appreciated, but the reality is that there are no hard-and-fast rules. Some firms give a week for each year worked, others give a month per year of work, while still others who have limited resources give whatever they can. At a minimum, your company should make sure the employee has the option of continuing any benefits you offer under COBRA (Consolidated Omnibus Budget Reconciliation Act). This allows them the chance to purchase the same medical and dental ben-

ENTREPRENEURSHIP ON THE FLY   *139*

efits for up to 18 months. At most, you'll have a small administrative role but will not incur any medical or dental expenses. Discuss the unemployment options your downsized employees can receive with your accountant.

It's important to have some business logic behind your decision of whom to layoff. You may have some legal challenges if you arbitrarily pick some people and not others. You may pick the weakest performers, as documented in the most recent performance review. Realize that people may raise eyebrows if all the downsized employees are of a single race, gender, or age. If you need to, get the input of an HR advisor or your lawyer. Many lawyers will suggest that you ask each downsized employee to sign a release waiving any rights to sue you in the future in exchange for whatever severance or benefits you have agreed to.

Address Rumors Quickly

Rumors spread quickly and distract employees when the company is most in need of their best efforts. Hold weekly meetings at which employees can learn about the difficulties the company faces. Make it clear that there's no place for rumors and that professionalism is expected at all times. While this certainly won't stop the rumors, it helps to set a professional tone. If rumors continue to be circulated by one or a few individuals, you may want to meet with them to address their unprofessionalism. You may also want to discuss their satisfaction with their job and their aspirations within the company. Make it clear that those who succeed will be those with positive, productive, and professional attitudes.

Lastly, set an example. Don't gossip or create rumors. Have a zero tolerance policy on this from day one. If your employees realize that they can't win your favor with juicy gossip, you'll help set a professional standard.

Hire Well, Fire Quickly

Hire well, fire quickly. This is easier said than done. There's probably not a single manager, let alone an entrepreneur, who has not at some point lamented the challenges of identifying and retaining the best candidates. Many entrepreneurs fire too slowly, concerned about any number of factors: loss of productivity or institutional knowledge, personal friendship with the employee, legal reasons, or simply concern over their ability to replace a person or skill set without losing critical time and revenues.

If someone's performance has been lagging or if it never made it to par, meet with him or her at regular intervals for at least a period of one to six months. Help him or her improve by outlining clear objectives. However, if the employee continues to perform poorly, be quick to let the employee go.

You may also find that despite your best management efforts, some employees are simply negative and will spread their negativity to others in the office. Young companies are small, and people work in close quarters. Get rid of bad apples quickly, as they are certain to create a bad working environment for other employees. Despite what you might think, the other employees are likely to be grateful for your decisive action. Don't hire till you've gotten rid of all of the negative energy. In the steps of the hiring and firing processes, you should work toward creating a positive work environment where employees feel valued and motivated.

If morale has been low for a while, you may consider bringing in an outside business coach to help you or your team members or both. If turnover and morale have been low for a while and they're not related to the outside economic environment, be ready to honestly assess your own management style. A business coach may be able to help you improve your management and communication styles.

Don't Get Isolated

A challenge for entrepreneurial managers is discovering how and when to interact with others in their company. In large companies, corporate executives are physically insulated from day-to-day interactions with their employees and so are shielded from suggestions, criticisms, and even ideas. They're usually on a different floor or area from others and don't always hear everything. They also tend to be physically situated around people who are likely to have the same frame of reference they do.

As you grow, don't let yourself get isolated. Encourage people to keep coming into your office to chat with you, to tell you their honest opinions and to hear about how products, sales, and processes are progressing. While you are probably busy, it's important to find time for informal information exchanges.

Stay in touch with all parts of your business. The early stages of the business are usually very taxing on entrepreneurs. By the time you can hire experienced managers to spread the workload, you may feel anxious to hand over work. Delegate; don't abdicate. Stay involved and know what is going on in each area of your business. This doesn't mean that you should micromanage. However, you should have a good sense of the workflow.

Additionally, as you enjoy your company's growth phase, don't get too caught up in your success. Stay in touch with the most common elements of your business and remember what helped get you where you are. Don't buy into your good or bad press. Keep in touch with employees, customers, colleagues, and investors. Keep talking to just about anyone who has an opinion or comment on your business, product, or market. Everything is worth listening to at least once—you never know what new opportunities you may uncover.

The Buck Stops Here

Many people don't pay enough attention to the spiritual side of entrepreneurship. Entrepreneurship is a constant soul-searching exercise. When you're not at the top of a corporation or organization, it's much easier to find a scapegoat to blame for any business shortcomings. However, as the founder of your company, you bear full responsibility. As your company grows and experiences the peaks and valleys most young companies experience, be ready to take on all tasks and accept responsibility. Your attitude will guide your team by example.

Recognize and Accept Differences

Give 10 people the same problem and you're likely to have 10 different solutions. Even if the solutions seem similar on the surface, the execution and tone will differ. Managing can really make you realize the extent to which this is true. We're all unique individuals, and we respond differently, guided by any number of factors including our personality, our upbringing, our experiences, and our perspectives. This applies to entrepreneurs, managers, and employees alike. Recognize that you'll need to manage based on an appreciation of different peoples' unique skills, strength, and challenges.

Learning to Trust Your Business Instinct

Don't get intimidated by competitors, investors, or customers. Trust your instinct and have faith in your ability to listen, analyze, and learn.

We all know that moderate, sustained growth is preferable to explosive growth. Growth that's too fast or too slow is probably not the healthiest, although both kinds of growth can still lead to success in the long run. The pace of growth differs for each type of business and depends on you as well. You need to trust your instincts and also be clear on your personal philosophy as I covered in Chapter 1; both will help you determine the right pace for your company, market, and timing. It's certainly helpful to have input from seasoned, experienced, and knowledgeable professionals, but at the end of the day, you'll have to learn to trust your own judgment and your own sense of business goals.

Make an effort to lift your head above the daily grind and sniff for new opportunities. Think boldly and be willing to constantly reinvent.

Join or Form a Network or Peer Group

Many entrepreneurs face a feeling of aloneness. There's a limit to what an entrepreneur can share with employees, and while friends and family may mean well, they don't necessarily understand the multiple hats and roles you play or what it really takes to grow a young company. Also, in the early years, most entrepreneurs do not know other entrepreneurs or have trusted and experienced confidantes.

There are two basic types of groups that many entrepreneurs find useful. The first is the more common: networking groups that focus on businesses' needs. The second is peer mentoring networks that focus on the entrepreneur's unique position as owner and executive.

Formal and informal peer mentoring is becoming more common as entrepreneurs seek out others who have successfully steered young and growing companies through start-up phases and growing years. Entrepreneurial support groups function like business peer mentoring, where you can freely discuss and exchange issues and receive experienced input from other entrepreneurs. Peer groups are invaluable places to discuss and exchange ideas on managing growing companies, as well as obtain introductions to advisors, customers, and possibly investors/venture capitalists.

Networking groups tend to be organized by industry, geography, and type of company. You need to be practical about how many organizations you can join. It's not a productive use of your time to spread yourself too thin. Consider joining a couple of networking groups and one or possibly two peer mentoring groups.

Some of the more popular peer groups for entrepreneurs are the Entrepreneurs' Organization (EO), which consists of YEO/WEO (Young Entrepreneurs' Organization/World Entrepreneurs' Organization) and YPO (Young Presidents' Organization). To join YEO, you need to have $1 million in sales and be under 40 years of age. WEO is the "graduate" level of the organization. Members can join WEO between the ages of 40 and 46 and remain members for life. YPO membership requires members to join prior to their 45th birthday and to meet a number of business requirements that are listed on their Web site at www.ypo.org.

Both organizations have chapters in almost every major city in the United States and around the world. While they are technically different organizations, they work closely together, and many entrepreneurs move from YEO to YPO as they become eligible. One of the more valuable parts of these organizations is what they both refer to as the "Forum."

Every YEO/WEO/YPO member has the opportunity to join a Forum group. The groups meet monthly for a couple of hours, and entrepreneurs have the opportunity to discuss a personal or professional issue that is pressing for them and/or their company. In essence, as the YPO Web site (www.ypo.org/network.html) notes, these Forums provide a "safe haven where young leaders faced with similar personal and professional challenges gather to share experiences and consult each other in absolute confidence." These groups provide a unique opportunity for peer mentoring and networking. While the value of your particular Forum can depend on group dynamics and the individual participants, many entrepreneurs who join these organizations find Forums to be invaluable and one of the key motivators of membership. (More information can be found in Appendix B, "Entrepreneurial Resources.")

Some entrepreneurs prefer to create their own informal peer mentoring group based on factors like compatibility, personal interests, or geographic proximity. For example, some women find that many of the other peer groups have predominantly male members, and as a result, most of the issues discussed tend to exclude work/family and personal issues that are often experienced by women entrepreneurs, such as pregnancy and the need to take time off or bringing babies to work.

As a result, some women have formed formal and informal peer mentoring groups to exchange information on their diverse entrepreneurial businesses, customers, management issues, and personal lives. Some of the formal groups for women entrepreneurs are the Women Presidents' Organization (WPO), the Committee of 200 (also known as C200), and the National Association of Women Business Owners (NAWBO). The informal groups are often very local and get started by friends and colleagues. Whether you prefer formal or informal groups, make an effort to make them a part of your regular schedule. Even if you just meet monthly for dinner, you have an opportunity to discuss issues, learn new strategies, and get critical advice. More resources are listed in Appendix B.

With all of the groups, you need to determine what you're looking for. Some provide industry insight, and others are general business peer groups. Some of the organizations are open to membership from entrepreneurs who founded their companies as well as to people who have inherited family-run firms or who are senior executives at large companies. Clearly, this combination results in a range of issues and focuses. If you're looking for a group of fellow entrepreneurs, then be sure to check the background of others in your peer group. For example, at the YPO level, there's a mix of people with ownership or executive responsibility. As a result, you may be more focused on growth issues and on developing your senior team, whereas a fellow senior executive may be more interested in understanding how to deal with his or her president or board. Further, some of these corporate professionals may have ascended quickly without working in all the roles that you, the entrepreneur, have likely had. In a productive scenario, you'd both learn from each other's perspectives, but you should recognize that each peer group may have a slightly different viewpoint.

Industry groups provide a great opportunity to get to know your competition on neutral turf. These groups serve as networking opportunities rather than as peer exchanges and are likely to be your best source of information. Seek out your competition's executives and get to know them informally. You may want to hire them one day as you grow. Use industry groups as a way to scout out other talent as well.

Finance

Assessing Progress

Most entrepreneurs will tell you there are some "magic milestones" that, when achieved, will improve your company's long-term viability. These often include achieving $2 to $3 million in sales, having at least 5 to 10 employees, and making it past the three-year mark. These milestones are impacted by your industry and market. It's more important to focus on profitability than on the number of people you employ, and knowing your company's profitability per employee can be very useful. Identify which benchmarks are valuable for your company.

There's also a certain amount of education that comes with early bootstrapping. Even as you grow and have more disposable income, try to not rush to throw money at either opportunities or problems. Analyze and strategize with your team for creative solutions.

Also, as you grow, continue to review what processes you can outsource. The fact that your revenues are increasing does not mean that your expenses need to increase as well. Not all functions need to be performed in-house. For example, it's common in today's world to outsource payroll and other HR functions.

Cash Flow Challenges: Yours and Your Customers'

Yours

Just about every entrepreneur has spent a sleepless night or more worrying about his or her ability to make payroll and payables.

Even companies that are doing well and experiencing increasing sales face these issues. Often, when companies grow rapidly, their expenses also grow quickly, and the need for cash increases. Entrepreneurs tend to focus more on sales than on cash. As a result, they're caught short when payments from customers take longer than expected and employees and bills need to be paid. Focus on cash and know your daily cash position. We have done daily cash reconciliation in all of my companies. Further, we do a cash budget alongside any other financial projection. This tells us exactly how much is coming in per month and what is needed to cover expenses for the same month, without tapping reserves. This way we can anticipate shortfalls and incentivize customers to place more orders and make payments more quickly.

Cash flow and profitability should drive your financial analysis more than revenues alone. Sure, you need to increase sales, but if you're not making money and your cash flow is poor, you'll face far more troubles and more quickly than you're likely to anticipate.

When cash flow gets poor, companies often slow down the pace at which they pay bills. Don't just avoid your vendors or ignore bills. Communicate with vendors if payment cycles change. Not all will be willing to work with you, but those that are will deserve your long-term loyalty. If you need to wait until your customer pays you before you can pay certain related expenses, let the vendors know. Again, most will work with your firm in the hopes of increasing long-term opportunities.

Another way to manage your cash flow cycles is to have a standby line of credit to dip into during critical months. If you find that you are using this line monthly, then you may need to determine if you are absorbing this cost or if it is being passed on to your customers. You may also want to consider giving your larger customers incentives like preferential pricing or discounts to pay faster. Ideally, you want to get to a point where you have at least one or more years of expenses in liquid reserves, not including the company's fixed or investment assets or your personal assets. Remember that as you grow, so will your expenses and the amount needed for your annual reserve. In Chapter 3, I reviewed using a factor or accounts receivable firm as an alternative short-term financing tool. Keep in mind that all of these options have a cost. The best option is to strive toward building your company's own reserve.

If your business takes a severe and sustained downturn, acknowledge it as soon as you can. Know your financial and legal options at every stage. Being prepared and knowledgeable will help you avoid nasty surprises. Many companies have to restructure at some time in their corporate histories, even including Chapter 11 reorganization. Doing so earlier rather than later will help you rebuild your company. Neither bankruptcy law nor your customers and vendors will let you restructure often, so make sure to plan carefully and get good legal advice.

Your Customers

Similarly, take a look at your inflow to see if your accounts receivables are taking longer to collect. It's always wise to be in touch with your customers quickly if you detect any changes in their payment cycles. You should monitor your key customers on a regular basis and monitor changes like restructurings, layoffs, mergers, acquisitions, new debt, or equity offerings, all of which could impact payment cycles.

In the interest of building good customer relationships, you should make every effort to work with your clients through any challenging periods. They are likely to be grateful and to perhaps give you more business when their circumstances improve. However, if your customers stop paying, are nonresponsive to your efforts to work with them, or appear to be ready to close or file for bankruptcy, consider using a collection agency as soon as possible. For example, you may consider using Dun & Bradstreet, which offers a very cost-effective and credible collection program. For just a couple of hundred dollars, they will commence with collections. They are only paid a success fee if and when they recoup any or all of your receivable.

Your accountant or banker may be able to suggest other collection agencies as well. Some law firms do this as a service. Determine how difficult the collections will be before using a law firm, as law firms tend to cost more. Also, shop around for the most reliable and least expensive option. Make sure that you hire a professional and reputable agency. There are very strict laws governing what and how companies can collect from customers. You don't want to be accused of harassment because your collection agency uses questionable tactics.

In a worst-case scenario, the quicker your efforts, the more likely you'll be to collect even a fraction of what's owed. You should note that if a company does file for Chapter 7 or 11 bankruptcy protection, any payments it makes in the 90 days prior to the filing may need to be returned to the courts. Usually this occurs if the bankruptcy trustee determines that certain creditors received preferential treatment and were paid ahead of other creditors. You'll be advised if this is the case. Just don't be surprised. Additionally, if a customer files, note that you are not allowed to contact them regarding any outstanding invoices.

Getting Robbed

Being cheated by your bookkeeper or accountant is more common than you think. Embezzlement is unfortunately a common occurrence in many young entrepreneurial companies, which often have insufficient controls, despite their best efforts. It's not enough to say that you will be the only signator on checks, as check forgery is a common form of embezzlement. In addition to being the only signer on accounts, have an independent outside accountant do the monthly bank reconciliations, or at a minimum, do them yourself. For example, it's the only way you'll find missing checks that may never have been entered into the accounting system.

A good accountant or finance manager should be able to help you set up critical systems and processes. Consider establishing at least two bank accounts: one for deposits and one to write checks from. This will limit access to the deposit account where you should have more of your money. Transfer money to your checking account on a weekly basis to cover payables. Also keep sizable funds in investment accounts, and diversify your banking relationships. You'll be able to determine which of your relationships will provide you with the best and most cost-effective services as you grow. Most banks will waive or adjust your fees when they review the combined relationship. Get to your know your branch manager so that you can identify your options.

It's not just your finances that risk robbery. Equipment, products, and supplies can also be taken by employees or outsiders. Establish procedures early on for things like who can order supplies or equipment. Also, limit access to inventory areas, and depending on your industry, do periodic reconciliations.

Contingency Plans

Contingency plans are essential. You should plan for a range of possible outcomes, including the worst-case scenario. Everything that can go wrong with your business probably will at some point or another.

Contingency plans are not limited to managing through a systems crash, although that is one possible hurdle and is covered below. Contingency planning refers in its broadest sense to thinking about what might go wrong or just differently than anticipated and then planning for it to the best of your ability.

For example, what if your major customer, who represents 40 percent of your revenues, files for bankruptcy? Your contingency plan will need to address how and under what conditions you might still sell to them. You will need to figure out how to find new customers to replace any lost revenue. Your plan will also need to assess how and when you may need to cut staff and expenses to stem any losses. Ideally, you will have already been working on getting new customers long before the crisis, as your business should never be dependent on just one or two major customers. Diversifying your customer base is essential to long-term survival, but it can take time to achieve.

Systems do crash, and you need to plan for this possibility. Young companies with tight budgets often don't have backup systems or off-site data recovery. You need to determine how critical your systems are to your business and prioritize accordingly. If your systems are a core part of your product or service, you may want to consider having your network backed up daily or weekly. If you can make a copy of critical information on a regular basis, you can then physically store it off-site as a backup in case something happens to your office. For example, you could rent a bank locker or bring it home for off-site storage.

If you hire systems people, strategize with them on the most cost-effective solution for a backup. If you do not have these skills in-house, consider hiring a systems consultant to help. Often, even the major computer sellers like Dell, Gateway, Microsoft, IBM, and Apple can provide some very basic insight on backup systems that are appropriate for your stage of business. Of course, these companies are trying to sell you the system, so ask more than one for an opinion. Keep in mind that their business is selling systems and that their suggestions will be far from complete. If your core product or service does not rely on technology, you may only need good systems for backing up sales and finance records. Also, many young companies use online resources for data management in areas like sales and HR. These serve as backups as well, although they may take longer to retrieve. When selecting a data management resource, review online resources as an option.

It's also important to note that contingency planning doesn't always imply planning for a negative scenario. You also need to plan for unseen windfalls or for outcomes that exceed your expectations. For example, you will probably want to plan under what business conditions you would need to hire another sales account manager or more product development people. Sometimes if you get a new piece of business quickly, you may not have enough time to search for the right hires. Planning ahead and keeping a database of potentially qualified people can help you manage in times of sudden growth. Contingency plans help you identify which variables can impact your business, positively or negatively.

Legal

All young companies encounter a range of standard legal issues as they grow. Protecting your business, products, and know-how is essential. Additionally, almost all companies get sued at some point. Understand how these legal scenarios can impact your business.

Protecting Your Intellectual Property and Confidentiality

It's important to protect your intellectual property (IP) and confidential information. In addition to filing for patents as applicable and registering trademarks and copyrights, you need to protect your intellectual property from full-time and part-time employees, consultants, investors, board and advisory members, as well as anyone else to whom you disclose information. Your confidentiality agreement is separate from any employment offer, contract, or retainer agreement. The latter two may include a confidentiality clause. Many institutional sales and distribution agreements include a confidentiality clause along with noncompete clauses. Make noncompete provisions standard in all of your agreements, although their term and scope may differ. More senior employees definitely need a noncompete clause that extends a couple of years beyond their involvement with your company. You may want to consider providing a formula for the penalty so that if someone does breach this provision, you do not have to spend an enormous amount of money to prove how much your business suffered.

Most lawyers have templates of these agreements that can be customized for your company quickly and cheaply. You need to protect your company, especially when competitors try to poach your sales, marketing, and product teams. In your agreement, it's important to clearly state that "confidential" information includes everything about your product, customers, business model, and company know-how. While this may seem overly legal, a good definition actually protects you by being comprehensive. There are many variations, and your lawyer can help customize a definition that best suits your company, market, and recipient.

An agreement won't prevent an employee from trying to take customers, but it may dissuade them if they understand that you intend to pursue legal action if they try. The more thorough your legal agreements, the better your ability to dissuade.

In addition to using agreements, many companies seek to limit employee and consultant access to different types of information, including customer databases, product specifications, and pricing models. For example, some companies simply restrict computer access.

Today's office networks make this relatively easy to accomplish. It's best to protect your IP with a combination of legal documents and daily operational processes.

Getting Sued

Almost all businesses are likely to get sued at some point, rightly or wrongly accused of a business, personnel, or related infringement. For many first-time entrepreneurs, this can come as a shock. Most people never encounter the legal system on a personal level. In large companies, legal issues are dealt with separately from the business, and as a result, most employees are not even aware of these occurrences.

Get good and appropriate counsel. Make sure your lawyer has experience in the area of law you need. For example, get a labor lawyer if an employee is suing you. Get a good intellectual property lawyer if your product patent or trademark is being challenged by another company. Most importantly, don't take the suit personally. Lawsuits are just a part of business. Focus on responding professionally and consistently, particularly if you are being sued by an employee.

Issues with Investors, VCs, and Partners

Building Trust

As you navigate bumps in the road and experience growth, you'll find that some bigger and more complex decisions would benefit not just from the input of experts but also from the input of trusted confidantes. Good confidantes are people who have experienced many growth challenges and opportunities in your industry, with whom you can share details of the company's financial and market status. For some people, this may be one or more members of their board or advisory council; for some, it may include their company's senior managers; and for others, it may be a business consultant or fellow entrepreneur. Just be sure that you understand your confidante's varying motivations, strengths, and weaknesses.

One of my institutional investors potentially fit the category of a good confidante. As an astute and seasoned owner and manager of profitable businesses, he had some critical and valuable experiences that would have helped me navigate some entrepreneurial bumps in the road. However, his previous professional (and personal) dealings with my other institutional investors complicated the company dynamics, and their mutual mistrust made his advice suspect, even when it was sound. I resolved the situation by looking outside and bringing in a senior and experienced advisor, who became a reliable and trusted business confidante. Knowing who to trust can be challenging, but it's essential to nurture your own small team of business confidantes.

Reassessing Your Role

As your company grows, you'll need to transition from an entrepreneur who is involved in doing everything to more of a strategic role. As we all know, the role of a CEO in a start-up and growth phase is different than the same role in a larger, established company. You'll need to honestly ask yourself if you are willing and able to make that transition. If you have outside VC capital and a board, they may very well be asking the same questions. By addressing the issue proactively, you can determine the roles you want to take on and are best suited for. You can then develop a senior team to complement your position and role. For example, if you're a creative person who enjoys being close to the product or service and the customer, you may want to be the chief executive officer (CEO) and head of creative. You can then search for a competent chief operating officer (COO) to run the company's operations.

Managing Issues with Partners

If you're in a partnership, at some point you'll encounter issues with your partner. Even if you have a partnership agreement, it's the day-to-day issues that can make partnerships frustrating as well as rewarding. While it's useful to share responsibilities and workloads, many entrepreneurs don't clarify roles until conflicts arise. The more successful partnerships iron out responsibilities and clarify roles early on and acknowledge that these roles may need to evolve as the company grows.

There are also many partners who do not enter into partnership agreements when they first start their companies. Years later, they may recognize the need for an agreement, but the stresses of running the company together may make it harder to agree on critical points such as exit strategies and valuing the company. If you have not had the time to create an agreement, aim to address this problem within the coming year. If your company has grown significantly, you'll both probably need lawyers to ensure that the full range of issues is adequately and fairly addressed. This is also a good way to put the agreement on a schedule; though, of course, if you can't reach consensus, no amount of scheduling will produce an agreement.

Aside from agreements, there may be differences in how you see the organization and its future. If neither of you wants to exit the company, you may want to consider splitting the business in two, with each of you heading one part. It may be better to divide the company by product lines or markets as customers can come and go. Some partners actually start new related businesses in an effort to address management and control issues. This strategy simply allows you to continue operating. At some point though, you will still need to address how you can both exit the business. However, if you both are running successful related businesses, there's a better chance of reaching an agreement on your combined holdings.

Some partners hire business consultants to come in and assess the partners or team for strengths and weaknesses, in an effort to determine the company's best structure. Ask other partnerships how they have addressed their issues. They'll probably have some good suggestions and perhaps referrals for business consultants and coaches.

Delaying/Deferring Your Compensation

You may opt or be asked to defer your compensation for a short or extended period of time. Doing so for several months may be in the best interests of the company. However, even if you can handle a deferment, think carefully about doing so if it's a condition of your investors, particularly if they have sale, merger, or liquidation preferences over you. What are they really asking you to do? If you have external investors, it's important to realize that your rights are different than if you owned the company outright. You should consider protecting your interests by negotiating your willingness to defer compensation. You may want to ask for additional equity or a cash bonus once the company's performance improves. Any conditions should be documented to protect your interests. If you own your company 100 percent, then your ability to repay yourself in later months or years is completely your decision, although you should review any tax consequences with your accountant.

Having said that, many entrepreneurs defer compensation for one or more months, sometimes even a year, to help their companies get through challenging periods. Always be sure you have incurred the "pain" of deferred compensation before passing it on to others on your team.

Growth

Planning as You Expand

As you expand and grow, planning continues to revolve around three basic questions.

1. What is the new unique opportunity? It may be a new product version or new market.
2. Who is going to tackle the new opportunity? Do you have the team in place? How quickly can you hire?
3. Do you have what you need to engage the new challenge in terms of other resources?

Each of these core questions requires attention to details. Entrepreneurs occasionally get caught up in the lingo. Every industry, including entrepreneurship, has lingoes and cultures uniquely its own. Don't get caught up in the lingo. Focus on the underlying concepts and opportunities.

For every new product or market extension, you should plan to develop a mini business plan complete with financial projections. You should treat these new opportunities as their own separate profit and loss center. This will enable you to measure success, and if your new venture doesn't work out, it will help you decide how soon to pull the plug.

Even as you experience fast growth, you don't need all your resources immediately. Focus on achievable short-term, monthly, or quarterly goals so you can assess progress and continuously adjust your planning.

Growth Through Acquisition

Many young companies grow by acquiring other firms. We read about high-profile large acquisitions everyday. In reality, there are many more small acquisitions that occur routinely and give growing companies faster access to products, markets, and customers.

In Chapter 9, I talk about exit strategies and hiring investment banks and business brokers. You may want to review that chapter with the reverse in mind. You may consider hiring either a broker or a banker to help you identify potential acquisition candidates.

If you're a young company, it's likely that you will know who you want to buy based on your own industry research and knowledge. You may have also gotten to know the other business owner through the industry, and he or she may have approached you, offering their company for sale. Take your time and do a full legal and financial due diligence. Also check to see if you have compatible and complementary businesses in terms of products, services, employees, culture, and operational style. Before you finalize an acquisition, it's very helpful to complete a full business plan for the new company. In preparing the plan, you'll be able to identify any weak areas and address them. Even just being aware of the weaknesses will help avoid nasty surprises post acquisition.

One of the critical issues is the ongoing role, if any, of the other company's senior executives and, if applicable, entrepreneurs. Before you decide who stays and who doesn't, you may want to hire a business consultant to help do a team assessment of capabilities, strengths, and weaknesses. You'll need to address ways to integrate the work teams from both companies so they all feel essential to the company's growth and clearly understand the company's vision and mission. All of the other company's team should sign new confidentiality and noncompete agreements with your firm.

Growth Through an Inital Public Offering (IPO)

For some entrepreneurs, going public through an initial public offering (IPO) provides a financial exit strategy from which they can cash out some of their gains. However, for most entrepreneurs, the IPO is more of a financing strategy through which they can fund expansion as well as reap some financial benefits from what's likely to have been years of hard work. There are limits to how much money an entrepreneur can take out in an IPO. For one thing, it may imply low confidence in the business if you sell a majority of your stock in the days after going public, just when you're asking others to invest in the company. In most situations, the entrepreneur is limited in how much stock he or she can sell over the course of one to two years.

Regardless of which exchange you go public on, you need to plan for at least around $1 million in expenses, including investment banking and legal fees as well as marketing, administrative, and investor or public relations. The expense increases with the amount of your IPO.

To complete an IPO, you will need an investment bank. Your best bet is to start by asking for referrals from lawyers and accountants. You'll want all of your advisors to have completed successful initial public offerings, and you may need to switch lawyers or hire a new additional team to complete this growth strategy. You'll also need a public relations (PR) or investor relations firm that has experience in communicating effectively with shareholders and analysts. Some young companies that go public outsource the shareholder's relations for several years until it makes sense to hire an in-house person.

As you go through the IPO process, you should remember a few things. First, you are likely to be distracted by the fund-raising process, which includes meetings and the actual road show, when you travel to meet with prospective shareholders and analysts to encourage them to purchase your stock as well as view it favorably. Post IPO, you'll also spend a great deal of time communicating with these stakeholders.

Further, if you are going to go public in the next few years of your company's growth, consider spreading the potential gain, establishing an options plan, or giving stock as an incentive. This will motivate everyone toward the IPO goal. Once you have gone public, and if it's successful, you may have to think about how you are going to retain your employees. Fostering a good work environment will help stem any employee losses in the post-IPO world. While you are preparing to go public, consider hiring an HR consultant to specifically address the impact on employees and the resulting impact on the company. You'll need to think about how to keep employees focused and productive as well as address disparities among people who benefited more than others from an IPO. Develop a plan for retaining and motivating post-IPO employees, although if it's very successful, you're bound to lose some who now have the financial freedom to pursue different personal dreams.

Tales from the Trenches

Rosalind Resnick built her Internet marketing company, NetCreations, Inc., from a two-person home-based start-up to a public company in just five years. She cofounded NetCreations by pioneering opt-in e-mail marketing. Unlike many of its competitors, NetCreations generated *both* revenues and profits. Resnick initially resisted pressures to raise capital, but eventually saw going public as a way to expand as well as harness some of the company's value in the strong public markets.

Further, with so many of her competitors raising capital through VCs or through the public markets, Rosalind and her partner had few options if they wanted to remain a leader in their market. They also wanted to retain management control of their business and preferred to go public instead of being acquired. Resnick and her partner made their final decision to go public when their biggest reseller raised significant VC money and became their biggest competitor almost overnight.

At the start of their efforts, Resnick and her partner were turned down by every New York investment bank, all of whom saw them as too small and lacking in critical VC support, which was considered essential at the time. In the end, they chose a smaller boutique investment bank, Friedman Billings Ramsey (FBR), because the firm was smaller and "hungrier" for the business.

As is typical for IPO companies, their road show lasted three weeks. They visited 13 cities and had 71 meetings. The company successfully went public, reaching the astronomical heights that were standard for the dot-com boom. On the first day of trading, they had a market capitalization of $300 million, and three months later it was almost $1 billion.

More telling, though, are Rosalind's personal observations about running a public company, which she equates with doing business in a fishbowl with a gun pointed at your head. Managing employee, investor, and public expectations can be very demanding, as there's a constant expectation that CEOs and their team can somehow predict the future. There's no room for error in earnings predictions and forecasts, and the company is inevitably forced to think very short term.

For Rosalind, going public is only a strategy; not the end game. There are other ways to raise money, expand your company, compete with other larger companies in your market, and, of course, cash out value from your firm. More than a year after going public, Rosalind and her partner accepted a generous offer to buy NetCreations.

Successfully navigating the entrepreneurial bumps in the road and taking advantage of market timing proved a financial boon for Resnick and her partner. They walked away from the IPO and acquisition ready to start their next ventures . . . with their own money.

Changing Directions

It's very possible that despite your best efforts, something in the market, the product, or the timing didn't fit. It may be that while your company is profitable, you don't have significant growth or see long-term opportunities within your current business model or product line. Should this be the case, you don't necessarily need to close the company. Instead, you can opt to change directions. This is one clear reason why many successful entrepreneurs say it's a good idea to focus on creating a company, not just a product or service.

Usually the hardest thing about changing directions is, quite frankly, attitude: yours and that of your team. We all get set in our ways, and it's even tougher to challenge our assumptions when business looks okay or even good. But every type of business has to challenge its foundation and business model in order to survive the long term. Even more successful and established companies challenge their assumptions about their market and business models.

In an ideal world, you would have time to plan a new product or new direction without having to meet other obligations. In the real world, you'll have to plan while you are running your business in its current form. Time will be limited, as resources and even your energy has its bounds. One way is to take a day or a half day every week to focus on researching new strategies, markets, and products. In essence, you are creating a new business plan and may even need to test a few assumptions before you finalize. For example, you may think you sense a new market, but you'll need to gather research and talk to potential customers. You may even need to build a demo product to test customer interest. Likewise, it can be difficult to change business models when your customers have certain expectations and when the pricing models of your industry are well entrenched.

The key is to stay open and flexible and to be willing to challenge your own assumptions. Focus on your company's survival, not on a favorite product or service. Be willing to reinvent your entire approach, including your products and services as well as your business model and strategy.

CHAPTER 7

GLOBAL EXPANSION STRATEGIES

Today, expanding to new global markets is a more readily available option for young companies than it was before. The Internet, easy travel, and the gradual distribution of wealth to more people around the world have increased the number of opportunities for younger companies overseas.

Approach overseas markets the same way you approach domestic markets, using the planning process we reviewed in Chapter 2 and the marketing and sales plan we covered in Chapter 4. Each new market should in essence be viewed as a separate "company" or profit and loss center. Most larger and well-established firms conduct an internal analysis before entering any new market. The key difference between their analysis and yours is that you are likely to have fewer resources and less room for error. Nevertheless, thanks to the Internet and the focus on global trade, there are ample resources to use when researching and entering new markets.

The first way many younger companies sell globally is through their Web sites. We'll cover this approach and then discuss the ways companies enter new markets. Finally, we'll discuss how local culture impacts marketing and business interactions.

Global Web Sites

By default, if your company sells to customers around the world through your Web site, your company is global. You may not have dedicated sales and marketing efforts in key countries, but people anywhere can buy from your Web site, provided they have Internet access and a credit card, or even, in some cases, just the ability to make a bank transfer. However, selling over the Internet does have some limitations and added costs that you need to be aware of.

First, if you are selling a tangible product, there are a number of factors related to the cost and fulfillment. If you only accept U.S. dollars or a major currency, that's fine, but you may want to have a currency converter link so that buyers can easily see what the cost equivalent is in their currency. Additionally, you need to account for the added cost of shipping. If you have an online store, your site should automatically calculate shipping and handling to other countries. If the quantity gets large or you want to be sure to cover all costs, you can have some sales completed by customer service via e-mail or the phone. Many countries charge duties or value-added tax (VAT) for goods coming into their country. You'll need to calculate for these as they are usually paid at the point of entry by your shipping firm. All of these costs will need to be passed on to the customer in order for the sale to remain profitable. Most people who buy online are aware of these added costs and are aware that they'll need to pay them if they opt to purchase online.

You should be clear that shipments overseas may take longer and provide your customer with a projected time frame, though not a specific day, for your product's arrival. Many firms select reliable carriers such as FedEx or DHL, the latter of which has a reputation for being more reliable for international deliveries.

Second, if you expect to sell primarily from your Web site, you must decide if your site needs to be localized into foreign languages and terminology to make it more user-friendly. Your user is no longer from a single market or country, and you need to appeal to a wider segment. Later in this chapter, we'll talk more about understanding the impact of culture on marketing and business interactions.

Also, people around the world still access the Internet over varying connection speeds. Make sure your site loads quickly, and skip any introduction pages. They're a waste of valuable time, and you may lose potential customers who have to wait till they reach your home page.

Going Global

Going global as a young company requires you to use many of the same strategies and thought processes a larger company would use with the caveat of more limited resources. There's no room for mistakes, and you need sales results faster, with a smaller marketing budget.

Many companies, and even young firms, are attracted by global markets for two main reasons. The first is that they are in search of cheaper manufacturing or outsourcing service options. Young companies are acutely aware of the need to keep costs down and maximize profitability. As a result, they often follow their larger competitors to cheaper offshore production. Emerging markets have large, well-educated, and inexpensive labor and provide cheap options for manufacturing, technology development, customer service, and back-office operations.

The second reason companies look globally is that they are searching for potential sales markets. Many major markets as well as some emerging markets represent sizable populations, all of which have increasing disposable incomes. Companies are finding active interest for a wider range of products and services overseas.

It's clear that how companies do business globally is changing. One approach no longer fits all, and companies need to keep in mind the cultural nuances that impact all aspects of life in a country—whether they're selling to locals or hiring them or both. The keys to doing business in a new market are flexibility, patience, and persistence, some markets requiring more than others.

In this chapter, we'll cover the following:

- Choosing your global markets
- Options for researching the local market
- Determining the more optimal structures and ways to enter the market
- Understanding how culture impacts business practices

Choosing Your Global Markets

It's common to find people who are interested in doing business with a country simply because they have read that it is the new "hot" economy.

They know little or nothing about the market or country, its history, evolution of thought, people, or how things are generally handled there in business and social contexts. Young companies look at new global markets often because they're approached by potential customers or partners. Occasionally, companies see global markets for their products early on and incorporate them into their business plan.

When you begin to consider expanding globally, research the local market thoroughly and learn about the country and its culture. Understand the unique business and regulatory relationships that impact your industry.

Early in your research and planning process, take a look to see where your competitors are already selling. You can't enter multiple markets at the same time. You need to prioritize. By studying others' successes *and* failures, you'll be well positioned to determine which markets make the most sense. You may, for example, decide that Asia is a good place to do busi-

Tales from the Trenches

Liz Elting, of TransPerfect/Translations.com, was determined to enter global markets. When one of her successful U.S.-based salespeople brought a British salesperson to her attention, she began to plan how to actually enter the market. Staffing was a challenge, and she needed a good, reliable, and capable salesperson on the ground. Trusting the recommendation of her own very qualified salesperson, she hired the Brit, and within one year, the U.K. office was profitable. Liz utilized the same compensation structure as she used with the U.S.-based sales team. (Please refer to the Tales for the Trenches in Chapter 4, titled "Building a Direct Sales Force.")

Liz's experience illustrates that despite the many ways to find partners or local employees, most companies tend to succeed when they use their own network and referrals. Once established, she was able to turn to more standard recruiting options online and offline, using Monster.com as well as local publications and newspapers. The firm tends to hire foreign nationals. She now has a London-based international sales director who oversees the global sales team.

ness. Within Asia, you should pick two to three countries and plan to enter a new one only once every two to three years. Regional strategies have the added value of marketing synergies. But as with domestic channels, don't try to take on more than one new market or distribution at a time.

Some younger companies tend to choose countries closer to home and their time zones. Conducting business can be harder if you're on opposite time clocks, unless everything is done via e-mail. Some companies highlight several countries and then choose their first market based on available sales or distribution options. For example, they may have a salesperson eager to start working in a specific market. Often, local partners and salespeople will approach you even before you have formally decided to enter a new global market. It can seem easy to simply let the person start selling, but before you give this person the green light, make sure you have a plan in place. It will help to set goals, to manage everyone's expectations, and to determine what a success or failure will look like in terms of revenues, profitability, and time frame.

Researching the Local Market

A number of resources are available to companies considering new global markets. Some resources may be more useful than others, depending on the country and on whether the new market is for sourcing or for selling into. The Internet is often the best place to start any research, and e-mail is the best way to contact some of the offices noted below. Many of these organizations operate online exchanges where companies can find partners, customers, and suppliers.

1. Develop a relationship with your own country's embassy and commercial service office in the target country. Many governments realize that large companies have multiple options and that the companies most likely to need their services and insight are smaller or midsize. Some offices charge modest fees for researching lists of potential partners or distributors. Whether you need this list or not, the added insight from an experienced country expert can be quite useful. These commercial service officers will be able to tell

you about the track records of other companies within a specific industry or with specific distributors. Even learning about a lack of other companies entering the market may be helpful, as you may identify the reasons for their lack of success or interest.

In the United States, the Department of State publishes *Key Officers of Foreign Service Posts: Guide for Business Representatives*, available online at http://foia.state.gov/MMS/KOH/keyoffcity.asp. The site also provides more general country information.

2. Contact the target country's commercial office within its embassy or consulate in your home country. If the country does not have a trade office, contact the respective diplomatic offices. Even tourist offices can provide you with general information. Most country offices are eager to promote their local economies, even on a small scale. If you're considering sourcing from the country, they're usually even more eager to provide you with resources and lists of potential companies as partners or manufacturers.

3. Contact the chamber of commerce for that country in your home country. These are different from the commercial office noted in 1 above, as they tend to be funded by private sector companies. Many smaller or still emerging countries may not have a chamber of commerce office yet. You may also want to contact your home nation's chamber of commerce in the foreign country of interest.

For example, in the United States, there are two types of chambers: American Chambers of Commerce (located in numerous countries) and binational Chambers of Commerce offices (located in the United States). The primary difference between the two types of chambers is their location. Both organizations seek to facilitate business interactions between the United States and the respective country, often collaborating on specific projects as well as lobbying governments for protection of U.S. business interests. The American Chambers of Commerce (AmCham) are affiliated with the U.S. Chamber of Commerce and tend to focus on American business interests in the target country. A list of overseas AmCham offices can be obtained by contacting the United States Chamber of Commerce in Washington, D.C. (www.uschamber.com/chambers/international/international_directory.asp).

The binational Chambers of Commerce located in the United States promote both American business interests and other countries' interests in the United States. Note that these are not the International Chamber of Commerce or its World Chambers Federation division, which has a mission focused on creating a business and legal environment that encourages global trade. Instead the binational chambers of commerce are focused on bilateral issues. For example, the American Indonesian Chamber of Commerce is located in New York. These binational chambers tend to be run by executive directors who really know the countries well and have excellent networks of both American and local companies to supplement any needed information or facilitate business introductions. Offices run by people who have been in country for a lengthy period of time will more likely be useful and full of rich information.

Both AmCham and the binational organizations tend to be dominated by large and well-established companies, but they can be enormously useful in research and information gathering as well as in obtaining introductions to possible partners. Again, the strength of any of these organizations usually rests with the executive director.

Chambers of commerce are also great places to get in touch with others who are experienced in dealing with a country, either as advisors, as consultants, or as hires. Utilize the expatriate community located within that country, as well as those who have recently returned to your home country, as sources for valuable information about the country and its business climate and practices.

4. Contact the U.S. Department of Commerce's International Trade Administration office in your state and in Washington, D.C., or the respective trade office in your home country, and speak with the desk officer for the country of interest. In the United States, general trade information can be obtained by going online at www.ita.doc.gov or www.usatrade.com. Government trade offices also provide an export programs guide that lists resources available at www.export.gov/exportamerica/index.html.

5. Find out if your home state or city has a "sister" state/city relationship with specific countries and what promotional opportunities are available.

6. If possible, conduct a fact-finding trip to your country of interest. Participate in any delegations or trade missions that the U.S. Commerce Department, your local chamber of commerce office, or other trade organizations sponsor. Always review the agenda and list of meetings carefully. Make sure that they not only fit the needs for your industry and company, but also that the people are decision makers and not just political figureheads.

7. Attend trade shows in the country or region of interest. Trade shows have become particularly popular for smaller companies, as many organizers offer smaller booth options with lower fees or allow companies to share both space and costs. In many cases, country trade offices also facilitate trade trips to a target country or trade show. The delegation often shares exhibition space to minimize cost. Most of these shows are organized by industry; schedules are available online and through the country's trade or diplomatic offices.

8. Be creative. Find common connections with companies in the country. Also seek connections with individuals who have experience doing business in the country or with the specific company with which you are dealing. For example, perhaps a supplier or client company or individual that you interact with also does business in your target country. Talk to natives from the country who live in your home nation. Even if there is no direct business application for the information you glean from such sources, you will be able to gather a great deal of cultural and social information that you may be able to put to good use.

9. If you are hoping to win local business through government contracts, you may want to approach the larger vendors who are more likely to obtain the overseas contracts. Many of them have blanket government contracts and look to subcontract for specific goods and services. Further, they often have a requirement

to utilize small businesses, particularly those that are women- and minority-owned. The entire government contracting industry is very time-consuming and will require resources up front to cultivate the necessary relationships and process the required paperwork. Unless you're sure that your product or service is required or have established buying relationships, it's not the best first sales prospect given the lengthy sales cycle.

Many service companies start to work in new markets through project contracts for specific tasks and time periods. It can take longer to build a sustainable business in a country, but the projects allow you to learn about the country and its business practices as well as identify local partners. Most young companies initially choose to partner with a local service firm rather than try to establish their own office.

Recognize that some embassies, offices, and individual officers are better able to assist you in your efforts. For example, junior-ranking career people who have spent more time in the local country are often more insightful and knowledgeable than senior and politically appointed officers with less in-country experience. Over time and through research and references, you will learn which officers and professionals have the most experience and knowledge. As a safety measure, double-check all information with at least two independent sources. Also, be aware that the embassies in your home country may differ in their degree of responsiveness to foreign interest. Do not automatically assume that the embassies or trade representatives of the larger and/or more economically advanced countries are more efficient or helpful.

Determining the Best Structures and Ways to Enter the Local Market

How to enter a local market really depends on what you're hoping to accomplish—outsourcing or sales.

Using Overseas Markets for Offshore Production and Operations

Accessing cheaper production and service options is one of the primary reasons younger companies venture to a new country. You can find local vendors through the research process noted above, as well as by identifying your competitors' sources. Often, if you have work experience in the same industry in which you're an entrepreneur, you may already have access to this information and the contacts.

If you haven't worked closely with companies in other countries, it may seem daunting at first to consider sourcing from a new country. Ask fellow entrepreneurs, employees, vendors, and suppliers for possible sources in key countries. You can even talk to people who may be in a completely different industry but have experience with a particular country. They can help you understand the macro level issues.

If you are researching countries for sourcing, pay attention to language and culture. Make sure you have a comfort level even if you do not speak the language or know much about the culture. Some people prefer to have a minimum common ground of language and business culture; others are not as particular. You need to know your own operating style to determine this.

When you are sourcing from another country, you'll need to consider a number of factors including the following:

1. **Payment terms and currency.** Which currency? Will the payment terms work for you? Keep in mind that you may have to pay the manufacturing source well in advance of receiving payment from your customer. Can a line of credit help bridge these gaps? What options are available for your firm?
2. **Provisions for damaged goods.** Usually agreements specify that payments will not be released until goods are "accepted" by you.
3. **Intellectual property protection.** You've given the local firm access to your business processes, select product information, and so on. How can you manage this legal issue before it becomes a problem?
4. **Customer service.** If you are outsourcing any aspect of customer service, keep in mind that the overseas firm will be the point of

contact for your customers. Are they trained on your products and services as well as on the cultural expectations of your customers?

Selling to a New Global Market

If you've decided to sell to a new market, you'll need to consider a number of factors.

Legally, you'll need to think about the need to obtain trademark and copyright protections. For example if you sell to one or more countries in Europe, it may make sense to file for a Community Trademark (CTM), which covers all of the EU (European Union) member states. Doing so ensures that you will most likely only need to pay one set of fees and fill out a single application. Many industries, like the food, pharmaceutical, and cosmetic industries, also may require local governmental permissions.

In sales and marketing issues, you'll need to think about how the local culture will impact your marketing and sales strategy. Do you need to change the packaging or the product in any way, and if so, is it justified from a profit and loss (P&L) perspective? Will you need to adapt your marketing materials to highlight the features and benefits in a more culturally appropriate manner?

Many of these types of considerations can be addressed depending on how you choose to enter the local market and if you have a local partner or distributor. You have to determine the best way to enter the market based on the stage of your company, product, and resources. Most companies utilize some form of collaborative arrangement with local firms when entering a new market.

There are four key ways to enter a new market:

- Exporting
- Licensing, including franchising
- Equity joint ventures
- Wholly owned foreign enterprises

These are not mutually exclusive ways to enter.

It's clear for those experienced in doing business internationally that there isn't one best way to enter a new market. Companies have to consider a number of financial, operational, and resource factors. For example, some companies start by considering how much control they wish to retain, while for others, the primary concern is how much of their own resources they're willing to commit. As companies develop more experience doing business within a specific market, they're likely to reassess the way they do business in the country, particularly in terms of collaborative arrangements. Companies that aim to have a stronger and more profitable presence in the market may need to increase their commitment of resources over time.

When researching and selecting partners, exercise caution and make sure that there is mutual business compatibility. Make sure that your potential partner is credible, reputable, financially sound, and technically capable of living up to their side of an agreement. Pay close attention to the local business history, as well as to the political relationships of your potential partner. In most cases, your local partner will be responsible not only for day-to-day operations, but for the management of your company's reputation. Failure to select carefully may lead to the failure of the venture and a squandering of resources.

Every culture has its share of unscrupulous businesspeople. Maintain your business sense, and listen to your instincts. Posture yourself in a culturally acceptable manner in terms of your communication style and verbal and physical gestures. Understand the trigger points or "hot buttons" for that culture. If you are dealing with government officials, take the time to research their political priorities and objectives before you seek a face-to-face meeting. The more you are able to address *their* objectives and concerns verbally or in the terms of a proposal, the easier it will be for you to gain their approval and their contractual commitment. Remember to be discreet and tactful in any verbal discussions, particularly with government officials.

Exporting

Exporting may be effective, especially for smaller and midsize companies that can't or won't make any significant financial investment in the local market. Companies can sell into a new market either through a local distributor or through their own salespeople.

Use the research suggestions above to find a local distributor or producer. Increasingly, the Internet has provided a more efficient way for foreign companies to find one another and enter into commercial transactions. If you do come across a potential partner via the Internet, use a commercial office or chamber of commerce to check them out more thoroughly. Sources like Dun & Bradstreet can help provide references and more in-depth credit checks, primarily in the major markets.

Using distributors can have its own challenges. For example, some companies find that if they have a dedicated salesperson based locally or who travels frequently to the country, they're likely to get more sales than a single local distributor. Often, distributors sell multiple products and sometimes even competing ones. It can be difficult to make sure that the distributor favors your product over another.

Further, in some countries, companies often find that consumers are more likely to buy a product from a foreign company, particularly an American or European company, than from a local distributor. This is often the case with complicated, high-tech products. Locals are simply more likely to believe that an overseas salesperson knows his or her product better.

You can certainly learn a lot about the local market through exporting. Nevertheless, there are long-term risks associated with relying on the export option. If you merely export to a country, the local distributor or buyer might switch purchases to a cheaper supplier or even just threaten to in order to get a better price from you. Or, someone might start making the product locally and take the market from you. Also, local buyers sometimes believe that a company that only exports to them is not very committed to providing long-term service and support once a sale is complete. Thus, they may prefer to buy from someone who is producing locally. After entering the market as an exporter, many companies begin to consider acquiring a local presence, which moves them toward one of the three other entry options.

Export management companies and international trading companies can also be good partners if you want to export. Export management companies tend to also be small companies who are experienced in the logistical, legal, and financial aspects of exporting. Like freight for-warders, for a fee they can help you with the logistics of shipping and customs. Export management companies can also help with local dis-tribution advice. Both export management and trading companies make their money by a markup or commission on your products. Trading companies differ in that they do both exporting and importing.

In addition to the export financing options that the above compa-nies offer, the SBA provides some options through its Export Work-ing Capital Program and the International Trade Loan Program. The Export-Import Bank of the United States (Ex-IM Bank; www.exim.gov/) also provides a range of financing tools for small businesses. Like the SBA, they often provide guarantees enabling your local bank to assist you more readily. Start by checking with your bank to see what options they may offer. In essence, all of these financing options act as a line of credit enabling you to fill an overseas order. You'll need to adjust for the financing cost, as it is likely to impact your bottom line on the orders.

Licensing and Franchising

Under a licensing or franchising agreement, your company would grant rights on some well-defined intangible property, like technology or a brand name, to a local company for a specified period of time. In return, you will receive a royalty. While your company usually has no owner-ship interests, you'll be expected to provide ongoing support and advice. This option makes the best sense if you have a unique product or a strong brand name, but do not want to incur up-front costs to establish a company in the country. You can always add a provision in any agree-ment that gives you the option to buy out your local franchisee, although you may get some pushback if you try to define the price or a formula for determining the price. At a minimum, you should at least have the first right of refusal should the local franchisee decide to sell at some point in the future.

You may want to consider a royalty chart that changes depending on the total volume of business transacted. You want to create incentives for your local franchisee, so a percentage that decreases slightly at higher revenue levels incents your local franchisee while still increasing your net royalty.

Define not only the exact geographic boundaries for your license, but also a finite time period for the initial license with revenue benchmarks. For example, you may decide on a three-year license with a defined minimum annual license revenue paid in U.S. dollars or another major global currency. Since it usually takes time to establish a new product or service, the license revenues may start low for year 1 and increase annually. If the local company meets this target, then the agreement may automatically renew for another two years, or you can renegotiate.

Franchising usually requires your firm to provide more marketing and sales support. This may be a welcome option if you are closely managing brand and quality. Be sure to charge for support, as that is a new cost that should not be part of the base franchise or license fee. While many companies try to license or franchise, you'll want to be sure that you have a local market before you start down this path. An enthusiastic local partner is not sufficient proof of a local market. Research the intended target market, and prepare your own business plan for that country. You can waste quite a bit of time and money chasing new markets that may not deliver. Also, if you are sure that the local market is viable and strong, be sure you have the right partner before you give a license or franchise. Most of these agreements have some type of exclusivity, either by geography or by being first to market. You may miss a new market because you're stuck with the wrong partner. Be clear in defining the rights and obligations of both companies.

You'll need well-prepared legal documents. Consider getting legal advice from a law firm that has direct experience in the country or an affiliate relationship with a local firm. You can find a list of law firms through the chambers of commerce or the commercial desk.

Most companies still consider the market entry option of licensing and franchising—it's a low-risk option because there's typically no upfront investment. However, foreign companies are sometimes concerned about protecting their intellectual property. There are wide variations on how well countries protect intellectual rights.

If you consider licensing, be sure that the local company has the will and the ability to develop, market, and sell the products. Have revenue targets that if not met in a certain time frame release you from the agreement. For example, you may license the concepts for a line of toys to a company that specializes in the children's market for that country. If that company gets another more lucrative license contract from another company, they may opt to invest their energies in that line of toys over yours. While good legal documents can help you navigate such scenarios, really knowing your local licensee is essential.

Licensing is an interesting option for companies who are willing to license only select intellectual property or items. For example, a company that has a new hot electronic game player may license the right to design and manufacture adaptable game cartridges to local companies as a way to grow quickly in new markets. Companies like Nintendo have used this growth strategy very successfully.

Equity Joint Ventures

The next option for companies entering a new market is some form of equity joint venture, including wholly owned local subsidiaries. Many countries have regulations in place to oversee these types of local investments. Some countries do not allow wholly owned subsidiaries in certain industries, while other countries have financial and legal controls that may make it difficult for younger companies to establish local offices.

Equity joint ventures pose both opportunities and challenges for the companies that choose this option. In some countries, particularly those that have heavy government involvement in business, equity joint ventures are seen as a great way to gain access to the technology, capital, equipment, and know-how of foreign companies. The risk to your company is that if the venture sours, the local company might be able to keep some or all of the assets they acquired from you. In these cases, the local companies probably only contributed things like land or tax concessions—things that you can't keep if the venture ends. While this practice continues in some countries, like China and India, it's of less concern than it was in the past, as more governments try to observe global standards for intellectual property rights.

A key challenge to joint ventures is finding the right local partner—not just in terms of business focus, but also in terms of compatible cultural perspectives and management practices. We'll talk more later about these kinds of considerations.

Wholly Owned Foreign Enterprises

The most intensive entry option requires the highest commitment by your company, as you are to assume all of the risk, financial and otherwise. In some countries, it may seem easier to own your own operations than to deal with a local partner. This is particularly true if you have new technology, trade secrets, or unique business processes that you don't want to disclose to a partner. On the flip side, local companies understand the local culture—both that of the customers and workers—and are often better equipped to deal with bureaucracy and regulations.

Even if you establish your own subsidiary in country, you're likely to hire local professionals and will need to understand the cultural nuances of managing and operating.

Regardless of which entry strategy a company chooses, several factors are always important:

- **Cultural and linguistic differences**. These affect all relationships and interactions inside the company, as well as your interactions with customers and the local government. Understanding the local business culture is critical to success.
- **Quality and training of local contacts and/or employees.** Evaluating the skill sets and determining if the local staff is qualified is a key factor for success.
- **Political and economic issues**. Policy can change frequently, and companies need to determine what level of investment they are willing to make, what is required to make this investment, and how much earnings they can repatriate.
- **Experience of the partner company**. Assessing the experience of the local company in the market, with the product, and in dealing with foreign companies is essential in selecting the right local partner.

- **Managing channel conflict.** Are your products priced differently among distributors and different countries as well as within countries through different channels? How can you manage this conflict in today's wired world where customers are likely to access that information more easily than ever before?

Understanding How Culture Impacts Local Business Practices

It is difficult to make generalizations about any culture, as there are always exceptions.

To conduct business with people from other cultures, you must put aside preconceived notions and strive to learn about the culture of your counterpart. Often the greatest challenge is learning not to apply your own value system when judging people from other cultures. It is important to remember that there are no right or wrong ways to deal with other people, just different ways. Concepts like time and ethics are viewed differently from place to place, and the smart business professional will seek to understand the rationale underlying another culture's concepts.

For younger and smaller companies, there's no room for error or delays—both of which may result from cultural misunderstandings and miscommunications. These miscues can and often do impact the bottom line.

In reality, understanding cultural differences is important whether you're selling to ethnic markets in your own home country or selling to new markets in different countries. Culture also impacts you if you're sourcing from different countries, as it impacts communications.

Your understanding of culture will affect your ability to enter a local market, develop and maintain business relationships, negotiate successful deals, conduct sales, conduct marketing and advertising campaigns, and engage in manufacturing and distribution. Too often, people send the wrong signals or receive the wrong messages, and as a result, become tangled in the cultural web. In fact, there are numerous instances where deals would have been successfully completed if finalizing them had been based on business issues alone. Just as you would conduct a technical or market analysis, you should also conduct a cultural analysis.

It's critical to understand the history and politics of any country or region in which you work or with which you intend to deal. It is important to remember that each person considers his or her "sphere" or "world" the most important and that it forms the basis of his or her individual perspective. We often forget that cultures are shaped by decades and centuries of experience and that ignoring cultural differences puts us at a disadvantage.

In general, when considering doing business in a new country, there are a number of factors to consider. Make sure to learn about the country's history, culture, and people, as well as determine its more general suitability for your product or service.

What Is Culture? Values, Customs, and Language

We often underestimate how critical local culture, values, and customs can be in the business environment. We assume, usually incorrectly, that business is the same everywhere. Culture does matter, and more and more people are realizing its impact on their business interactions.

What exactly do we mean by culture? Note that culture is different from personality. No doubt one of the highest hurdles to cross-cultural understanding and effective relationships is our frequent inability to distinguish the influence of culture from that of personality. Once we become culturally literate, we can more easily read individual personalities and their effect on our relationships.

In essence, each of us is raised in a belief system that influences our individual perspectives to such a large degree that we can't always account for, or even comprehend, its influence. We're like other members of our culture—we've come to share a common idea of what's appropriate and inappropriate.

Culture is the beliefs, values, mind-set, and practices of a specific group of people. It includes the behavior pattern and norms of a specific group—the rules, assumptions, and perceptions, the logic and reasoning that is specific to a group. Culture is really the collective programming of our minds from birth. It's this collective programming that distinguishes one group of people from another. It impacts our business interactions, and it defines our customers.

There are a number of factors that constitute a culture: manners, mind-set, rituals, laws, ideas, and language, to name a few. To truly understand culture, you need to go beyond the lists of dos and don'ts, although those are important too. You need to understand what makes people tick, what's impacted their mind-set and how it has been influenced over time by historical, political, and social issues. Understanding the "why" behind culture is essential.

Much of the problem in any cross-cultural interaction stems from our expectations. When we say *cultural*, we don't always just mean people from different countries. Cultures exist in all types of groups. There are even subcultures within a country or target market. The challenge is that whenever we deal with people from another culture—whether in our own country or globally—we expect people to behave as we do and for the same reasons.

When you're dealing with people from another culture, you may find that their business practices, communication, and management styles are different from what you are accustomed to. Understanding the culture of the people with whom you are dealing is key to successful business interactions as well as to accomplishing business objectives. For example, you'll need to understand the following:

- How people communicate
- How culture impacts how people view time and deadlines
- How likely are people to ask questions or highlight problems
- How people respond to management and authority
- How people perceive verbal and physical communications
- How people make decisions

Sure, you may think you've all agreed on a project scope and timetable, but often people realize that there were missed communications and the project isn't going as planned. Further when you're dealing with an overseas vendor, it's not always the same as your local domestic vendor-supplier relationships.

Language is a secondary, but still important, factor. It is impossible to become fluent in any language overnight, and you should not be overly concerned about your language capabilities. However, it helps to learn some phrases and to show an interest in your host country's language. If you do business in several countries, it is unlikely that you will be conversant in each language. However, if you are focused on one country, it will give you a significant long-term advantage to learn the language.

Verbal language aside, body language and the "packaging of information" must be treated with sensitivity. How you gesture, twitch, and scrunch up your face represents a veritable legend to your emotions. Being able to suitably read—and broadcast—body language can significantly up your chances of understanding and being understood.

People may not understand your words, but they will certainly interpret your body language according to *their* accepted norms. It is *their* perceptions that will count when you are trying to do business with them, and it's important to understand that those perceptions will be based on the teachings and experiences of their culture—not yours.

Cross-cultural understanding then requires that we reorient our mind-set and, most importantly, our expectations, in order to interpret the gestures, attitudes, and statements of the people we encounter. We reorient our mind-set but do not necessarily change it.

When trying to understand how cultures evolve, we look at the factors that help to determine cultures and their values. In general, a *value* is defined as something that we prefer over something else—whether it's a behavior or a tangible item. Values are usually acquired early in life and are usually nonrational—although we may believe that ours are actually quite rational. Our values are the key building blocks of our cultural orientation. In business, we may often note the ways in which we apply values to marketing, advertising, and understanding our target market. When we're dealing with other cultures at the business level, it's the same process, although for a different purpose.

Odds are that each of us has been raised with a considerably different set of values than that of our colleagues and counterparts around the world. Exposure to a new culture may take all you've ever learned about what's good and bad, just and unjust, beautiful and ugly, and stand it on its head.

Precisely where a culture begins and ends can be murky. Some cultures fall within geographic boundaries; others, of course, overlap. And cultures within one border can turn up within other geographic boundaries looking dramatically different or pretty much the same. For example, Indians in India or Americans in the United States may communicate and interact differently from those who have been living outside of their home country for a few years.

Political and economic philosophies impact the way people's values are shaped. Formed by our education, religion, or social structure, our cultural base of reference impacts our business interactions in critical ways. It's also very important to recognize that cultures are not static entities. They're constantly evolving: merging, interacting, drawing apart, and reforming.

Human nature is such that we see the world through our own cultural shades. Tucked in between the lines of our cultural laws is an unconscious bias that inhibits us from viewing other cultures objectively. Our judgments of people from other cultures will always be colored by the frame of reference we've been taught. As we look at our own habits and perceptions, we need to think about the experiences that have blended together to impact our cultural frame of reference.

Conducting Business and Negotiating

The following are some tips on how to equip yourself for success and avoid some cultural pitfalls.

One of the most important cultural factors in many countries is the importance of networking or relationships. Whether in Asia or Latin America or somewhere in between, it's best to have an introduction from a common business partner, vendor, or supplier when meeting a new company or partner. Even in the United States or Europe, where we like to think that relationships have less importance, a well-placed introduction will work wonders.

Even if you have been invited to bid on a contract, you are still trying to sell your company and yourself. Do not be patronizing or assume you are doing the local company or its government a favor. They must like and trust you if you are to succeed. Think about your own business encounters with people, regardless of nationality, who were condescending and arrogant. How often have you given business to people who irritated you?

In some countries, it can be almost impossible to get through the right doors without some sort of introduction. Be creative in identifying potential introducers. If you don't know someone who knows the company with which you would like to do business, consider indirect sources. Trade organizations, lawyers, bankers and financiers, common suppliers and buyers, consultants, and advertising agencies are just a few potential introducers. Once a meeting has been set up, foreign companies need to understand the local cultural nuances that govern meetings, negotiations, and ongoing business expansion.

Make sure you understand how your overseas associates think about time and deadlines. How will that impact your timetable and deliverables?

You need to understand the predominant corporate culture of the country you are dealing with—particularly when dealing with vendors and external partners. What's the local hierarchy? What are the expected management practices? Are the organizations you're dealing with uniform in culture, or do they represent more than one culture or ethnicity? Culture affects how people develop trust and make decisions, as well as the speed of their decision making and their attitudes toward accountability and responsibility.

Understand how you can build trust with potential partners. How are people from your culture viewed in the target country, and how will it impact your business interactions? How are small or younger companies viewed in the local market? Understand the corporate culture of your potential partner or distributor. More entrepreneurial local companies may have more in common with a younger firm in terms of their approach to doing business.

How do people communicate? There are also differences in how skills or knowledge is taught or transferred. In the United States, we're expected to ask questions—it's a positive and indicates a seriousness about wanting to learn. In some cultures, asking questions is seen as reflecting a lack of knowledge and could be considered personally embarrassing. It's important to be able to address these issues without appearing condescending. Notice I said *appearing*—the issue is less whether you think you're being condescending and more about whether the professional of the differing culture perceives a statement or action as condescending. Again, let's recall that culture is based on perceptions and values.

Focus on communications of all types, and learn to find ways around cultural obstacles. For example, if you're dealing with a culture that shies away from providing bad news or information—don't ask yes/no questions. Focus on the process, and ask questions about the stage or deliverable. Many people get frustrated by the lack of information or clear communications. You certainly don't want to be surprised by a delayed shipment to your key customers.

There are no clear playbooks for operating in every culture around the world. Rather, we have to understand the components that affect culture, understand how it impacts our business objectives, and then equip ourselves and our teams with the know-how to operate successfully in each new cultural environment. Once you've established a relationship, you may opt to delegate it to someone on your team. Be sure that your person understands the culture of the country, and make sure to stay involved until there is a successful operating history of at least one or more years. Many entrepreneurs stay involved in key relationships on an ongoing basis. Be aware that your global counterparts may require that level of attention.

Make sure in any interaction that you have a decision maker on the other end. On occasion, junior people get assigned to work with smaller companies, and you could spend a lot of time with someone who is unable to finalize an agreement. If you have to work through details with a junior person, try to have that person get a senior person involved early on so you run fewer chances of losing time and energy.

When negotiating with people from a different culture, try to understand your counterpart's position and objectives. This does not imply that you should compromise easily or be "soft" in your style. Rather, understand how to craft your argument in a manner that will be more effective with a person of that culture.

Entrepreneurs are often well equipped to negotiate global contracts or ventures. They are more likely to be flexible and creative in their approach and have less rigid constraints than their counterparts from more established companies. Each country has different constraints, including the terms of payment and regulations, and you will need to keep an open mind about how to achieve your objectives.

Even in today's wired world, don't assume that everyone in every country is as reliant on the Internet and e-mail. You may need to use different modes of communication with different countries, companies, and professionals. Faxes are still very common, as many people consider signed authorizations more official than e-mail, although that is changing.

As with any business transaction, use legal documents to document relationships and expectations. Many legal professionals recommend that you opt to use the international courts or a third-party arbitration system in case of a dispute. Translate contracts into both languages, and have a second independent translator verify the copies for the accuracy of concepts and key terminology. But be warned: No translation can ever be exactly accurate, as legal terminology is both culture- and country-specific. At the end of the day, even a good contract has many limitations in its use. You have to be willing to enforce infractions.

Tips on Using Interpreters and Translators

Even if you know the language, it is always advisable to hire an interpreter. In addition to minimizing misunderstandings, an interpreter provides you with additional time to prepare a response while the discussion is being translated. Following are some tips for using interpreters.

Whenever possible, educate your interpreter beforehand about the intricacies of your product and/or service. The interpreter's accuracy in translating may depend on the product/service knowledge that you provide him or her with beforehand. If you start to travel to a country frequently, you may want to hire the same interpreter so that over time he or she will become more cognizant of the technicalities of your business. In essence, your interpreter will be your most valuable marketing and presentation tool.

Always use your own interpreter. Never rely on the interpreter of your counterpart, because that person works for your counterpart and is more likely to protect his or her business interests. It is common and preferable to have a different interpreter represent each side during negotiations and meetings.

Always face your business counterpart, not your interpreter. The interpreter is only there to facilitate your business interests. Your goal is to develop a business relationship and personal rapport with the local businessperson, despite your language differences.

Recognize that the audio level in some countries is lower or higher than in other countries. If your interpreter is speaking softly, it may be considered normal. Do not ask him or her to speak louder, unless necessary. Similarly, make sure to speak at the same audio level as the others in a discussion. Often, people speak very loudly when interacting with people who communicate in another language, subconsciously forgetting that there is a language barrier, and not a hearing one.

Use short, simple sentences. Avoid use of slang, clichés, analogies, or idiomatic expressions that are specific to your language or culture. Westerners, particularly Americans, should be careful not to use sports analogies, as not all American sports are popular in other countries. Analogies can be misinterpreted by your listeners and should be avoided.

Pause after each sentence to give the interpreter time to translate it; otherwise, he or she may try to summarize groups of sentences. Speak about only one concept at a time.

Avoid buzzwords and explain concepts thoroughly. For example, words like "empowerment" may not have a direct translation, and therefore the translator may translate parts of the word separately and most likely incorrectly. Instead of saying "MBO" or "management by objectives," explain exactly what you mean. This does not imply that your counterpart does not understand terms and concepts, but rather that these concepts may have different names in his or her culture. More importantly, the interpreter may not understand the intention or concept and may translate the words incorrectly.

Ask direct questions and avoid double negatives to minimize confusion. It may be valuable to verify the cultural suitability of certain direct questions with your interpreter before the encounter. You may need to simply reword a question. The key to success is making sure that your interpreter understands the intention behind your questions.

If you are having marketing and sales materials or corporate information translated, use the same guidelines as above. Also, you may want to consider having the materials translated in your own country rather than relying on your local partner. If the materials are done in-country, make sure to have them professionally reviewed by your own translation firm to ensure accuracy. Many firms will check translations by translating them back into your base language.

In general, the key words to entering any new market successfully are "patience," "patience," and "patience." Flexibility and creativity are also important. You should focus on the end result, and find unique ways to get there.

CHAPTER 8

KEEPING THE FAITH

O kay, for some this chapter may seem corny, simplistic, or filled with clichés, but the reality is that every entrepreneur goes through ups and downs. Finding ways to keep the faith is essential to your company and to your personal long-term survival. By faith I am not referring to religion, although for many that may certainly be an essential component. How you keep your faith is tied more to your personal and managerial philosophy. It will shape how you deal with problems, people, and challenges.

Entrepreneurship is certainly not for the faint of heart. You need to determine before you get into it if you have the stomach for the often rapid ups and downs. The more you talk to fellow entrepreneurs, the more you'll see that just about everyone has their own ways of keeping the faith and moving forward during challenging times. This chapter highlights many ways that people keep the faith, professionally and personally. During your entrepreneurial ride, it's important to keep an eye on both your spiritual and physical health.

In essence, there are two distinct scenarios in which your entrepreneurial faith may feel challenged. The first occurs during the normal course of starting and growing your company and is related to the problems, issues, and challenges that just about every company faces. Even when you know you're not alone in confronting these problems, keeping focused, committed, and positive takes effort.

The second is the unfortunate but very common scenario of closing your business. In Chapter 9, I'll talk about the mechanical issues regarding knowing when to close your business and how best to accomplish this difficult step. In this chapter, I'll focus on how to move past closing your company to the next step. Successful career entrepreneurs learn from their failures, and closing one company doesn't mean you won't be successful with the next. Learning how to keep the faith will help you in both scenarios.

It Happens to Everyone

The first thing to realize is that everyone, including entrepreneurs, experiences challenges and makes mistakes. The key is to learn from them. In fact, many professionals find that their challenges, mistakes, and hardships help them find future successes. So, the key to keeping faith is figuring out how to go through the fire of challenge and emerge, scathed, but not destroyed, ready to move toward the next opportunity.

Failure is a part of life for just about everyone. What starts to differentiate people is our ability to respond to failure—our degree of resilience. Whether it's a politician with one or more previous election losses who keeps the faith and comes back to win an election, an actor who endures a pile of rejections before getting a prized part, an athlete who never gives up hope of being number one, or a career entrepreneur who keeps believing in a vision and comes back to start a successful company, a resilient person remains open to future success. Entrepreneurs need to find ways to cope with adversity and overcome the professional and personal challenges associated with their ventures.

An essential first step is to stop feeling sorry for yourself, determine what went wrong and why, and then move on. It's important to distinguish that it was the company that failed. The entrepreneur as a person is not a failure.

Some Common Reasons a Project, Idea, or Company Stumbles

Not every venture will succeed. Sometimes, the business model isn't right, the product doesn't meet the need, or the market timing is not right. These things can occur for reasons beyond the entrepreneur's control. The following will help you begin to dissect your own experience. Keep in mind that you can't be afraid to make mistakes. If you are, you will most likely hold yourself back in either your current or future ventures.

- **Not enough planning.** Did your plan get enough market input from customers and users? Were the financials thorough, or did you underestimate expenses and overestimate the timing of sales?
- **Not enough resources.** Did you have what you needed to execute your plan in terms of people, money, skills, and supplies? Were you able to reach your customer or was the marketing budget too small? Were you capitalized in a way that was productive for your company or that was disincentivizing for you and the other senior team members?
- **External factors (economy, market, or industry not yet ready).** Did you launch in a recession or at the end of an up cycle? Would your product have fared better in a booming economy? Often, for price sensitive, nonessential products, market timing is everything. Did you have enough resources to ride through a tough economic cycle? How could you have planned for it? Did you need to raise VC money in a weak market? Can you put your idea/company on hold for a short while till the market improves? Are you ahead of the market or behind it?
- **Incorrect team.** Did you hire the wrong senior team, or did you lack the resources to even have a senior team, forcing you to take on roles that you were not as strong in? Did you duplicate rather than complement your skills? (See Chapter 6.)
- **Partnership and ownership disputes and changes.** Did differences in strategy or management direction become irreconcilable? Did one or more partners cease to be involved with the company, or did ownership change and the company's prospects take a turn for the worse?
- **Inability to fulfill demand or grow quickly.** Did you actually succeed in getting orders, but fail to have enough resources to fulfill them? Products need parts, and if you can't buy the parts,

you can't make the products to fill the orders. Not having short-term cash to cushion growth is as much a challenge as not having the orders to begin with.

Listen, Analyze, and Learn

Everyone, including employees, colleagues, investors, customers, family, and friends, will undoubtedly have their own opinion about why a product, marketing campaign, or your business failed. It's normal to feel down and to not want to be bothered by others, no matter how well-meaning. But it's important to review scenarios, processes, and decisions. There may be some information that, if processed differently, may have helped you to make different decisions. If you can't examine your mistakes and failures, you're likely to make the same mistakes again.

Having said that, you should avoid listening to people whose criticism is too vehement or, worse, too personal to be productive. Amidst useful business and market information will likely be nestled a strong dose of unproductive blame, most likely from investors or others who had a vested interest in the business. Block that out. Yes, of course you probably made some errors. Who doesn't? If you accept responsibility and learn from your mistakes, you're likely to operate differently and more likely successfully in the future.

Decisions can be hard to navigate. We make decisions based on information we know at that moment in time, without the benefit of a crystal ball (though wouldn't that be nice?). The information we evaluate comes from inside as well as outside our company. The silver lining in making a mistake is that our learning process is made easier. We can analyze cause and effect so we're better equipped next time.

For example, imagine a scenario in which to increase sales in a down economy, a company drops its prices. When the economy improves, the industry and customers won't allow the company to raise them again, and as a result, the firm loses revenues and profitability. The next time around, that company will know to think of better ways to generate revenues and won't drop its prices quickly, if at all. That's one example of a lesson that could only come with experience or from a seasoned entrepreneur.

Don't wallow in your errors or misfortunes. If you made a mistake, recognize it and then get on with your life. We all learn more from our mistakes than from our successes. Determine what aspects of your business model or corporate structure didn't work. If you decide to start a new venture, you need to be careful to not just rebuild what you lost, but to build with newer and wiser information. If you're unable to truly listen and analyze, you're likely to keep making the same mistakes, no matter how great your idea.

Also, realize that you probably did some things right and that the company had a few successes. Isolate these so you can consider how to use these nuggets of information in your next venture.

Focus on Positivity

Get rid of negativity. If this sounds like a mantra from a new-age self-help book, it probably is. However, I have watched it work beautifully, both in my own experiences and in that of many around me.

Corporations spend millions on team-building and coaching, but at the end of the day, it's about being focused and positive. You can't do that if you have one or more people in your world who are negative. Particularly if that person is you or someone on your team.

Start with yourself. Are you a glass half-full or a glass half-empty kind of person? As discussed in Chapter 1, knowing your personal philosophy and your personal temperament can help you understand how you approach stress. Every new and growing venture goes through stressful periods. You need to think about how you respond to stress and if your response is generating the right, positive energy for you and your company.

Negative energy on your team can be disastrous for a young company. I have heard entrepreneurs talk about "flushing" their teams. This may not sound very pleasant, or even very polite, but it refers to "flushing" or letting go of people who are negative and unproductive. "Flushing" is the easiest way to get everyone back on track and moving toward positive growth. Negative people will spread their negativity. In young companies, which are typically still small, bad energy can spread faster than the speed of light.

Now, this does not mean that you should surround yourself with "yes" men and women either. Find people whose experiences, attitudes, and opinions you respect and who complement you, not copy you. You want people who can identify problems and challenges—hopefully before they happen. While positive people are likely to recognize both the problem and its potential solutions, a negative person is likely to dwell on the problem without pushing past it toward a solution.

As part of focusing on positive energies, take a look at the extended network of your family and friends. Some may inadvertently pass their fears on to you. Remember that these fears result more often from their own discomfort with the world of entrepreneurship than from other, more legitimate sources. Beware of negative energies, which may distract you. Once your have heard the message, separate constructive criticisms or projections from the purely negative energy. Remember what's constructive, and throw the rest away. If you don't, negative energy will impede your ability to creatively think your way out of tough situations. A positive and open-minded attitude will help you tackle the toughest adversities.

Your Attitude Is Contagious

Your employees will glean a great deal about the company from your attitude and perspective. There's certainly no need to hide the fact that your company may be experiencing challenging times. In fact, quite the opposite is true. Your employees will know about the challenges whether you tell them or not; but if you recognize the issues openly, they will more likely respect and appreciate your professionalism, candidness, and leadership.

In stressful periods, it's common to be down or even grumpy. But if you genuinely believe that your firm can turn around, then your employees need to see and hear that energy. If you have resources, you may want to bring in a motivational coach to help find ways to get everyone excited and focused. If it's likely that your company will need to close and you don't have resources, small gestures will go a long way in recognizing an employee's effort. Even during difficult periods, find something positive to note. It might be an employee's work or attitude or a product or new customer.

Letting Go of Anger

As your company goes through a closing, your anger and resentment are likely to increase, particularly if they are directed at a particular person or entity. Of course, you are more likely to assign the blame to someone other than yourself, although some people habitually accept more blame than may be due them. It may seem easy and comforting to be mad at investors, employees, customers, the market, and even family or friends for any variety of reasons, not the least of which is their failure to provide support. It should be no great surprise to hear that left unchecked, anger can be self-defeating.

A truly remarkable story of moving past anger comes from the life of Nelson Mandela, a man who was warranted in feeling more than just a little angry at his jailers. Instead, Mandela realized that if he remained angry, it would be like leaving one kind of imprisonment for another. By letting go of his anger and resentment, he set himself free. Try to find your own inspiration in people who overcome and go on to achieve their visions.

Keeping Perspective

One essential part of keeping the faith is keeping perspective. We get so caught up in the crisis of the moment that we're unable to detach and focus on solutions. We torment ourselves with needless stress. Keeping perspective is essential. I learned this early on. In college, when I would call home stressed about the semester's series of exams, my mother would walk me through a soothing exercise that calculated the number of exams per semester, multiplied by the number of semesters over the four-year period. Suddenly, when it was one of about 160 exams, the pending test seemed much less stressful.

The lesson here is that you should take any complex and challenging issues and break them into smaller parts that can be handled one by one. Avoid becoming overwhelmed into inaction. Try to break every issue into "bite-size" pieces. Often, it's helpful to work backward when contemplating a particularly difficult problem. Determine the worst-case scenario, and work backward to identify solutions.

Don't Take Yourself Too Seriously

By now, it should be clear that all businesses, including entrepreneurial businesses, experience cycles. We've all known plenty of successful, arrogant professionals who were later humbled by life's ups and downs. Stay consistent and stay humble—it will endear you to your employees, customers, and investors alike. As my folks always say, "Be nice to everyone on your way up. You never know when you'll meet them on your way down."

Keep a Sense of Humor and Find Inspiration

Laughter is truly a great medicine. Find ways to bring it into your office, even in the worst of times. Find a Web site that has acceptable jokes or inspirational sayings of the day or week, and pass them through your office. Find ways to laugh at yourself. If you tend to be stiff and proper, your team will likely appreciate the effort even more. You may even break away to see a funny movie or bring one in and have an office video lunch on a Friday. It will help everyone relax. And who knows? Some creative solutions may creep in.

The most important thing to keep in mind is to avoid "hiding." No doubt, you can't see much to laugh about or even to be grateful for. But it's important to lighten the atmosphere of the office. You need people to stick around and be productive, whether you're just going through a prolonged slump or whether you have to close your company. You may find that some people respond better to humor and others to words of inspiration. As a manager, use whichever works best to keep your team energized and focused, no matter which direction your company is headed.

Get a Hobby and a Charitable Interest

Having a balanced personal life will make you a better entrepreneur in any situation. Having a hobby will keep you balanced, and having a charitable interest keeps you humbled and focused on what matters most in the long run. Don't wait until times are tough to develop your interests. As your company grows, having outside personal interests will round out your perspective, keep your outlook positive, and keep your ideas fresh and creative. Even with entrepreneurial pressures, it's worth carving out time for personal activities.

If your business stumbles, your family and friends are your likely support and lifeline in the first few months. Having a long-term hobby or charitable interest will continue to give you a sense of purpose and meaning as you regroup and move on to your next venture.

Keeping the Faith in Yourself and in Entrepreneurship

Many entrepreneurs launch and grow several companies before reaching real professional and financial success. Knowing when to move on is a real challenge for most entrepreneurs. After all, our companies are very often extensions of ourselves, children of sorts. It's very difficult for most entrepreneurs to clinically assess when their companies have lived out their useful lives and when termination is best. External confidantes can be very helpful in helping us honestly and accurately assess the moment at which a company must be closed. Pay particular attention to counsel from people who have no vested interest in keeping the company alive. Employees and angel investors have much to lose as well and may also hesitate from making a tough call. Most VCs, on the other hand, are quick to cut their losses, although many are happy if someone else continues to sustain their investment in the slim possibility of a turnaround.

While deciding to close may be one of the hardest steps, it's also one of the most essential skills required. Companies are sometimes kept alive by "artificial measures"—through the entrepreneur's passion and resources and possibly through outside funding. You need to focus on why your company is not self-sustaining and how long you should keep it going. Just as strategies need to evolve and move on, sometimes you may need to actually move on from the entire company.

Career entrepreneurs often find that their natural determination and resilience enables them to overcome the bigger bumps in the road.

Closing a Business

Closing a business in our success-obsessed society can be very hard, yet many entrepreneurs are faced with this predicament each year. It's tempting to see the entrepreneurs facing this situation as failures or perhaps quitters. The reality I have observed is that it takes more courage and wisdom to know when to close a business and when and how to do it as best as possible. Accepting the situation, addressing it, and moving on is key to long-term survival and resilience. If you have to close a business, think carefully about who you take along to any subsequent ventures. This includes employees, investors, and advisors. Negative energy is not worth transferring, and you're not obliged to take anyone you don't want to take.

Experiencing the failure of an entrepreneurial venture can feel like the stages of bereavement. The resulting grief can last from a few months to several years, often depending on how personally impacted you are as well as how well you learn to keep the faith and move on. Allow yourself to feel each emotion, such as anger, sadness, and frustration, but don't dwell on them.

In fact, despite the initial pain, going through the closing of your company can actually help you emerge as a stronger and more competent entrepreneur. You have to be willing to analyze your mistakes as well as recognize which factors were beyond your control. The humility and new sense of purpose often makes career entrepreneurs more open to new opportunities.

Optimism and Resilience

Entrepreneurs are an incredibly optimistic lot. We'll always find that one hint of light peeking through even on the dreariest days. Stay focused on that optimism, resilience, and determination. Certainly, don't let it blind you to the real problems, but let it help motivate you to find creative solutions and persevere to your next venture.

EXIT STRATEGIES

A t some point, every entrepreneur thinks about a day when they may not be running or even owning their company. It's never too early to think about exit strategies, although in your early growth years these thoughts should not dominate any decision making or planning.

The exit options for your company may, however, impact how you choose to fund a company, the types of partnerships you may be willing to consider, and how you decide to incent your employees. For example, if your company is not likely to go public, you may not need to or want to give your employees options in the early days. Rather, you may prefer to incentivize your team with bonuses along the way or upon an acquisition.

There are really two exit strategies—sell or merge the company, or close or liquidate the business. I'll cover both options in this chapter. Ventures that have prospered well will have stronger prospects for merging with another, but even companies that have poor revenues or profits but unique products or services can also be ripe acquisition candidates.

Some view going public as an exit strategy, and it is for the investors, but not really for the entrepreneur. While everyone can get some money out, the entrepreneur is likely to remain involved, serving as the CEO and/or president. I reviewed going public as a growth strategy in Chapter 6. In this chapter, I'll review the two exit strategies and the variations on each. Sometimes the entrepreneur cashes out fully, and other times, it's partially and perhaps over time. I'll also review issues to consider when passing on your business to offspring or other family members. Passing on your business is unlikely to provide you with an immediate financial exit, but it may allow you a day-to-day management exit.

Determining your exit options and how you choose to plan for them will depend in large part on your evolving personal philosophy. Entrepreneurs who expect to grow their company for five years and then sell may be surprised when they reach the four- or five-year mark and don't want to sell. They're enjoying running their company and may opt to acquire for growth rather than be acquired. Be prepared for the fact that your motivations may change. The key issue here is that if others are involved, particularly if those others are outside investors, they will undoubtedly be expecting an exit strategy, and you'll need to think of one for them. Some entrepreneurs consider buying out existing investors. If you consider this option, be sure to get an independent valuation. You can structure a payout over time or finance the buyout and use long-term debt.

Regardless of which options you choose to pursue, planning is essential. Just as you planned how to grow your company, you'll need to think about how to transition it, either by selling it to outsiders, by passing it on to family members, or by closing it.

Sell or Merge

There are various kinds of sales and mergers. Your options will vary based on your company's structure, stage of growth, and industry standards, as well as your own personal needs and motivations.

Phased Sale

A phased sale is more common for service companies in which the entrepreneur is likely to be perceived as a "core asset." Companies in advertising, public relations, consulting, law, or accounting may have been founded by entrepreneurs who are essential to the business. Clients may rely on that person's involvement. As a result, if you have a service company, you may find that any buyer wants to structure the sale over two or three years. The value of the firm may also be determined in phases. The rationale behind this is simple. The acquiring firm wants to be sure that the clients will remain and the company can survive and grow without the original entrepreneur; otherwise, they will have spent good money to buy a shell of a company.

Sale of the Assets

Selling the assets of a company is an interesting concept, one that many entrepreneurs are not initially familiar with. In essence, this means that one company can buy the assets of another company without acquiring that company's obligations, like its loans, for example. Many acquisitions are actually structured this way so that the company that is buying the assets doesn't face any surprises from any outstanding liabilities.

You can use the money received from the assets to repay any obligations. Some companies may actually go through a Chapter 7 liquidation to ensure that there are no outstanding obligations that could come back to haunt the entrepreneur or the company that purchased the assets. Lawyers are quite familiar with this process and can guide you step by step.

Merger

For entrepreneurial companies, a merger usually means the sale of the company, particularly from the point of view of control. Unless you want to stay on indefinitely, which is not often part of the merger agreement, you will probably be offered a management contract for 1 to 3 years to facilitate a smooth transition with an added noncompete caveat for 3 to 10 years. No one wants to buy your firm only to have you start a brand-new potential competitor. Some entrepreneurs may opt to stay with the merger entity and take on larger roles. If you are acquiring another company, you will be running the expanded company and won't be provided with an exit strategy. This scenario was discussed in Chapter 6.

Mergers are often completed as stock swaps rather than cash transactions, although many are both. It's hard to value stock in a nonpublic company. By accepting this kind of stock, you may be preempting any short-term exit strategy and may also tie up your money for years. Even if you expect the other company to be bought or to go public in the near future, you are still taking a risk, as even the best of transactions do not get completed for any number of reasons. However, receiving stock in a public company with solid trading volume could be beneficial in bringing you long-term value and more upside potential. For example, if you don't need cash immediately, you could hold the stock and let it appreciate, which might reduce any immediate tax liability and enable you to increase your gain.

Knowing When to Sell

For entrepreneurs of hot growth companies, knowing when to sell can be quite confusing. There's no right answer. It depends on your industry, the stage of your company and its long-term prospects, your personal goals, and the stage you are at in your life. Everyone would love to sell when their company is doing great and they are ready to exit the business. Selling is not just a financial decision, but an emotional, spiritual, and lifestyle one as well.

Some entrepreneurs miss the financial opportunity to sell because they are convinced they will receive an even higher offer. In the early 1980s, the head of a hot, new medical products firm with new technologies and $30 million in revenues turned down early offers to buy his company at almost $100 million. His firm was attractive because of its new innovative products, and the offer came from a large firm that saw rapid growth potential with integrated products and distribution. Fifteen years later, this same entrepreneur realized that his company's growth had peaked in a fast-changing industry. The value for his company was less than it had been 15 years ago, and potential buyers were few and far between. The industry had adapted new technologies, and while his firm's products still had a market, it was diminishing, no longer growing.

Selling can be either reactive—you decide to respond to an offer to buy your firm—or proactive—you decide it's time to sell your firm. Either way, you'll do best if you start thinking about the possibility of selling early in the life of your company.

Some companies have unique products, patents, or intellectual property, sometimes with research and development efforts to support future developments. These companies may also develop an internal marketing, sales, and distribution organization to get their product out to market. Both parts of the organization are valuable, and as a result, some entrepreneurs may keep the two separate, sometimes even as two distinct legal companies. This enables them to sell either the product company or the distribution company, but not both. The decision on how best to structure two companies starts very early in the entrepreneurial process—usually years before the value is recognized. In this scenario, the company may operate as two separate companies working together through exclusive sales and distribution agreements.

This structural option may work if you envision selling one part of your company but not both. However, if you want to consider venture capital, be aware that external investors are unlikely to invest in only one part. Often entrepreneurs try to expand their sales and distribution organization and look for investor funds. However, investors are likely to focus on the fact that ownership of the core assets—the patented product, for example—is owned by a separate company that they have no ownership or control over.

You may opt to split the company in two much later in the game. You may decide to keep the company with the assets and sell the operating company that has the sales and distribution. This option makes particular sense if you are selling to a third party or handing over control to family. The assets are leased to the operating company, providing you with a steady stream of license revenue but no operating responsibilities. Of course, your income is dependent on how well the operating company is doing.

Tales from the Trenches

Selling your company can seem like the ideal entrepreneurial exit strategy. It is for many entrepreneurs. Along the sale process, there are many issues to consider as well.

Rosalind Resnick, founder of NetCreations, was fortunate to receive an offer for her firm after taking it public. Faced with the choice of going it alone after the dot-com bubble burst or accepting an acquisition offer, Rosalind chose the latter and walked away with millions. While a glowing financial success story, Rosalind is quick to advise entrepreneurs that acquisitions come with issues that need to be successfully navigated.

Rosalind advises many entrepreneurs that great deals don't happen in a day. They take time, patience, preparation, and often years of negotiating and building relationships with potential buyers—who may also be your biggest competitors. That's why, if you want to get a great price for your company five years from now, you've got to start planning your exit strategy today. Unlike many other Internet companies, NetCreations had both sales and profits, enabling Rosalind to achieve a successful sale for her company, regardless of the unique time in history.

Structurally, entrepreneurs need to pay close attention to the terms of a deal. She recommends against taking payouts over time if possible to reduce risks. Cash or publicly traded stock up front is the best because you know exactly what you are dealing with. Management contracts are also a double-edged sword, as most buyers need the entrepreneur's involvement to transition the company, but it can be hard for the entrepreneur to watch their "baby" be absorbed into a different entity, and not always smoothly.

There's never a perfect time to sell, and often the best offers come when your company is at its peak, making it even harder for many entrepreneurs to sell. Many erroneously assume they'll get more money later or that they can continue to take money out of their companies at the same rate. They forget to anticipate downturns, market changes, and industry pressures, all of which can impact future personal financial gains. Rosalind is grateful that she and her partner had the market sense and timing to accept the acquisition offer and walk away with roughly $40 million each.

Based on her experiences, Rosalind has identified five key steps for business owners to help maximize the chances of a successful sale:

1. **Build a scalable business model.** This means creating a great product, assembling a solid management team, and putting together long-term contracts that kick off a recurring revenue stream. If the company is nothing more than you and your partner and the services that you personally provide, you don't have a company that's worth buying.

2. **Get your financial house in order.** Before NetCreations went public in 1999, Rosalind was acting as her own CFO and, by her own admission, her books and records were a mess. It took the company's auditors nine months to clean them up. But by the time NetCreations was acquired, it was a public company with audited financials, and the company was able to put together deals with DoubleClick and SEAT in record time.

3. **Network with your competitors.** While it may seem counter-intuitive to invite your competitor over for lunch, it actually makes sense. Your competitors—especially the larger ones—are the ones most likely to buy you. DoubleClick had already tried to acquire NetCreations three times before the smaller company's stock collapsed. Consodata, the French direct-marketing company that led the SEAT deal that succeeded in acquiring NetCreations in 2001, had expressed interest in merging with NetCreations the previous year. Rosalind knew the CEOs and M&A executives at both companies.

4. **Know when to hold 'em and when to fold 'em.** It's better to walk away with some cash and start another company than to be saddled with a worthless business that you'll never be able to sell. That's why NetCreations quickly entered into a merger agreement with archrival DoubleClick after the company missed its numbers

and its stock collapsed. You've got to be able to park your ego at the door when the time comes to pull the trigger.

5. **Get liquid fast.** Many privately held companies get acquired in earnout deals that leave them with very little cash or liquid stock. NetCreations avoided that fate by going public and letting the public set a price for its stock that bidders had to match. However, even a private company can boost its chances of liquidity by attracting multiple bidders, letting the marketplace set the price, and creating a sense of urgency for the sale.

Buyers

There are, in essence, several potential buyer groups, either related or unrelated to your business: strategic buyers; financial buyers; and "company insiders," such as partners, family, friends, and employees.

Selling to a Strategic Buyer

In Chapter 3, I talked about strategic investors. Strategic buyers follow the same reasoning and in many cases may be the strategic investor you brought on earlier. If your strategic buyer is an existing investor, the original agreement may give him or her a first right of refusal, which means that if you put the business up for sale, the person or institution is first in line to buy it if he or she chooses.

Strategic buyers may be interested in a good fit between products and/or services, or they may be interested in accessing your distribution capabilities. They may pay a higher price if the business generates positive cash flow and is profitable. If the business continues to need financial support, that may impact the price and terms. When discussing a sale or merger with a potential strategic buyer, be careful how much information you disclose. If the deal does not close, you don't want them to have too much information about your operations. Even if they sign a confidentiality agreement, enforcing the agreement would not reduce any market damage that may have already occurred.

Selling to a Financial Buyer

A financial buyer may be a buyout firm that looks to purchase companies, integrate them, and then resell the complete group of companies for a premium, or it may be a company looking for an investment or an entrepreneur interested in owning and operating his or her own business. Which financial buyer you attract depends, in large part, on the size of your company. Financial buyers are almost solely interested in the cash flow your business generates. Therefore, they are most interested in self-sustaining businesses.

If your business is not performing well, you may attract interest from financial buyers who specialize in turnarounds or restructurings, or in just purchasing companies' assets. In this scenario, you're not likely to get a premium price and more likely will have to sell at a discount.

Selling to Partners, Family, Friends, and Employees

A common exit strategy is to sell your business to a company insider, including other partners, family, friends, and employees. This group knows your business well and is likely to be clear about the value and benefits. If selling to an insider is likely to be the best option for your business, you'll need to plan for it. You may need to hire senior people and give them time to get to know the business and become comfortable with the idea that they can own and run it successfully. If it's a family member, you'll want to bring him or her on for a few years to learn about all aspects of the business. I'll talk more about succession later in this chapter.

The challenge in selling to this group may be in how best to finance the deal, as they may not have enough cash for an outright purchase. There are several options. One option is that they could take out a loan through the company or individually. Another option is that you could help finance the purchase over a period of time and receive a steady stream of payments. There is usually a down payment. Many entrepreneurs find that this financing option better meets their tax considerations. Some sales are based on an earnout where there is a minimum purchase price to be paid on mutually agreed terms. Additionally, you can receive more money if the company meets certain mutually agreed upon terms. In such cases, the minimum price is likely to be low, because otherwise the buyer has minimal incentive to give you the upside potential.

As you consider selling to insiders and debate to what extent you should self-finance the purchase, there are several issues to bear in mind:

- Be sure that the cash flow from the business will enable the buyer to pay you over time. Otherwise, you may want to suggest that the business take out a loan and pay you up front. The new owners can repay the bank loan over time. You no longer have a future risk in this scenario.
- If you opt to finance, the down payment should be at least around 25 percent to ensure that the buyer won't have a change of heart without consequence. Even family members can change their minds.
- Be sure that the buyer understands the business well enough to run it without you, that he or she won't lose key customers, and that he or she will take advantage of existing and new opportunities.
- Address what recourse you have if the business fails and liquidates before you are fully paid. To mitigate this risk, for example, you may want to have secured a perfected lien on all assets. You can only collect the outstanding unpaid purchase price, but if your lawyer files a Uniform Commercial Code (UCC) filing immediately at the closing of a transaction, you will likely have rights ahead of other creditors, except in some cases the IRS.
- Address your options in case the buyer is unable for any reason to continue operating the business before you are completely paid. For example, to cover unfortunate situations, you may want to designate a term in which the buyer will purchase life and disability insurance with you as the beneficiary.

Selling to employees using an employee stock ownership plan (ESOP) is another financing option. In essence, the company forms a trust fund that takes out a loan that is used to pay you. The company makes tax-deductible contributions to the ESOP trust fund to repay the bank loan. ESOPs are used by many companies to sell partial or complete interest in a company. A couple of key points about ESOPS. First, you must have at least 25 employees, have over $5 million in sales, and annual payroll requirements of at least $500,000. ESOPs are considered tax-qualified pension plans and are governed by ERISA, which is the Employee Retirement Income Security Act. Accordingly, routine paperwork and tax filings are required. Plus, the company will need to appoint an ESOP trustee, all of which can add $10,000 to $20,000 or more in annual ESOP expenses.

Many people who start their companies with a partner create a partnership agreement that governs scenarios in which one partner leaves the business. Partners may leave for any number of reasons, including in the event that one of you wants to get out of the business or wants the other person out of the business, or in a situation where one of you dies or is incapacitated.

Often called buyback clauses, these may outline how a purchase price would be determined. For example, a partnership agreement may require a company to hire one or more valuation firms or appraisers to come up with a value. Much of the success of a sale to a partner really depends on the state of the relationship prior to the sale. If the sale occurs because you are both squabbling about everything and want to pursue incompatible directions for the company, then it's likely that the sale terms will seem poor to both of you. The agreement may also provide you with ways to use the proceeds of a life insurance policy to buy out the living spouse of a dead partner.

Hiring Investment Banking, Business Broker, and Other Key Advisors

It's best to hire an investment bank or business broker in addition to your legal and accounting and tax firms to advise you on the sale process. If your sale is relatively small and straightforward, you may only need an experienced lawyer and an accountant. If you're selling to management or employees, you are not likely to need an investment bank, but should plan to use your accountant and lawyer as well as consider a valuation appraiser to help determine a value for the firm.

Business Brokers and Investment Bankers

Business brokers, investment bankers, and other intermediaries represent a category of people who can help you sell your business, including finding buyers, setting the price, and negotiating the terms. Often the names of brokers and bankers are loosely used. Sometimes people who do nothing more than introduce you to a potential buyer may try to charge you a much higher investment banking fee. Everyone charges a fee, so be sure their fees are commensurate with their efforts.

Business brokers tend to do smaller sales in terms of sale price. You can find brokers online or through business broker directories. However, if you've been in business for at least a few years, you have probably already received unsolicited marketing materials from brokers offering to help you sell your business. Some specialize by industry or geographic region, while others may target companies of a certain size. Some hold informational meetings for a small fee. It may be worth attending one to educate yourself, even if you're not quite ready to sell. As with all sales pitches, don't sign up with the first one that contacts you. Do your research and take your time in selecting the firm that's right for you. You can only sell your company once, and given all the time and energy you've spent growing your company, you want to be sure to do it right.

Investment bankers tend to do larger deals, usually over $5 million. Many business brokers may prefer to call themselves investment bankers, as there can be a market belief that bankers can get a higher fee. There are many small boutique investment banks who work with companies to help raise capital, finance expansion, and facilitate exit strategies. Investment bankers will also do valuation analysis and related consulting work, all for fees. Business brokers tend to only focus on selling companies.

Almost all brokers and bankers will charge you a fee up front, which can sometimes be applied to the final sale commission. This up-front fee, which is sometimes over $50,000 if your company is large, but is usually around $25,000, covers the preparation of a formal memorandum of offering, which is similar to a business plan but includes historical information but not always projections. It may also include a valuation analysis that gives you a possible price range. Many will tell you that charging a fee helps them assess the seriousness of the seller's intent. Perhaps.

Keep in mind that business brokers can act like real estate brokers. They are more interested in business turnover than in getting the best possible deal for your company. In other words, they would rather get some commission quickly rather than wait for a high number. They do not want your deal to take an excessive amount of time. As a business themselves, business brokers are concerned about the time involved and their profitability. Accordingly, do some of your own research so that you know what would be a reasonable sale price for your company given the industry and stage of your firm. Do be reasonable. Adamantly sticking to some astronomical figure will not produce results.

Also, as happens with a house that's on the market too long, interest in your company may dwindle over time. This is one reason that many business brokers and investment bankers will conduct what's called an auction. They will send the offering memorandum to a target group of buyers, offer to hold presentations, and ask for bids at the end of a time period, usually 90 or 120 days. This helps to keep everyone's interest focused. The risk is that the bids may be lower than what you had hoped for. In most cases, you are not obligated to accept a bid unless your business is performing poorly and you need to be bought in order to get the cash to remain operational or to take care of any liabilities.

Brokers and bankers also receive a commission in the event of a sale. This success fee can range between 10 percent and 15 percent depending on the sales price. Often there is a sliding scale, where the percentage decreases as the sale price increases. If you do the math, you can see that they are still making money. Most brokers will apply any up-front fees against the success commission. If they don't, ask them to. Further, when negotiating your broker agreement, make sure that the fee is paid when you receive the purchase monies, not when the deal is "legally closed." This will protect you in the situation that the purchase price is paid over a long period of time. You will not have to pay the broker cash up front. All of these terms should be negotiated up front and be documented in a brokers' agreement. Be sure to have a confidentiality clause, as you're going to have to disclose valuable information about your business.

When interviewing potential brokers or bankers, be sure that they know your industry well and have access to likely buyers. Generalists may not have the reach to find the best buyers for your firm. Also, ask them for referrals, and speak to companies who have gone through the merger and sale process with the broker or banker. You're not just looking for how well they did on the sale price, but also on the entire process. Did they represent the entrepreneur and the company well? Negotiate favorable terms for the entrepreneur? This will help you determine their strengths and weaknesses so you can round out your team of advisors properly.

Tax and Legal Advisors

You'll need to hire expert tax and legal advice. Your day-to-day account-ant or law firm may or may not have the experience necessary to review all the issues that would need to be considered in the event of a sale or merger. Ask your advisors if they have assisted companies through sim-ilar processes. Gauge their experience with your industry and size and the complexity of the sale.

Any sale or merger could trigger tax consequences. You need legal and accounting experts who are well versed on reducing your tax exposure. Reducing tax exposure can be accomplished in a variety of ways, for example, phasing the sale over time or providing for partial payment in stock. The latter option is favorable if it's an actively traded public com-pany, for example, a Fortune 500 firm. An experienced tax advisor can help you determine if the deal should be structured as a stock sale or an asset sale, as the tax implications could be different for corporations. Ide-ally, these specialists should have experience in your industry. They're more likely to be aware of industry nuances that could work in your favor.

Planning for the Sale

While most advisors will tell you that you need to think about exit strategies from the very beginning, the reality is that many entrepre-neurs don't have the time to do so. Further, in the early years, many are more enthused about the opportunity of owning and growing a com-pany and can't anticipate that they will one day want or need to exit a business. Some career entrepreneurs, particularly those who have founded multiple companies, may have potential buyers in mind. As you get closer to pursuing an exit strategy, you'll need to focus on a few key areas that can enhance your prospects and terms.

Improve Revenues, Profitability, and Cash Flow

As you prepare to sell, plan to firm up major contracts for at least two to three years after the anticipated sale closing date. This will help ensure a higher value. Many buyers are focused on revenues, profitability, and cash flows. Unlike when you are accessing financing to start or grow, as I covered in Chapter 3, buyers will focus on historical financial results as a base case. Unless they are willing to invest in your company after the purchase, they want to be sure your company is self-sustaining. Occasionally, if a company buys an early-stage firm for its products or technology, they will be willing to support or invest in the operations to get it to break even. More often, they will look to buy the assets and integrate them into their larger company.

Get rid of legal liabilities and other problems to the best of your ability. Your goal is to make the company's financials look straightforward and free of any red flags that may scare a potential buyer. For example, any lawsuits involving your products or services should either be handled prior to starting the sale process or disclosed completely. Have your financials recast by your business broker, accountant, or investment banker to exclude expenses and assets that will not be part of the sold company.

After making their interest known, potential buyers may provide you with letters of intent outlining key terms. You should plan to negotiate the terms, even though the letter of intent is nonbinding and is subject to a satisfactory due diligence. The due diligence stage is similar to the stage in which you raise capital, in that everything about the company—its market, customers, books, records, and actual offices—can be reviewed by the prospective buyer. The buyer will likely conduct an exhaustive financial and legal review to make sure there are no hidden skeletons.

As you prepare documents and company information for a prospective buyer, disclose with integrity. Any misleading or missing information is bound to come back and haunt you, at, no doubt, the most inopportune time—during the negotiation phase, for example. If you're a career entrepreneur and hope to start more new businesses, you'll also want to be sure to preserve your credibility and market reputation.

Your Role

Think about your own involvement. How long would you like to be involved? Most buyers will want your involvement for anywhere from a few months to a few years to facilitate smooth transitions. Most entrepreneurs who sell their company find the sale or merger honeymoon to be short-lived and want out quickly.

On the flip side, there are many buyers of businesses who are actually looking to actively run the company who may not want you to be involved or obligated by contracts. Your role, if any, should be clearly outlined as part of the negotiations.

Additionally, particularly if you are a service company, pay yourself a market competitive salary for at least two to three years prior to the sale. This will be critical if you need to negotiate a management contract. Many entrepreneurs take money out of their companies in ways other than direct salary. However, in the event of a sale or merger, most buyers or acquirers will use your salary to determine your post-buyout compensation. Additionally, clean up your books and get nonessential family members off the payroll and end excess insider perks and benefits. Eliminate all factors that will reduce your profits. You need to show the best numbers possible for valuation purposes.

Management Contracts

As you grew and possibly took on outside funding, you may have had to enter into a management contract with your own company. Many venture capitalists require this of their entrepreneurs. Key terms include regular and termination compensation as well as a noncompete for a certain number of years after ending involvement with the firm.

Use the merger or sale as a way to get rid of any terms that are cumbersome to you. For example, the noncompete would limit your future earnings potential. If the firm that buys your company wants you to have a noncompete for three to five years, as is often the case, you can ask for compensation to cover that time period. It's also common during a sale or merger for the entrepreneur and senior management to be asked to stay on to facilitate a smooth transition. This transition period is usually one to three years. If your management role does not work out, as is often the case, the acquiring firm would still have to pay you the compensation or negotiate a mutually agreeable amount; in essence, "buy you out of your contract." While the entrepreneur usually benefits financially, it can be heart-wrenching to watch others tamper, sometimes destructively, with something you've spent years building and nurturing. As a result, many entrepreneurs and wiser, more experienced buyers opt for short management time periods, recognizing the point of diminishing returns after which the involvement of the entrepreneur can be negative for all involved. On rare occasions, the entrepreneur transitions smoothly to the new environment and becomes an integral and long-term member of the new company's management. This is more often the case with earlier-stage companies that are acquired by large companies. The entrepreneur has probably had fewer years running the show and is not as entrenched.

In addition to management contracts, many use consulting arrangements to ensure the entrepreneur's role for period of time. Consulting arrangements should clearly state the scope of work, responsibilities, and terms. These can be easier to dispute than management contracts, although the latter are likely to be more binding on the entrepreneur in terms of the noncompete.

In addition to thinking about your own role and management contract, you should spend time thinking about the senior team that your buyer will probably want to retain, either permanently or for a short while to ensure a smooth transition. When you place your company for sale, you may find that senior managers and key skilled employees are concerned about their long-term employment prospects. You may want to enter into a contract with valued and essential employees to cover the sale period and up to two or three years post acquisition. This will reassure to the buyer that the management and technical know-how will remain with the company long enough to facilitate the transition. Further, your key people will feel secure knowing that even if the new company does not need them, they have a financial incentive to remain as long as possible.

Determining Value

Companies may conduct valuation analyses of their company at different stages and for varying reasons. Keep in mind that a valuation assessment completed for the purposes of a sale or merger is very different than an assessment done for tax purposes. Obviously, for the latter, most people want the value to look smaller.

If you hire a business broker or investment banker, he or she should be able to conduct an appraisal or valuation analysis. If you opt to hire an independent valuation firm, look for one with expertise in your industry. Ask the firm for recently completed valuations within a certain range and the resulting sale price so you can assess their track record. If they tend to value companies substantially higher or lower than the price for which they sell, you may need to look for more reliable appraisers.

Valuations can become complex, and it's best to have experienced advisors assist you with this process. However, you should understand the key principles of how your appraisal was conducted, as it can help you a great deal in your negotiations, especially when the price and related terms come under intense negotiation.

There are a number of ways that people calculate values, some more useful than others. Some valuation firms use a combination of methods to arrive at a range of values, which is probably the soundest approach. At the end of the day, beauty or value is in the eye of the buyer. No matter what value you or your advisors assign to your firm, it will be meaningless unless a buyer agrees.

Asset-based valuations are not commonly used for a sale or acquisition, and you should steer away from them, as they are likely to bring you a lower value. Book value and liquidation value are the two approaches used in asset-based valuations. These approaches might be more useful for tax purposes. Book value is arrived at by looking at the balance sheet and using shareholder's equity. Liquidation value is the amount remaining after a quick sale of the business or of all the assets and after paying all of the business debts.

Assessing historical earnings is a more common approach for valuing a company. In this method, a company's most recent two to three years of earnings are used to calculate a price. Buyers look at this number to assess the cash flow a business is most likely to generate in the first few years after a purchase. They also do projections to see what the company's growth potential might be. This is particularly relevant if you're being bought by a larger company that sees its distribution or sales and marketing clout as a way to harness value and growth.

Values are also determined by looking at industry averages and comparables within your industry and perhaps, if applicable, geographic area. These approaches evaluate the most recent transactions to determine the appropriate earnings multiple. For example, your industry may be experiencing a multiple of two to three times earnings, usually defined as earnings before interest and taxes (EBIT). Knowing this will help you determine the sale price range.

Assessing future earnings potential is also a common evaluative method. The earnings of three to seven years are calculated, and then each is discounted back to the present to determine the net present value (NPV). The sum of the net present values provides a current value for the company. This option often results in a higher value, but it is also the hardest to calculate, as a number of assumptions have to be made about future projections. During the heady dot-com days, sales prices were determined by using incredibly aggressive future revenue projections and/or using a multiple of *revenues* (sales), not earnings.

One of the most important things for entrepreneurs to remember as they negotiate a price and relevant terms is to make sure that the proceeds can cover any outstanding debt. If they can't, when the business is sold, you will not only end up with nothing but may still be liable for remaining obligations. If your business was generating enough cash flow to cover debt payments, you may want to consider keeping the business longer until the debt is reduced. Alternatively, you may want to make assumption of debt part of the negotiations. This is more likely to happen in larger deals with big companies who are eager to acquire your product, technology, or service.

Tips for Making the Business Broker and Investment Banking Role Valuable

As noted, your advisors will play a key role in your sale or merger. The following are key ways you can ensure that they will play a valuable role and help achieve your exit strategy objectives:

1. **Be clear about your objectives—your financial as well as your managerial and personal objectives.** Don't be vague or "shop" your company just to see what the market will bear. While you certainly can refuse an unacceptable offer, you should proceed down the path of a sale or merger with a clear intent to complete a transaction. Not only will this keep your advisory team incentivized, but it will ensure that you have the right approach and attitude during meetings and negotiations. Further, by disclosing sensitive information during the process, you may place your company in a less market-competitive position. If you are only curious about market pricing, invest in an appraisal from either a valuation firm, a business broker, or an investment bank. All will provide this service for a fee.

2. **Let your selected advisors do the buyer search for you.** You can certainly provide them with potential companies or financial buyers, but let them make the first contact. This will keep a level of objectivity and, in the early stages, confidentiality about your firm. Many brokers and bankers are experienced at soliciting interest by describing a business vaguely without disclosing the name of the company.

3. **You may want to consider preparing a draft business plan that your advisors can use to create the selling or information memorandum.** If they are charging you a fee for this first step, you may be able to negotiate a lower one by doing some of the early work. Also, if you complete the first draft, the tone and structure will more closely resemble your company. Once the memorandum is complete, have it reviewed by a lawyer.

4. **Be clear about your timetable.** If you are an early-stage company and are running out of money, let your brokers or bankers know that the clock is ticking. They may adjust their strategy to meet your specific needs. For example, an auction may be more appropriate if you need a transaction completed by a certain date.

5. **Get early legal and tax advice on how the sale might impact you personally, and discuss the range of terms that you would be willing to accept.** With this information, your broker and

banker will be better equipped to shift and direct negotiations one way or another to benefit you the most.

Passing It On

Most entrepreneurs, who run their companies for extended periods of time, do not spend any or enough time thinking about *how* they will pass their business on to their children or other family members. It's not as simple as many would like to hope. Passing on ownership or management control to the next generation does not always give you an immediate financial exit strategy. Above, in "Selling to Partners, Family, Friends, and Employees," I discussed the financial concerns you should consider when selling your business to family members. You also need to consider the actual succession process for management.

It is also important to plan for emergencies that may occur along the growth path. You may want to plan, early in your company's growth, about how your offspring or other family member could take over the business if you were suddenly not around to run it. Having a plan in place could help someone take over customers and key operating issues as well as avoid a fire sale of assets and a closing of the business. A good succession plan outlines what happens to both ownership and management issues in certain situations and over the course of time.

There are many sources, including legal, accounting, and consulting companies, dedicated to assisting entrepreneurs pass on their businesses with careful succession planning and estate management. A critical aspect of any sale or merger, especially one in which your firm is passed to a family member, is minimizing your taxes. If you plan to give your business to a son or daughter or other family member, the business will need to be valued. That value will be used by the IRS for determining the gift tax. For example, one strategy might be to give partial, minority interests to family members. The IRS will allow minority discounts when determining the value. There are many strategies, and it's best to use a good tax attorney, who is likely to be up-to-date with new laws and business strategies.

Management Issues

If you've been planning to transfer or sell your company to a family member, most likely your adult child or other adult relative, you have probably already brought the person in as an employee so that he or she can learn the ropes. Often, the company and family member benefit most if the family member is rotated to all departments and junior and senior roles over the course of a year or more. This ensures a thorough understanding of all aspects of the business. If you've got a couple of family candidates for the top job, have them all go through this "training" approach. Some family companies also try to have one rotation with another company to broaden the experience. Eventually, as the family members all become established and experienced in the company, one will likely shine more than the others.

Don't consider having two family members share the top management job—it's not likely to work. It's an incredibly rare company that can succeed with co-CEOs or co-presidents. Give kids or relatives who are not involved or who are not professionally suited to work in the business an equity interest. You do not have to transfer ownership and management equally. Further, if you are in any way financing the sale of the company to your family members or if you expect to continue holding shares, you have a vested financial interest in picking the person most likely to succeed and grow the company.

If you want to pass on ownership of your company but can't identify the right family member, or if a member is not yet ready for a senior role, consider hiring outside professional management. Many family companies opt to have professional management preserve the value of the company for all involved. It's important in these situations to be clear about both family members and the outside professional's roles and responsibilities. Conflicts arise when a family member tries to override the outside manager on key issues when it's not warranted.

Closing or Liquidating the Business

Deciding to close or liquidate your company may be one of the toughest decisions you've made. You've spent considerable time, energy, and resources nurturing the company, and it may feel like an extension of yourself. There are any number of reasons, internal or external, a business can be unable to continue operating. In essence, companies consider closing down for two primary businesses reasons:

1. The company is in financial trouble, and liquidating or Chapter 7 bankruptcy is the only viable option to properly close all outstanding business issues.
2. The value of your firm is nearly equivalent to the company's net assets and there's no likely buyer. Closing is your only exit option.

Even successful companies with quality products and customers can find themselves having to restructure or liquidate. If your reasons for closing your business fall more under reason 2, and you find yourself without willing successors to take on the business, you'll be faced with the difficult challenge of closing down your hard-earned efforts.

There are a number of legal, tax, and financial considerations that will require your attention if you need to close or liquidate. It's best to use your accountant and possibly a lawyer to assist with the process. The key is to make sure that there are no residual liabilities that will fall to you personally.

Knowing When and How to Close

There's a right and a wrong way to close a business, and I will candidly tell you that I've done both. My first business I successfully merged the business, clients, and employees into my next company. In my second company, I was guilty of entrepreneurial blind optimism and closed the business a year too late. Impacted negatively by 9/11 and the resulting business and funding climate, I should have heeded early advice to simply close shop. But as any entrepreneur knows, it's never simple. Knowing when to close is the hardest thing for any businessperson, let alone an entrepreneur who is far more likely to be emotionally as well as financially attached to their company.

Most entrepreneurs consider their companies an extension of themselves. You're likely to keep it alive longer than is profitable. It's helpful to have a trusted advisor who can help you draft your corporate DNR policy—"do not resuscitate." It should be one or more people who objectively understand your business, industry, and stage of growth and future prospects. You may have a family member as part of this, but don't rely on an "internal" person alone, as he or she may bring forth his or her own exaggerated fears or hopes. In Chapter 8, I dealt more with the spiritual side of closing your company and keeping faith. Below are some of the mechanical ways on how to close your company.

If you can close the business and take care of all of the company's obligations, you may be able to avoid a formal bankruptcy filing. Despite the emotional challenges of this period, you'll need to have a plan for closing. Otherwise, you may be forced to address some of them well after the closing or liquidation. Further, a plan can help you make the right decisions if your resources are limited.

- Review all outstanding obligations and make a timetable for resolving them. Address all personal guarantees as soon as possible. Implement a plan for resolving these before other obligations.
- Address any outstanding legal and tax issues.
- If you have an active board or advisory group, they should know about the company's closing as soon as possible, if they haven't been involved in the decision to start with. This is a group that can help both with the closing plan and with life after it.
- Let your tax, accounting, and legal advisors know that you need to close or liquidate as soon as possible. There are many small issues to address. For example, there are tax filings that need to note that the business is terminated; otherwise, you may incur obligations in later years for not filing payroll taxes or income tax forms. While these can usually be resolved, it's a cumbersome issue that can be easily avoided.
- Inform key customers. If you are selling a product that doesn't need your company to be in operations, you may find some last-minute sales that can at least add to the company coffers. If you're in a service industry, you'll build goodwill with potential future customers if you communicate with them about the closing process.
- Inform employees soon after you decide. They are bound to find out, and they are more likely to view the closing in an unfavorable

light if they don't hear about it from you. It's always best if it comes from you in a straightforward and honest manner. Further, you may need some of them to help close or liquidate. In such situations, you may need to incentivize them to stick around with a monetary bonus and/or severance pay if you can afford it. Your plan should also spell out the process for transitioning their medical and dental benefits. Most likely, they'll be eligible to continue insurance coverage under COBRA, and you'll need to start the paperwork one to three months before they need to switch. Any pension plans will also need to be terminated and distributed to employees. Get appropriate legal, accounting, and benefits guidance to avoid any problems.

Bankruptcy

After your initial review of your plan and obligations, you may need to address a formal liquidation of your firm. No one likes to think that they may ever have to file for bankruptcy protection. However, bankruptcy can be a lifesaving process for many companies, large and small, as well as their owners.

There are two kinds of bankruptcy: Chapter 7, which liquidates, and Chapter 11, which restructures the company. Individuals restructure under Chapter 13. If your company is a legal corporation, you will need to use a lawyer for either type of filing. Bankruptcy law does not allow an officer or any other non-lawyer to represent a corporation. When you look for a lawyer to assist with this process, make absolutely sure that you hire one who is experienced in bankruptcy law, on both the personal and professional sides. Do *not* retain the services of your general lawyer. Bankruptcy law is a specialty, and an expert is worth the extra expense. In an effort to save a bit of money, you may add exponentially to an already very difficult situation and eventually spend even more money to respond to problems that the bankruptcy expert would have known how to avoid.

There's a great deal of required paperwork. Work closely with your lawyer to make sure everything is filed properly and accurately. In general, when in doubt, consider disclosing. Most lawyers will tell you to do the opposite, and while you should follow their direction, as they know your case best, keep in mind that even inadvertently failing to include information or complete paperwork properly can complicate your filings.

The bankruptcy courts will appoint a trustee to oversee the liquidation process. As an officer of the company, you'll be asked to assist in assembling information and answering questions about the business and its operations. Interestingly enough, if your company owes you any money, you'll then actually be a creditor of your own company. Before you file, make sure you have had a full briefing with your bankruptcy attorney. You'll want to be sure that there are no areas of conflict, particularly on the financial side.

If you have to file Chapter 7 to liquidate and close the company, you may unfortunately need to assess whether a personal filing will also be required. Many entrepreneurs have had to, along the way, personally guarantee bank loans, equipment leases, most credit cards, and similar kinds of debt. If the company files for Chapter 7 and there is not enough money to repay the creditors, then you are personally liable for anything you guaranteed.

It's important to keep this fact in mind as you start and grow your company. The entire reason many people choose to incorporate is to protect themselves personally. Yet, during normal operations, entrepreneurs are forced to take on a range of personal obligations in order to enable the company to grow. If you must take on equipment leases or credit cards with personal guarantees, be sure to take care of these obligations as early as possible. As you grow and the company establishes its own credit, you may be able to negotiate away any personal guarantees. However, keep in mind that even Donald Trump has had to personally guarantee bank loans and other debt for his companies. This was one reason why, when his companies fared poorly in the late 1980s, he was forced to file personal bankruptcy as well.

If you have provided such guarantees on behalf of your company, see if you can resolve the outstanding obligations prior to closing. If you can close the business without filing Chapter 7, you'll save yourself both money and a big headache. Amounts due to the IRS, particularly for payroll taxes, are a key obligation that entrepreneurs are still liable for, even if the corporate and personal bankruptcies are properly discharged. Your lawyer can best navigate you through this maze.

Some companies have managed to avoid Chapter 7 filing through a good-faith effort by reaching out to creditors. The companies informed their creditors in writing that the company had ceased operations and would not be able to pay its bills. It may work if your creditors do not believe that pursuing legal action against your company will net any financial results. If you have personal guarantees and your creditors are determined to pursue you personally, then you'll probably have to file to protect yourself. On the corporate side, it takes three creditors to legally force a company to file bankruptcy. As the most recent corporate officer, you'll not only have to cooperate with the trustee, but more importantly, you'll most likely have to incur the personal expense of hiring a lawyer for the company. Clearly, the entire liquidation and bankruptcy world can be very confusing, and it's critical to understand the personal and corporate ramifications. Even if you're short on resources, it is worth hiring a lawyer for a brief consultation to help you understand your options at the outset.

Under Chapter 11, your company has the opportunity to restructure its obligations and enable it to continue operating. It can be a yearlong process, depending on the amount of discussion and negotiation with the company's key creditors. Recognize that you may lose majority ownership of the company in the process. If you're a creditor of your company, you may emerge with a stake in the restructured company. Again, you'll need a corporate bankruptcy lawyer to help you navigate this process. As the company will continue to operate, any personal guarantees that you made on behalf of the company will probably not come due to you. These liabilities will be restructured alongside other liabilities. On occasion, you may encounter a creditor who will seek to have you meet a corporate obligation. You'll need to have your lawyer review the terms of the guarantee to assess when and how the obligation can be called on you.

CHOOSING A CORPORATE STRUCTURE

Deciding on the right structure for your company can seem a bit tricky, but most entrepreneurs pick between an S or a C corporation or a limited liability corporation.

A corporation is basically a company, which is a distinct legal entity from the person(s) who formed it. Many people opt to incorporate in Delaware because corporaPte taxes are lower, but check with your accountant before you finalize your choice, as it will depend on the type of business you have and where it does business.

Many entrepreneurs also who choose to be a corporation opt to elect to be a subchapter S corporation. This means that any profits are passed through to the individual shareholder(s) and taxed at their personal rate. Electing subchaper S status can work in the early days. There are a few points to consider.

An S corporation cannot own a C corporation. This is important if you intend to set up related companies or make an acquisition. Further, if you choose to be an S corporation, you can elect to switch to a C corporation at a later date, but not vice versa.

A limited liability corporation (LLC) is a hybrid corporate entity that has some benefits and qualities of both a corporation and a partnership. It has become the structure of choice for many entrepreneurs; however, you should do your own research before finalizing on a structure. The best structure will depend on your business, geographic location, intended markets, and financing expectations.

All three options (LLC, S corp, and C corp) give you limited liability protection for business debts. This means that you won't be personally liable for business debts. To illustrate, if you didn't incorporate and your business was sued, the other party could sue you personally. Given how cheap and easy it is to incorporate these days, there's no reason not to.

The critical difference between all three is in how taxes are treated. In a subchapter S corporation, there's no risk of double taxation, as your company is not a separate *taxable* entity (it is a separate legal entity). All profits or losses are passed to you and the shareholders, and taxes are paid at the individual levels. In a C corporation, profits are taxed at the corporate rate and then any distributions to you are taxed again at your rate (hence the term "double taxation"). In an LLC, profits (or losses) are passed to shareholders and not necessarily in the same proportion as their ownership interests. Profits are taxed once at the individual shareholder level.

While an S corporation can have up to 75 shareholders, it can only issue one kind of stock. As a result, if you plan to raise investment capital, most investors and VCs prefer the flexibility of a C corporation, which can have multiple classes of stock. If you intend to immediately raise capital, you may want to consider first consulting with your lawyer and accountant. One structure may be more suitable than another in terms of the number and type of shares. If you set up correctly on day one, you can avoid the need and expense for changes a few months later when you're ready to accept investment capital. Instruct your lawyers to keep it simple, as a junior associate may get overly ambitious and structure your company in a way that will trigger more annual filing fees than necessary.

To incorporate, you can find many online options, including The Company Corporation (www.incorporate.com) and Business Filings (www.businessfilings.com). Check out a few, and see which one has a package that works for your budget, as fees can differ by state. Many of these sites also have information on how to choose the best structure for your firm. Your accountant is probably the best source for this information as he or she probably knows your company and your personal matters. Even if you incorporate in Delaware, you'll probably still need to file to do business in your state. Simplify this by using one service if possible. They should also send you annual reminders for filing fees and any additional paperwork if required. You also don't file for subchapter S at the time of incorporation. You can do that later on with the IRS directly at www.irs.gov, although you need to elect subchapter S before the end of your first tax year. All of the business structures require annual paperwork, which is important to maintain.

The following site contains a useful chart comparing all of the common business structures from the state of Delaware:

www.state.de.us/revenue/obt/business_structures_table.htm

ENTREPRENEURIAL RESOURCES

The following are some useful resources on a range of topics that I've covered in the book. This list is by no means comprehensive, but it provides additional organizations, books, and Web sites.

Peer Mentoring Organizations

www.c200.org—Web site for the Committee of 200; for companies that are too small for membership, offers a mentoring program for women-owned-and-operated business

www.fwe.org—Web site of the Forum for Women Entrepreneurs and Executives

www.nawbo.org—Web site of the National Association of Women Business Owners

www.wpo.org—Web site of the World Presidents' Organization (graduate level of YPO)

www.eonetwork.org—Web site of the Young Entrepreneurs' Organization and World Entrepreneurs' Organization (YEO and WEO are now the Entrepreneurs' Organization)

www.ypo.org—Web site of the Young Presidents' Organization

Books

Allen, Kathleen, and Courtney Price. *Tips and Traps for Entrepreneurs*. New York: McGraw-Hill, 1998.

Arredondo, Lani. *How to Present Like a Pro*. New York: McGraw-Hill, 1991.

Boudreaux, Bill. *The Complete Startup Guide for the Black Entrepreneur*. Franklin Lakes, NJ: Career Press, 2004.

Brown, John H. *How to Run Your Business So You Can Leave It in Style*, 2nd ed. Denver: Business Enterprise Press, 1997.

CCH Consumer Media Group. *Start, Run, and Grow a Successful Small Business*. Riverwoods, IL: CCH Incorporated, 2002.

Collins, Jim. *Good to Great*. New York: HarperBusiness, 2001.

Duck, Jeanie Daniel. *The Change Monster*. New York: Crown Business, 2001.

Grabhorn, Lynn. *Excuse Me, Your Life Is Waiting*. Charlottesville, VA: Hampton Roads Publishing Company, Inc., 2000.

Greco, Susan, and Mary Naylor. *Customer Chemistry*. New York: McGraw-Hill, 2004.

Hawken, Paul. *Growing a Small Business*. New York: Simon & Schuster, 1987.

Lesonsky, Rieva. *Entrepreneur Magazine's Start Your Own Business*, 3rd ed. Entrepreneur Press, 2004.

Stralser, Steven. *MBA in a Day: What You Would Learn at the Top-Tier Business Schools*. New York: John Wiley & Sons, 2004.

Timmons, Jeffry A., Andrew Zacharakis, and Stephen Spinelli. *Business Plans That Work: A Guide for Small Business*. New York: McGraw-Hill, 2004.

Wolff, Michael. *Burn Rate*. New York: Simon & Schuster, 1998.

Web Sites

Government

1. www.dol.gov—Web site for the Department of Labor, with a wide range of information and links to state sites

2. www.irs.gov—Tax forms and information
3. www.mbda.gov—Web site for the Minority Business Development Agency
4. www.sba.gov/sbir—Information on the Small Business Innovation Grant program
5. www.uspto.gov—U.S. Patent and Trademark Office Web site
6. www.women-21.gov—Department of Labor Web site for women entrepreneurs

General Business

www.dnb.com—Dun & Bradstreet for company information and collections services

www.entrepreneur.com—Web site of *Entrepreneur* magazine, with a wide range of articles and resources for entrepreneurial companies

www.hoovers.com—Information on a wide range of companies and business topics

www.inc.com—Web site of the *Inc.* magazine, with a wide range of articles and resources for entrepreneurial companies

www.kauffman.org/entrepreneurship.cfm—Entrepreneurial research organization; has relevant articles and resources

www.mbemag.com—Web site of *Minority Business Entrepreneur* magazine, with a wide range of articles and resources targeted to minority-owned entrepreneurial companies

www.womensbusinessresearch.org/index.asp—Web site of Center for Women's Business Research, including information and resources

COMMONLY USED
WORDS AND CONCEPTS

Accounts payable   Often abbreviated as A/P. Accounts payable are the amounts your company owes to vendors. At any given time, it's your company's outstanding, unpaid bills.

Accounts receivable   Often abbreviated as A/R. Accounts receivable are the amounts due to your company from customers and other debtors.

Accrual method of accounting   Under the accrual method, your company books a sale when you make it, even if the money has not been received. Your company records expenses when you receive the products or services even if you have not paid for them. The other accounting method is the cash method.

Asset   Anything of value that your company owns. It can be tangible, like property or equipment, or intangible, such as intellectual property. Assets are noted on the balance sheet.

Balance sheet   Shows a picture of your company's assets, liabilities, and equity on a specific date.

Capital   The money invested in the business; also referred to as equity.

Cash flow   Measures cash in and out of a business over a period of time. Positive cash flow means more cash is coming into the business than is going out, and negative means the opposite. It's an important barometer of a company's financial health.

Cash method of accounting   Under the cash accounting method, revenues and expenses are booked when the monies are received or paid.

Collateral   Assets pledged as security for a loan.

Control   The shareholder who has majority voting interest in a company.

Convertible debt   Debt that has the option, but usually not the obligation, to convert into equity at a certain price and/or under specified conditions.

Debt   An obligation of the company to repay a borrowed amount of money.

EBIT   Earnings before interest and taxes.

EBITDA   Earnings before interest, taxes, depreciation, and amortization.

Equity   The shares of the company owned by an individual or institutional investor.

First right of refusal   A concept found in an investor, strategic or partnership agreements. It means that if the company wants to sell itself, the investor or partner has the option to decide whether to buy it before it can consider outside offers.

Founder's stock   The entrepreneur's shares given at the time the company is founded.

Gross income   The total income or revenues booked by a company during its fiscal period, which usually coincides with a calendar year.

Gross profit   The total revenue minus the direct costs of generating that revenue. Gross profit is calculated by the following formula:

Gross profit = Total revenues (sales) – Cost of goods sold (COGS)

Gross profit margin   Also called gross margin or margin, it is a percentage that is calculated by dividing the gross profit by total revenues or sales. The more you pay for supplies or direct labor (the cost of goods sold), the lower the margin. The lower the margin, the less profitable your product or service. The gross profit margin indicates the efficiency of your company. Companies strive to have a higher gross profit margin than their competitors.

Gross profit margin by product is calculated by the following formula:

$$\text{Gross profit margin} = (\text{Selling price} - \text{Cost}) \div \text{Selling price}$$

To calculate gross profit margin for your firm, use the following formula:

$$\text{Gross profit margin} = (\text{Total revenues} - \text{COGS}) \div \text{Total revenues}$$

(To state as a percentage, multiply the gross profit margin calculated by the above formulas by 100.)

Income statement   A financial statement showing revenues, expenses, and net profits.

Inverted balance sheet   Scenario where liabilities exceed assets on a balance sheet.

Liabilities   The amounts that a company owes. Liabilities are noted on the balance sheet.

Line of credit   A loan that is available as needed by your company for up to a fixed amount and during a certain time period. There's often a small fee to secure the line of credit even if you do not use it. You can access the funds as you need them and repay them without penalty. There are variations on the terms for a line of credit.

Liquidation preferences   The order of priority in which secured and unsecured creditors of a business are paid in the event of a liquidation.

Liquidation   When the assets of a business are sold.

Long-term loan   A loan that is to be repaid on a term longer than one year.

Net income   The income minus expenses. It's also referred to as net profit.

Net worth   Assets minus liabilities is the company's net worth, also referred to as equity.

Operating income   Operating income equals revenues minus expenses for cost of goods sold, selling expenses, and general and administrative expenses. It does not include any expenses for interest and taxes.

Percentage mark-up   The gross profit expressed as a percentage of cost as opposed to margin which is a percentage of the selling price. Percentage mark-up is calculated by the following formula:

$$\text{Percentage mark-up} = (\text{Selling price} - \text{Cost}) \div \text{Cost} \times 100$$

To calculate gross profit margin by product, please refer to the formula noted above.

Preferred stock (equity)   A class of stock that usually pays dividends and has a preference over common stock in the payment of dividends and in a liquidation.

Revenues   Income from all sources before any deductions are taken.

Secured loan   A loan that is guaranteed by collateral that has been pledged as security.

Seed capital   Often refers to the initial investment in a company by the entrepreneur, angel investors, friends, and family. The aggregate amount is usually under $1 million.

Stock   Refers to ownership in a company.

Term loan   A loan that is lent in one or more lump sums and must be repaid according to specified terms. The funds cannot be reborrowed as with a line of credit.

Venture capitalist   Often abbreviated as VC. A venture capitalist is an individual who invests in a new or fast-growing company.

INDEX

INDEX

ABOUT THE AUTHOR

Sanjyot P. Dunung is president of Atma Global, a developer of innovative educational products for the corporate, higher education, and K–12 markets. The company's mission is to create engaging, best-of-class, global learning products for key markets around the world. Its solutions deliver high-quality knowledge to help people successfully interact with people from other cultures for business, academic, or leisure purposes.

Atma Global is Sanjyot's third entrepreneurial venture. With more than 13 years of experience as an entrepreneur, she's enjoyed wonderful successes but has also seen the darker side of midnight. Sanjyot communicates the insights she's gleaned from her business experiences and observations of fellow entrepreneurs in this dynamic and practical handbook for entrepreneurs.

Additionally, Sanjyot is a recognized leader in the field of cross-cultural learning and has more than 15 years of extensive experience in developing and communicating cross-cultural learning products and programs. Notably, she is the author of *Doing Business in Asia: The Complete Guide* (Simon & Schuster, 1995 and 1998), which focuses on the cultural issues of conducting business in 20 Asian countries. Sanjyot routinely writes articles on doing business internationally. Further, she periodically appears on CNBC-TV, CNN International, Bloomberg TV, and various radio programs and is often a guest speaker at conferences and seminars addressing international business and entrepreneurship. Sanjyot also worked as a banker in New York with American and Japanese banks.

As an entrepreneur, Sanjyot was selected as a Protégé member of the Committee of 200. She's cofounder and president of the Dunung-Singh

Foundation, which is committed to providing educational opportunities and hope to underprivileged children. She also recently served as a member of the board of directors of the U.S. Committee for UNICEF (United Nations Children's Fund).

Sanjyot's academic history includes a BA from Northwestern University and an MBA with an emphasis in International Finance from Thunderbird, the American Graduate School of International Management. She is the school's 1997 recipient of the Distinguished Alumni Award. Sanjyot was born in India; was raised in Liverpool, England and Chicago; and now lives in New York City with her husband and three young sons.